Extinction

Extinction

Ron Meyer

ROUNDFIRE BOOKS

Winchester, UK
Washington, USA

First published by Roundfire Books, 2012
Roundfire Books is an imprint of John Hunt Publishing Ltd., Laurel House, Station Approach, Alresford, Hants, SO24 9JH, UK
office1@o-books.net
www.o-books.com

For distributor details and how to order please visit the 'Ordering' section on our website.

ISBN: 978 1 84694 865 7

A CIP catalogue record for this book is available from the British Library.

Design: Stuart Davies

Printed in the UK by CPI Antony Rowe
Printed in the USA by Offset Paperback Mfrs, Inc

Dedicated to my wife of over 25 years, Diane Evans,
who on our own spiritual journey has been
my beloved companion and trusted critic.

Acknowledgments

I want to recognize my spiritual teachers, Peter Ralston, Edrid Riddle and Genpo Roshi, and of course, Ken Wilber's monumental insights. Also, I need to recognize my paleontological mentors, Dr. William Reed and Stephen Jay Gould. I need to acknowledge my developmental editor Doug Kurtz and editor Heather Newton who made invaluable contributions to the text. Lastly, I need to thank Mark Reeder, my partner in crime in writing this book. He took my voice recognition messes and made them into literature. Without his brilliant work this book would never have been.

Prologue

Caernarfon, Wales

Lungs bursting for air, leg muscles on fire, Dr. Ray Howe ran out of the alley and into the bright arc of a streetlight. Recoiling, he flattened himself against the side of a building. Across the street was the lit-up entrance of the Tail of the Red Dragon, his favorite pub in Caernarfon. It sat on the waterfront across from the Menai Straits that separated northern Wales from the Isle of Anglesey. Howe swallowed, thinking briefly about going inside. But he knew his pursuers would find him there. He had to get away. He'd tried going home but Gentel's security was there when he stepped out of his car. He'd barely escaped. He needed a place where he'd be safe long enough to put his plan in motion.

A light, mist-filled breeze blowing in from the Irish Sea brought with it the creak of clew lines as waves gently rocked boats moored in the Straits—an idea struck Howe. It was so simple. Gentel's security wouldn't expect it. *I'll hole up on my boat. I'll take it out. No one will find me. Then tomorrow I can send the T-gene information to the National Institutes of Health and The New York Times.* The plan made him feel good, and for the first time since he'd left Gentel, Howe knew he was going to get away.

With renewed confidence, Howe followed the road fronting the waterway until he reached the entrance to the marina. His Glassair 24 Sloop was snug in its slip. He watched behind him the whole way but never saw a person or a car. Usually this area is packed this time of night on a weekend. He maneuvered carefully along the mist-slicked boards of the dock until he reached his boat slip. Untying the lines, he let himself into the cockpit and found the spare key to start the electric motor. His hand was shaking and it took him three tries before he could get it into the ignition. The key turned slowly and dash lights came on in a stuttering fashion. And then everything was green, showing that the sailboat's small engine was online.

He eased into reverse and the boat backed away. A few minutes later he was guiding silently to the end of the Straits. Out on the water, the fog thinned, letting through a glimmering quarter moon, just enough light for him to swing out of the Straits without hitting anything. He was glad he had the electric motor installed and his silent passage made him feel more secure. No one could hear him and without running lights, seeing him would be just as difficult. By morning Gentel would have no any idea where he was.

The Irish Sea lay just ahead, around a small headland on the Isle of Anglesey. Once there he could raise sails and take off for Liverpool or the Isle of Man. He could make either one in a couple of days.

"I'm safe!" he exulted.

"Safe is a relative term, Dr. Howe," a low voice out of the darkness replied.

Ray's heart clamored in his chest as he whipped his head from side to side, straining to see where the voice came from. A compact, African-American man stepped around the mast, and gripping the boom, swung easily into the cockpit beside him, landing without a sound.

Ray recognized him as Hawke, Gentel System's security chief. He was five foot eight, with wide shoulders and a wasp waist. Slightly slanted dark brown eyes hinted at an American Indian heritage. They seemed to see everything at once.

"How did you find me?" Ray blustered.

"It was the obvious choice, Dr. Howe. Please excuse my bluntness, but you scientists for all your intelligence, really don't have much imagination."

Ray grimaced at the insult. "You're here to kill me."

Hawke shook his head. "Please Dr. Howe, I'm not some

Mafioso type who disposes of difficulties in so crude a fashion. I'm here to make certain Gentel Systems gets its property back. For instance, I'll take that." He pointed to the smart phone in the holster on Ray's belt.

"It's information people need to know," Ray protested.

"And they will when Dr. Jurgenczak decides it's time. But for now you've stolen proprietary information and I'm asking you nicely to hand it over to me."

Howe watched Hawke leaning against the gunwale, rolling easily with the waves like a part of the boat. He had no advantage over the younger man. Resisting would just get him injured or killed. Besides the smart phone wasn't the only place Howe stored the information. He had backed up all the data on an imbedded holographic magnetic strip on the back of his I.D. card. *Gentel's lucky no one thought of this before or the T-gene project would have been exposed long ago*. He handed over his phone.

"Is this everything?" Hawke asked politely.

Howe nodded, unwilling to trust his voice lying to the security chief.

"See, this is all very simple and easy, isn't it?" Hawke smiled, though there was no warmth in it.

The cold sea air sharpened Ray's senses. He watched Hawke standing steadily through the growing swells of the Irish Sea that now rocked the boat violently and he wondered what the man really wanted.

"Does anyone else know?"

Suppressing a sudden flash of fear, Ray decided not to tell him about the USB flash drives sent to Derek Simon and Yoshi Yamato two of Gentel's division heads working on the T-gene project. The drives carried everything he had learned concerning the project's failed research efforts.

"Does any one else know?" Hawke repeated flatly.

"No one," Ray lied.

"Good," Hawke said. "Dr. Jurgenczak will be pleased."

Hawke pointed back toward Caernarfon. "You can turn back now and put me ashore at the marina."

Ray's eyes widened in disbelief. "That's all? Aren't you afraid I'll tell the world about the Terminator Gene."

"In truth, Dr. Howe, what could you really say? You have no proof."

"No proof." Ray laughed harshly. "Is that what Jurgenczak told you?"

Hawke remained silent. He waited, knowing that the doctor would eventually tell him everything. Howe didn't disappoint him.

"There's proof...thirty million anomalous miscarriages last year – thirty million that don't fit any of the medical literature, Thirty million that could have only been caused by the T-gene. And that number is growing exponentially. We have less than two years left before we reach a tipping point. Do you know what *that* means?" Howe said, jabbing a finger at Hawke.

Hawke nodded. "The point where the effect becomes irreversible."

"That's right!" Ray shouted. *For Chrissake, my daughter won't be able to have children unless we find a cure. No one's daughter will have children.* "We need to start a Manhattan-style project right now! Bring in the entire world to research and stop this thing. Otherwise humans are going extinct! You should be helping me not Jurgenczak!"

"Do yourself a favor, return to the states and forget about all of this."

Ray couldn't believe what he'd just heard. "That's it? You hear the human race is going extinct unless we do something now to stop it and all you can say is I'm free to go."

"Wherever you like - home, Liverpool, Isle of Man. All the way to Dublin. The only place you won't be allowed is back inside Gentel. Your days in the field of genetics are over."

Ray thought about arguing but Hawke's offer was actually a

stroke of good fortune. *I'll be able to convince someone what's going on.*

"Th...thank you," Ray said, meaning it. He turned the tiller and adjusted his course. He watched the sea and felt the sloop cut through the waves easily. Far to starboard, the Isle of Anglesey loomed in the darkness.

"I'm glad we had this little talk," Hawke said. He glanced at the nearing shore. "You're a little spent from this evening's events. I'd better take us in. Make yourself comfortable there." He pointed to the stern.

Ray nodded.

Hawke watched the American scientist make his way awkwardly to the back of the boat in the choppy sea. Reaching down, he released a fire extinguisher clamped to the side of the cockpit. He hefted it, feeling its balance. Satisfied he knew its weight, he looked at Dr. Howe standing six feet away at the stern, staring at the boat's wash. Hawke settled himself, until he was completely calm and he knew his muscles would act exactly according to his wishes.

Ray started to turn when Hawke threw the canister, but it was already too late. The extinguisher caught the geneticist in the temple, leaving a deep bloody gash just below the hairline.

Already dying from the impact, Ray toppled overboard, disappearing into the dark swirling waters.

First Division

...As microbiologists we should continually ask ourselves, "Are there other ways for complex life forms to replicate themselves?" No one really knows the morphogenesis which drives the human egg to split in its various stages, forming gills at one point and lungs at another. Watson and Crick theorized that it was DNA, but nearly seventy years later even after unlocking the human genome, we're as clueless about the miracle of life as they were. DNA's true function eludes us, but we continue to worship it with murky hopes on unyielding faith that it will reveal something immensely illuminating.

- Baron Derek Simon, Oxford Lectures

Chapter 1

Sioux City, Iowa

This morning Dr. Kira Taylor felt a moment of ultimate creativity during that surreal time between sleep and being fully awake. If she had to explain it to someone, she would have said she was paying attention to her right brain equanimity. But even that didn't really describe what was going on. It was like being pulled off a ledge into the abyss. The feeling lasted only a moment, but it was enough to make her stay in bed and ponder what it meant. How could she have such a profound moment of awakening and continue to live her life with a constant background tone of fear and dread; constantly play the victimization card, never quite feeling good enough; be so driven to seek the spiritual and the way, yet never really love or be loved; or truly empathize with the suffering of her patients and the world as a whole without understanding who she was?

Fuck!

Shaking off the doldrums, Kira rolled out of bed and headed into the bathroom. She slept only in a tattered pair of running shorts and an old running shirt. Twenty seconds later, Kira emerged, dressed like she had slept, only the new T-shirt and shorts had not yet lost their store freshness. Her running shoes, on the other hand, were old friends, worn down to where there was little more than a thin layer of sole between her and the ground. Grabbing her car keys and her smart phone from the clamshell bowl by the front door, she walked out of the house. It was Sunday and she didn't have to be at work, so she had time for a nice long run at her favorite place.

With practiced ease, which comes from being an E.R. doctor, Kira deftly coiled her shoulder-length, red-gold hair into a tight knot with one hand, while the other checked that her phone was secure in its clip at her waist. She left it on to keep in touch with St. Luke's Medical Center if an emergency came up while running.

As if reading her thoughts, Kira's phone chirped. She glanced at the display. The time: 6:35a.m. The number: Jeff Wheeler, the intern on duty all night. He was eager and bright, top of his class from Harvard. Jeff handled everything she threw at him and never phoned for routine problems. A call this early wasn't a good sign.

"Answer," she commanded her smart phone.

"Sorry to bother you, Dr. Taylor," Jeff's resonant baritone hummed in her earpiece. "What's wrong, Jeff?" she asked.

"Mrs. Jacobson."

Shit! The Jacobsons were a quandary. They had been trying to have a child for a year and a half now, and Mrs. Jacobson was on her fourth pregnancy. The first three ended in miscarriages, all within two months. They had come into the E.R. yesterday afternoon because of some spotting in her underwear. Bleeding was the most common symptom of a miscarriage. After a routine exam and ultrasound revealed the embryo was healthy, Kira prescribed human chorionic gonadotrophin – a glycoprotein hormone a woman's body normally made during pregnancy. *That should've stopped the bleeding,* Kira told herself. *If they were back this morning...*She didn't let the thought go any further.

"I'm at home. It'll take me about twenty minutes to get there. Who's the OB/GYN on call?"

"Dr. Kelberg, but he's not answering. What do you want to do?"

Kira took a nanosecond to decide. "A CBC, Chem-7 with uric acid and liver profile first thing," she ordered, as she walked swiftly to her car. "And get me an ultrasound. This time use the enhanced imaging software. I want to see everything as clearly as a photograph. Send everything to my phone as soon as you get it."

"Yes, ma'am."

"And have the receptionist keep trying to get Kelberg. Feed him the same information you're sending to me."

"Will do." The line hummed to silence.

Kira couldn't help but marvel at how science and technology had advanced medical care exponentially since her internship and residency in Tucson. Specialized monitoring equipment hooked up to a patient's arm got all the vital information without having to draw blood or urine. Then with her smart phone, Kira could be out of the hospital and still get all the information she needed in real time right from the patient's bedside. The smart phone's display even handled imaging. It was usually enough to make a diagnosis, and she could use the information to get the staff working on what was needed to help the patient before she arrived. It saved lives.

How did we make do in the bad old days of the early 21st century? she thought wryly.

The Toyota Highlander started right up and Kira was leaving the driveway before she had her seatbelt buckled. She drove as fast as she dared. Every second gained could mean the difference in saving the child.

Kira's worst nightmare was a miscarriage. Maybe it stemmed from her own five years ago. She pictured the thumb-sized embryo, the tiny face that was just forming...a face that would never smile up at her...a child she would never hold in her arms. Kira exhaled slowly, easing the hammering of her heart, and focused on the Jacobsons.

A sinking feeling grew in the pit of her stomach.

Chapter 2

The only concession Dr. Kira Taylor made to St. Luke's rigid dress code was to take thirty seconds to throw on over her running clothes the pair of hospital scrubs the E.R.'s receptionist had waiting for her.

"Mrs. Jacobson is in Exam One," the receptionist said. It was one of the private rooms.

"Thanks," Kira said, and hurried away. She pulled out her smart phone. The new ultrasound image was downloading as she walked through the E.R.'s main exam area, alcoves separated by curtains. The "Rodeo" the doctors and nurses liked to call it. At the far side were the two private rooms, where critical patients were held. One look at the ultrasound confirmed what Kira already feared. The embryo was dead.

Stopping outside the room, Kira took a deep breath. The worst part of being a doctor was giving bad news to good people. For Kira it was especially hard. Top of her class in med school in diagnosing patient maladies, she was used to curing problems or coming up with the answers so that the specialists could do the job. Emergency medicine was different. Good and bad news happened in a split second. And today, it was just bad news.

Kira put on her best doctor face, knocked then entered. She took a moment to orient herself to the scene. Dr. Wheeler and the head nurse, Mike Ellis, were finishing up from the ultrasound, cleaning the gel from Mrs. Jacobson's abdomen and making her comfortable. Mr. Jacobson stood beside his wife holding her hand and looking for all the world like he wasn't going to let go.

The room could have been an E.R. exam room in any modern hospital: porcelain white walls and brushed stainless steel cabinets and counter tops. Monitors were hooked up and they updated the patient's vitals every five seconds, which were then bluetoothed to a large interactive smart board on the near wall in letters big enough for everyone to read easily. Even so, Wheeler had his stethoscope to Mrs. Jacobson's chest and read the patient's stats aloud: "Temp 99.4; PulseOx ninety-five; BP 150 over ninety; pulse was rapid at eighty-three beats a minute when she came in, it's now down to sixty-five; respiratory sounds uneven. Mrs. Jacobson is still complaining of some mild cramping, but the worst of it ended a few minutes before you walked in." Wheeler adjusted his wire-rimmed glasses and smoothed his already immaculate beard with a slender, manicured hand. He didn't say anything but his hazel eyes confirmed what Kira already knew.

Kira thanked him and turned to the Jacobsons. In their mid-twenties, Paul and Jeanette were a young farm couple who had gone to college and were doing very well economically. They had been trying for two years to have a child. The beginning of each pregnancy had given them a surge of joy. Today, their faces showed a mixture of hope and worry.

To Jeanette, Kira said, "How are you feeling this morning? I heard you had some more spotting."

Jeanette looked at her husband. Paul's thin lips were pressed hard together. He nodded and she turned to Kira. "We want to know what's happening. You know, whether this is going to be like the last time...times. Whether we're going to have a child." Fear strained her voice. "We want to have a baby so much."

Paul squeezed his wife's hand. "We just want to know what's happening," he repeated.

Kira wished she had good news or could deliver an optimistic prognosis. But the Jacobsons were savvy and wouldn't tolerate any evasiveness. Summoning all the compassion she could, Kira said, "I'm so sorry. The ultrasound shows no heartbeat. You are having another miscarriage."

The couple looked at each other, and for a moment Kira thought they might begin crying. But they pulled themselves together, and Paul said, "We understand." Kira could hear the resignation in his voice and she could see that the fear in Mrs. Jacobson's face was not one of hopes dashed but the terrible acceptance that they were never be able to have children. Paul helped his wife off the table and the two of them stood there woodenly, their faces carefully neutral. Kira reached out with both hands and felt the tension in their shoulders. "I wish I had better news."

All at once the three of them embraced and Kira could feel the heartache drain out of them as though they didn't have the energy to hold onto the grief any more. "There's some paperwork to sign at the admitting desk. I'll be out in a few minutes to walk you through it."

Paul shook his head. "No need, Dr. Taylor," he said flatly. "We know the drill." The couple left holding hands and Kira hoped they would stay that way and not be torn apart by their bad fortune.

She turned to Dr. Wheeler and Mike Ellis. "I'll have the orderlies get this room ready for the next patient." Mike said as he was leaving.

Wheeler cleared his throat. He had a habit of doing that whenever he was uncomfortable. Kira knew why. She could see it clearly in the two ultrasound pics. The one from yesterday showed an embryo that was healthy and growing like any seven-week-old embryo should. The image from this morning was no longer recognizable as a small human being.

Wheeler shook is head and pointed at the second image. "Jesus, Kira. It looks like the embryo just exploded. It's nothing but mush now."

"Uh-huh," Kira answered. She tapped a long finger against her lips and studied the dead embryo. The enhanced ultrasound produced an exceptionally detailed image at the cellular level. *There's something about this picture that's nagging at me. I know I've seen it before.* Turning to Wheeler, she said, "Have you ever seen anything like this?"

Wheeler shook his head. "The enhanced imaging software is new this year, so we've never had this detailed a resolution."

"New here in Sioux City but not new at Tucson Memorial Hospital when I was a resident there. Memorial was the guinea pig where they tested this software for three years." Leaning in close, Kira's eyes narrowed to tiny dots. "I know I've seen this before."

Wheeler waited.

"Got it!" she exclaimed. It was like a light coming on and Kira would have smiled if the information she remembered wasn't so bleak for Mrs. Jacobson. "In Tucson, we used this new software on all the pregnancies that came into the E.R. Tucson's a big city – over a half million people – so we had a huge testing group for the imaging. One group in particular stood out over all the others. They were almost always younger women in their teens and early twenties from every social economic group. The most curious thing about this peculiar type of miscarriage, was that if they had more than one like this, the chances of them going on to have a successful pregnancy were very low. One in ten to be exact."

Wheeler whistled tonelessly. "That must have raised a red flag."

"Sure did. I remember our epidemiologist Dr. Ikeda suspected there was some contaminant that was screwing up the local water supply. If I recall correctly, he applied for a grant to look into it."

"Did you ever find out what was going on?"

Kira shook her head. "I didn't stick around long enough to find out what the results of the study were. And now with the Jacobsons, I wonder..." She let the thought trail off. Then tapping her smart phone, the pictures disappeared. "Jeff, could you go and check on the Jacobsons and ask Tonya to expedite their paperwork so they can get out of here as soon as possible? And I want you to stay on top of everything in the E.R. for the next hour or so."

Surprise flickered across the intern's face. "What're you thinking?"

Kira shook her head. "Don't know yet. But I want to check something out. I'll be in my office if you need me."

Chapter 3

Kira's office wasn't large and she liked it that way, preferring to be in the Rodeo rather than tucked away from the action. But Jeanette Jacobson's ultrasound images haunted her and she had to take some time and look into them. Maybe because of her own miscarriage, she was making too big a deal out of this, but her gut told her there was much more going on here.

Her desk was squeezed into one corner with room behind it for a narrow hard-backed chair. The surface was clear except for a silver laptop and a tablet with a Bic pen. Kira liked to jot notes, the touch of the pen making her feel as though she were writing the words indelibly in her memory. It was process she picked up in grade school when she learned that if she used this writing trick, she created an eidetic memory of everything she notated. There were a few file cabinets with copies of reports. Despite the computerized medical records, St. Luke's still demanded paper copies of doctors' notes. There were no other chairs for visitors, because Kira preferred people out of her office rather than in it. The only other piece of furniture was an interactive smart board that filled the wall across from the desk. Synched to Kira's computer and the Internet, it displayed everything from medical records to medical literature, even newspaper articles, and showed them clearly.

The world's literally at my fingertips.

Kira brushed her smart phone against the computer, wirelessly dumping the data from this morning into its hard drive. She pressed a command code and the ultrasound images appeared on the screen. "Computer, search medical docs," she commanded. "Give me the percentage of American women under twenty-five who experience miscarriages in their first pregnancy."

"31.8%," flashed on the smart board.

Kira's eyes widened. She was expecting a number in the low teens. *And that's the official figure. It's probably higher since many women who become pregnant for the first time don't even know they're pregnant, and when they miscarry, all they see is some spotting during their cycle. Or if they're teenagers, they're too relieved to report it.*

"OK," she said slowly, "how many of these women ever go on to have a normal pregnancy after the miscarriage?"

The computer clicked and whirred and the number went up on the screen. Kira gasped, not believing what she saw. She bent over her computer's keyboard, punching in the question manually. The same answer flashed on the smart board: 32.7%.

Kira's lips were suddenly dry. *Why haven't we been notified by the National Institutes for Health about this mini-plague?*

Kira glanced at the images of Jeanette Jacobson's exploded embryo and it was as if her mind made a mental click. "Computer, correlate these images with any others found in the medical literature."

Seconds later the smart board flashed the words, "No correlation found."

Impossible, Kira mouthed. *I'm sure these images are the same as what I saw in Tucson, and at the very least, those images should be available.*

Kira ran searches for the next hour, but found nothing. Coming away empty-handed left her frustrated, angry – and determined to find the answer.

Chapter 4

By the time Kira finished stretching, her running clothes were soaked through with sweat and her long hair was plastered against her neck. Sweat trickled between her shoulder blades to the small of her back. Iowa summers smothered you in a hot, wet towel.

One final stretch, fingers pointed up into the sky, back arched until the vertebrae popped along her spine. Kira let her breath out slowly and gazed out across Sioux City's tall grass prairie restoration project, a fifteen hundred acre park at the edge of the city. Big bluestem grasses covered the steeply rolling hills. By August they would be taller than her five feet six inches, but here in early June, they only brushed her mid calf. Their blue-gray color reminded her of a sea at rest, and she understood why 19th-century pioneers described America's prairies as a vast ocean to cross.

Kira quickly checked that her SUV was locked and the car alarm set. Even though Sioux City was a small community, it still had thieves who stole from unlocked cars just to stay in practice. And hers was the only car in the parking lot. She smiled. She had the prairie to herself this morning. She spotted a single compass plant, its bright yellow flower rising above the grass at the edge of the asphalt. She focused on the empty space around the flower and held that emptiness, letting it fill her. She hoped to hold onto that emptiness as she ran and achieve her ultimate goal – the state of no mind where everything arose and disappeared effortlessly.

With a final deep breath, Kira took off, leaving the asphalt parking lot behind her. Her stride stretched out and she moved easily in the sultry air. Topping the first hill, she loped down a narrow path among the big bluestem, that bit of emptiness held firmly in her consciousness. To her left she glimpsed the glaring scarlet flowers of the butterfly plant, unseen on these prairie hills for a hundred years and now vivid in their reclaimed beauty. The prairie restoration project was bringing back flora and fauna driven to the brink of extinction.

The vivid smells of the grasses and flowers and the hot humid air brought up memories of Tanzania's wet savannahs where she spent her childhood. She watched her memories unfold and let them slip away one by one. The vast plans of Africa...herds of wildebeest, zebra...the idle roar of lions in the evening...the enormous baobab trees, fruit hanging pendulously from the thick branches. Her ecologist parents studied chimpanzees. She shivered at her imagined terrors from when she was six years old of chimpanzees sneaking into her tent at night and carrying her off to be eaten. The fears returned just as acute thirty years later in the stark early morning light of the prairie – the bared teeth, the eerily humanlike screams. Then in a burst of insight she understood her childhood fear. When she was learning language, learning to use symbols. In her mind, she had been unable to distinguish properly between the symbol she had created in the chimpanzee and the reality of the chimpanzee – a childhood error. Today with ease she could let these childhood images float away into the dawn, never to return. Freed new energy welled up in her. Such was the beauty of the spaciousness created by her running practice.

Kira rounded a curve in the winding trail and another steep hill rose up ahead of her. She powered into it. Then she was at the top and down into the wide valley. The way stretched out ahead of Kira, empty and endless as though she were running deep into the past before humans came to this area, came even to the continent.

More thoughts rose up. Again the plains of Africa, the birth-place of hominids, ancestors of modern humans. At thirteen Kira told her parents she was going to become an evolutionary biologist and solve the mysteries of life. With all the grave pompousness of a teenager, she announced she would be the one to discover how a spinning world of dirt and rock became a planet teeming with life. Her first book was going to be titled *From Dirt to Computers.*

The memory turned sad and ripped her back to the present, into ordinary awareness. Her shoulders and back tensed up and threw her stride off until she nearly stumbled. The dream of becoming an evolutionary biologist ended at Yale ten years ago during her PhD defense. Kira slowed her pace, forced her thoughts away from the bad choices she'd made during that time, not willing to revisit it or her decision to leave academia for the busy life of an E.R. doctor. *Another time,* she told herself and once more focused her mind on the empty spaces around her.

Kira breathed deeply. Lengthening her stride, she felt the tension in her shoulders and lower back begin to ease. More thoughts rose up in her consciousness and evaporated into the morning's golden glow, sweeping over everything and turning the grass and trees greener. She reached the trail's turning point. Her legs still felt fresh and her breathing was even and deep, and an inner stillness washed through her, providing a rare moment of calm clarity. Pulling her phone from its clip at her waist, she brought up Jeanette Jacobson's ultrasound. As the rich sounds of the prairie settled over Kira, her mind opened to a pair of questions. "What aren't you telling me?" she said aloud. "What's really going on here?"

Chapter 5

Omaha, Nebraska

Kira eased her Toyota Highlander into heavy traffic south out of Sioux City on I-29 toward Omaha. Towering cumulonimbus clouds gathered on the western horizon. A storm was coming. To Kira's right, the muddy waters of the Missouri River rolled on relentlessly. On her left the white spire of the Floyd Monument rose into the partly cloudy sky. It was a much smaller replica of the 550-foot tall obelisk in Washington D.C., honoring the nation's first President, George Washington. Sergeant Floyd was the only member of the historic 1804 Lewis and Clark expedition to die during the journey, and he did so right here on the banks of the Missouri River during the first four months of the trip. Kira had had developed an interest in the Corps of Discovery, particularly the life of Lewis Meriwether. She had read the expedition's journals, written by Lewis and Clark, a number of times.

Mostly these men described events much like typical well-educated twelve-year-olds. The trip was one gut-wrenching experience after another and never a sign of internal emotion, internal struggle, internal pain. Then well into the second year, Meriwether made this most astounding entry: "This day I completed my thirty-first year, and conceived that I had in all human probability now existed about half the period which I am to remain in this sublunary world. I reflected that I had as yet done but little, very little, indeed, to further the happiness of the human race, or to advance the information of the succeeding generation. I viewed with regret the many hours I have spent in indolence, and now sorely feel the want of that information which those hours would have given me had they been judiciously expended. But since they are past and cannot be recalled, I dash from me the gloomy thought, and resolved in future, to redouble my exertions and at least endeavour to promote those two primary objects of human existence, by giving them the aid of that portion of talents which nature and fortune have bestowed on me; or in future, to live for mankind, as I have heretofore lived for myself."

Something happened to Meriwether that awakened his inner life. But that awakening seemed to have been more than he could handle. In 1809, three years after the Corps of Discovery returned to St. Louis, Meriwether Lewis took his own life.

Through the years Kira tried to figure out what had led Lewis to his highest moment of great insight and the lowest depths of great despair, but he left no clue. She was left with a deep sense that his thoughts could very well have been her thoughts. Except for paleontology, nothing had come easy for her. "Get better, work harder" had been her personal mantra. She was coming to realize that all her medical 'do-gooding' was just in service of bolstering her ego. Jack had once said. "Perhaps one day you'll see that your life really isn't your life."

That's why you're going to see Jack, Kira told herself as she texted her best friend. "O wise man of the East," she began. It was the nickname she had given to Jack after learning his American mother had left him when he was five in the care of his father, Khenpo Rinpoche, the abbot of a Tibetan Monastery in Woodstock, New York. She then disappeared and Jack never saw her again. "Cming to c u. Much to tlk about."

"Bring it on," Jack answered.

"Dn't u want to knw what it's about?"

"I follow your Facebook page. Your current E.R. posting's up and you haven't decided whether to go or stay."

Jack was right about that. Sioux City had worked some kind of subtle effect on Kira. Things were happening. Some good...some very good. Algebra used to be a bitch. One day a teen in her neighborhood asked for help with his math homework. Kira was surprised by how easily she understood the equations for the first time. Then there were those moments of distance from her own thinking...watching her own thoughts...seeing how her mind worked out her fears such as her childhood dread of chimpanzees.

Leaving Sioux City wasn't going to be as painless as with her other E.R. postings. But that wasn't all there was to it.

"There's much more," she texted.

Thirty seconds later, "Drop by in the afternoon. I'll meet you in the usual place."

Kira typed, "K." *Good old Jack. He can help me make sense of all that's happened.*

Jackson Everett Kelley was Kira's oldest and closest friend and the only person she trusted without reservation. She had met him while in graduate school at Yale, where he obtained a PhD in Zoology. Big, nearly seven feet tall, loud and irreverent, Jack was completely open about his homosexuality. He had spent two years intensely studying with the founders of the brilliant psychological technique known as voice dialogue. It made him very intuitive, good with people and a brilliant administrator. He always seemed to know the right questions to ask.

Three years ago Jack took a job with the Scott Aquarium in Omaha, Nebraska and turned it into a world-class exhibit. The aquarium's seventy-foot shark tunnel was unique and an oddly appropriate place for them to meet, which was why he suggested it. Kira let out a long sigh. If anyone could help her wrap her mind around the things puzzling her it was Jack.

Like the Jacobson's miscarriage. Kira had done an exhaustive search on the Internet, for images of the type of de-differentiated cells she had seen in Jeanette Jacobson's ultrasound. A search spider using key word combinations, including "apoptosis" plus "embryo," "de-differentiation"' plus "embryo," and "miscarriage" plus "de-differentiation,"' turned up nothing out of the ordinary. In the Digital Age where YouTube carried videos of everything, the absence of such images like the ones she recorded back at the lab was unsettling. But what had really unnerved Kira was her inability to contact Dr. Ikeda to confirm the same kinds of miscarriages had happened in Tucson.

The epidemiologist who had led the investigation was nowhere to be found.

"He returned suddenly to Japan two weeks ago," the receptionist at Tucson Memorial Hospital had explained. "We've been unable to contact him, even by cell phone. It's like he dropped off the face of the Earth."

Ikeda was practically anal about doing his work and finishing it on time. For him to leave abruptly and be out of contact was so out of character, Kira couldn't help but think that something suspicious was going on. She had tried other avenues to find his studies on the Tucson miscarriages, but everywhere Kira met with a dead end. *It's as if no one wants this information out there. But that's just weird.* These miscarriages hinted of something very wrong, and at the very least the National Institutes of Health should be involved. Kira had checked with her contacts at the NIH and the Centers for Disease Control in Atlanta. Neither of them had heard of anything even remotely close to what she described. A roaring growl of thunder snapped Kira's attention back to the road. Dark cumulonimbus clouds filled the sky and lightning ominously crisscrossed their bellies. *Damn! This is coming fast.* Kira grimaced. Another thunderclap crashed, the sound so deafening it actually shook her. Huge raindrops followed. Rolling up the driver's window, Kira 's eyes widened as she saw the first of the marble-sized pellets strike the semi trailer rig in front of her.

Shit! Hail!

All at once rain and hail smashed into her, the roar like hammers pounding the car! Anxiously, Kira looked for someplace to pull off under cover. But she was on a long straight stretch of I-29 with no overpasses and no rest stops.

No place to hide!

Kira's fingers gripped the steering wheel and the muscles in her shoulders tensed. More thunder crashed. She peered through the windshield. The torrential rain and hail were horizontal and the wipers could not keep up.

Damn, this is bad!

A car whizzed by her, the driver oblivious to the danger. Kira glimpsed another semi-trailer in her rearview mirror. It was close on her bumper. Trapped between the two big rigs, the idea of stopping or even slowing down was suicide.

The gloom thickened and Kira gripped the steering wheel with white-knuckled intensity. Lightning crackled incessantly, the brilliant flashes illuminating the cars surrounding her. Another flash and ahead she spotted the semi-trailer's brake lights come on and stay on. Through the pounding rain and hail, Kira heard the screech of tires and saw the trailer begin to fishtail. Gasping, Kira slammed on her own brakes. For a moment she slowed and then came a sickening feeling of floating. Kira's world began to spin. Ironically, her anti-lock brakes locked up and she was hydroplaning out of control. A glance in her rearview mirror showed the other semi-trailer hurtling toward her. The two trucks loomed over her and Kira knew she was moments from being killed.

At that moment, propelled by imminent death, Kira's mind lurched into a different perspective of no self, just naked awareness. Everything reduced to slow motion. The rain and hail fell so gradually that she could make out individual drops and pellets and could have easily dodged between them and never gotten wet or hit...the two semis, inched across the pavement...her SUV in control, turning in a very precise arc between the two big rigs.

Floating above...looking down at the accident as it was beginning to take shape...no one to die. Somehow, the violence of it had been like a lever in her soul, separating her spirit from the physical, giving her an out-of-body experience. The scene – the three vehicles nearly immobile as though they existed in a timeless bubble, where years passed inside, while seconds passed in the world outside. From this new vantage point, the way through the intersecting paths of the three vehicles was like a child's puzzle. Looking inside the SUV, there she was, acting without thinking, taking her foot off the brake and gently turning the steering wheel into the direction of the skid. When the car straightened out she was headed toward the median. The two trucks still converged on her, horns blaring and tires smoking on the wet pavement. Pressing down hard on the accelerator, the car shot forward across the berm and into tall grass between the lanes of the interstate, steering in a straight line down the median away from the trucks. The two rigs found their own balance and the forces of the accident petered out into nothing. They roared by as if nothing had happened.

Seconds later it seemed to Kira she awoke from this most unusual experience to find herself turned around in the median looking at the road. The rain and hail had let up and she watched dumbfounded as the traffic whizzed by. For a moment she had to think of how she got here, how she had survived being smashed between two semis.

The out-of-body state had produced her first true non-dual experience. *Novel profound oneness with everything no separation into me and other.*

But the scientist part of her, that part of herself that made her a good doctor, that part which observed the world around her and made decisions based upon an examination of those observations, made her question the reality of what had just happened.

She pulled out her smart phone, amazed that her hand wasn't even shaking. In fact, she was completely calm as though this kind of thing happened to her on a daily basis. Kira dialed Jack's phone but the number couldn't get though. *The thunderstorm must be creating too much interference for the broad bandwidth necessary for voice communications.* Texting used a much narrower bandwidth, so she typed in briefly, "Nrly killd in strm. Will b late."

Chapter 6

Kira slammed the door of her SUV and checked the time: 2:49. She hurried across the blistering hot asphalt. Ignoring the "Scott Aquarium Closed for Repairs" notice taped to the glass, she pushed on the wide, steel-framed door. It opened easily. Kira threaded her way among scaffolding and workmen, past the visitors' information desk and down three flights of steps to the shark tunnel. She never failed to be awed by the structure. The acrylic walled passage zigzagged for seventy feet past coral reefs, rocky canyons and caves, with large sharks and manta rays swimming right along side and overhead. Kira always felt as though she were strolling on the bottom of the ocean.

She spotted Jack leaning against one of the giant acrylic glass panels at the far end. A dark bushy beard covered his expressive face and his barrel chest seemed to take up most of the tunnel. From his right earlobe hung a miniature Tibetan prayer wheel. Known as a mani-wheel, written on it in Sanskrit were the sacred mantra *Omani Padme Hum*. Jack stared into the tank, seemingly oblivious of anything else going on around him. While Kira was certain she hadn't made a sound, he waved a large hand at her and said, "Kira, you have to see this."

Hurrying over to him, she peered into the tank. Kira gasped. Hundreds of small jellyfish congregated in a mini bloom, occupying one whole section of the tank. No other fish were anywhere near. The medusas floated ethereally, their translucent, silver-white bell-like bodies giving off an aura of benign peacefulness. They were, in fact, the oceans' most prolific predators. Their stings could even kill an unwary scuba diver if he ventured too close.

"Intense, huh?" Jack observed.

Kira nodded, mesmerized by the slight bobbing action of the jellies, their tentacles moving with a liquid grace.

"These particular beauties are Aurelias and they thrive in the 'dead zones' around the Mississippi River delta." Jack was referring to the huge swaths of oxygen-poor salt water in the Gulf of Mexico. Fertilizer runoff from Midwestern farms made its way down the Mississippi drainage basin every summer and flooded the Gulf. Nothing lived in these so-called "dead zones" except the adult form of these *medusozoa*.

"I love animals that metamorphose," Jack said. "My goal is to somehow display to the public all life stages of these beautiful creatures. It's too bad evolution went away from this lovely design. Imagine if we had three very different body forms in our lifetime." Jack smiled at her. "You once asked such questions."

"Speaking of evolving, how's your father?" Kira had met the Rinpoche once when Jack took her back to the monastery in Woodstock for a weekend. It was her first year in graduate school at Yale. Khenpo Rinpoche was the epitome of everything opposite she expected to find in a Tibetan holy man. He smoked, drank, was rude and even made a pass at her. When she slapped him, he laughed it off. A year ago the Rinpoche was diagnosed with brain cancer. From that moment on he gave up all his old vices and did nothing but sit.

Jack shrugged. "Still sitting. The monks place a little food and water by him everyday. His body has become wizened and his skin is translucent like these jellyfish."

"It's amazing he's lasted this long."

"I suppose it is," Jack said. "On the other hand, the monks say the divine is penetrating his body down to its very atoms and he won't die until he's completely pure."

Kira's knee-jerk reaction was *bullshit*. But almost at the same time she pictured the old man sitting there, and something about the image drew her back to her revelation yesterday morning and the evolutionary abyss. Was the Jacobson's miscarriage signaling something greater than a personal tragedy? Her expression darkened.

Misreading her frown, Jack added, "It's what needs to happen."

"Huh?" Kira said. "I'm sorry, I wasn't thinking about your father. It's something else, Jack. You gotta place we can talk out of the way of workmen?"

"My office." He led the way up the stairs to the third floor of the building. Kira had never been in Jack's office before, preferring to meet in the aquarium or have dinner at his place. When he opened the door, she did a double-take. The suite was huge and lavish. Thick merino wool carpet covered the floor. A conference table sat in front of floor-to-ceiling windows framing the Omaha city skyline. The wall opposite was curved. The upper portion supported a large interactive smart board, Kira had ever seen. Beneath it an aquarium flowed along the room's wall for over twenty feet. There was no coral reef or fish, just a layer of silt two feet thick on the floor. Kira suspected there must be hidden pumps because the water in the tank moved in a gentle wave.

"This is something else."

"It is," Jack said indifferently. He kicked off his shoes and they landed haphazardly – one against the windows and the other on top of his desk. The desk was bigger than Kira's office at St. Luke's. Kira knew his attitude was not a studied pose. Jack treated wealthy ostentation with the same indifference he showed to any lifestyle. "It's all the same stuff," he liked to tell her. "We just dress wealth up differently and give it a catchy name like 'lifestyles of the rich and famous.' The wealthy are almost like a different species."

He pulled a pair of chairs away from the conference table and faced them toward the window. He patted the one next to his. "Come here and tell your old uncle Jack what's really going on."

Kira laid it all out for him, beginning with her upcoming decision concerning renewing her contract at St. Luke's and ending with her near fatal collision driving down here. When

Kira finished, Jack said nothing right away. He stared out into the Omaha afternoon. Kira waited, not bothering to prompt him. He could have been counting leaves on the trees or recognizing shapes in the high cumulus clouds on the horizon, but all the while he appeared to be doing nothing, Kira knew he was sifting the information she gave him, finding the common thread through all of it until he could speak in a way that would tie it all up in a way that made sense.

Jack had listened carefully to Kira, never uttering a word, even when she showed him the high-resolution images of Jeanette Jacobson's ultrasound and posited her own questions about what the de-differentiating embryo really meant. In truth, Jack didn't know how any of the events were related, or if there was an answer of any kind that could satisfy Kira. But clearly she was on edge. Her blue eyes looked troubled and she had taken great pains to mask her feelings by discussing her problems as if she were talking to a patient. Her exaggerated objectivity told Jack that his best friend suspected this miscarriage heralded something very bad was about to happen, something she was afraid she couldn't handle.

How do I help you? Jack mused. *How do I help you get past your feelings of uncertainty so that you can wade into this mystery and solve it?*

A memory arose. It was about the trip home with Kira over twelve years ago. His father came to him and said in his Rinpoche voice, "Your friend is a Rinpoche but doesn't realize it. She will need your help. If you don't intend to help her, then drop her now and forget about her. Otherwise you must promise yourself to be there for her."

"Of course I will," Jack responded.

His father patted him compassionately on the shoulder. "This is a lifelong bond. You may have to go places friends don't normally wish to go." He left then and didn't speak to Jack except for innocuous conversation for the rest of the weekend. But when the two of them embraced, saying goodbye, the Rinpoche said, "Sometimes people don't need answers. They need a key to let themselves into the space where the answers are already waiting."

Jack had known for a long time this moment would come some day. Kira always prided herself on being a good-natured and cheerful person. However, Jack knew she was in fact a very angry person but denied it, denied it by putting her unwanted, immature anger deep in her subconscious. Kira had to work so hard and things never quite worked the way she wanted. She began saying, "Why me? This isn't fair!" and started blaming those who seemed to foil her success. She felt victimized by the world. At times Kira's anger would come out unconsciously. To those on the outside she looked crazed. But most of the time it only tormented her inner world, not letting her clearly see her motives and why her life turned the way it did. To free her, Jack had to take a big risk – trigger her anger and make himself the one who victimized her. She needed to do what psychologists called shadow work.

Jack eyed Kira. The first key to her problems lay in her own past, events that had shaped her when she was very young, events that in the past had left her crying on his shoulder. These events were buried deep in Kira's subconscious. It was in seeing them for what they really were that she would find the strength to face and solve the mystery of the miscarriages.

Jack glanced at the aquarium. It looked empty, but in fact was far from it. Tiny sea creatures, holdovers from Earth's ancient past thrived there. They were tiny tunicates, the simplest of all vertebrate families. They held the key that would open the door to Kira's shadow world. But first Jack had to lead her to the door.

Jack cleared his throat. Letting the corners of his mouth drift downward into a frown, he said bluntly, "You're always leaving, Kira, never staying anywhere long enough to put down roots."

Kira shrugged. "It doesn't bother me any and you know I like having new experiences."

Jack's frown deepened. "It's more as though you collect experiences so that you can claim them like trophies."

That's a little harsh, Kira thought, wondering why Jack was being so critical of her. It wasn't like him to be so unsympathetic to her problems. "At least I have experiences," she said defensively.

Jack snorted. "Your experiences are casual, like your affairs. A one-night stand here and there, but nothing permanent."

Kira found herself leaning back in her chair. It was difficult to keep her anger in check, but she managed. "'To exist is to change, to change is to mature, to mature is to go on creating oneself endlessly,'" Kira answered, struggling to keep her voice even.

"Wonderful quote. Henri Bergson, right?" Jack asked.

Kira nodded.

"Nice man. Did I ever tell you my grandmother knew him. She made me read his book, *Creative Evolution*."

"And?"

"Nothing," Jack said, deliberately baiting her.

"You never drop a name casually, Jack."

Jack hid a smile. *Got you hooked*. "You know me so well," he said. "Okay. Evolutionary biology is your reason for these experiences. You're looking for that edge that will give you the insight into figuring out how a ball of spinning gases and dust can turn out beings capable of computers and space flight. You won't find it by doing more, getting better. That's all you've ever tried to do since I've known you."

Kira could feel heat rising to her face. Even if Jack was her best friend, he didn't have the right to treat her this way. In fact it had been a long time since she had let anyone speak to her like this. The last time was graduate school at Yale. She choked back a feeling of inferiority that her graduate school days always invoked in her and glared at Jack. "Careful Jack, you don't want to go there."

Jack ignored the warning. "You've always got to work harder than most and for that you play the victim."

"Jack, stop it," Kira heard herself say, her anger palpable now.

He could see she was on the verge of going unconscious...of slipping into unconscious rage. *Good. Kira's bringing some fire to her problems. A little more so that she can focus that energy on what's really needed.* "Always the victim cheated by…"

"That's enough!" Kira shouted.

She's ready. Jack heaved himself out of the chair and went over to the aquarium, motioning Kira to follow him. "I had this installed three months ago."

The abrupt shift in emotional energy caught Kira off guard and she found herself following him in spite of her anger. To Kira, the aquarium appeared to be little more than a tank of seawater with a mud floor. The water moved back and forth like the waves of the ocean. "I don't get it. What's so special about it?" Kira said, her voice tight.

"I'm trying to recreate the evolutionary environment of the Cambrian Sea 500 million years ago. In this tank, the water is less salty, has less oxygen, there's no plant life but ..."

"In other words you've got a whole tank full of nothing." Kira laughed harshly. Jack's rebuke of her lifestyle still stung. It had gone beyond friendly rivalry or banter and she was more than a little eager for some payback.

Jack stared at her. "It looks that way, except for these little guys. They're the only creatures I've found that can thrive in this water chemistry." He pointed at animals so translucent that Kira almost missed them.

Like a jellyfish they moved in unison with the gentle wave action of the tank. The skin was semi-opaque. She squinted at one of the creatures and could just make out the precursor of a backbone. Then their scientific nomenclature came to her – *tunicatus, phylum Chordata, subphylum Urochordata. Tunicates* were a family of vertebrates which included salps, humans' oldest ancestor and the precursor to all vertebrate evolution.

But the name came tagged with a memory that hit her like a sledgehammer.

Tears came to her eyes. She felt helpless and lost. She reached out to Jack for help, but he stood there like an unfeeling block of stone. Then before she could clamp down on her feelings, for the second time that day, Kira was swept out of her body. Only this time it wasn't to safety but into a flashback so hurtful, she nearly collapsed in pain.

Chapter 7

Nevada 1996

A cold blast of wind showered Kira with fine particles of dust and pine needles. She closed her eyes and turned her face away, waiting for the blast to die down. Chuckling all around her. A gloved hand slapped her shoulder. Kira opened her eyes to narrow slits and recognized Pete Englund, a long-time family friend. As a favor to her mom and dad, Pete had agreed to let Kira come along on his latest fossil dig, even though she was only sixteen. A chance to go on a dig with America's leading Cambrian expert was everything Kira could have hoped for, and it fit nicely with her dream of becoming an evolutionary biologist.

Pete grinned at her. "That's why we all wear these," he said, pointing to his leather-clad sunglasses, the kind Arctic explorers use to cut down glare and keep out blowing snow and ice.

"And these," another man said, laughing. He doffed his colorful straw sombrero, the strings looped casually around his neck.

"And long pants." A third man shook his head disapprovingly and pointed at Kira's shorts. "You're going to burn like a piece of toast out here."

Kira swallowed and put on a tight-lipped smile at the hazing she was going through. It was the first morning of the week-long dig in the basin and range of northeastern Nevada. The area was mostly slabs of dull green and yellowish-brown rock. A few spindly mesquite bushes were the only areas of shade anywhere around for miles.

Kira gripped her hammer tightly and went back to pecking at the rock, slicing the slabs the way Pete showed her so that they broke along the planes and revealed hidden treasures inside. This nine-inch layer was remarkably rich in early Cambrian fossils. It was Pete's site, America's great fossil Lagerstätten, and he showed it off to his fellow paleontologists and fossil-collecting buddies like a proud grandparent.

Pete was the grand old man of the Cambrian period, founder of the Cambrian Institute at the University of Colorado in Boulder. He was tall and leathery and seemed to move nonstop over the landscape, more energetic than the others who were half his age. Pete had put together this little expedition by convincing America's most prestigious universities – Harvard, Yale, Southern Cal, University of Chicago, and Kansas – to fund it. It was the largest gathering of the greatest young paleontological minds in the world.

The first morning of the dig, Kira and Pete were the last ones to arrive. Kira was stunned by the frenetic activity. The scene was crazy, nearly twenty men beating away on rocks; some, like the Brits, singing at the top of their lungs; others squatting silently like they were praying; and everyone dodging a front-end loader that was ripping up the rock in a quarter-mile long trench to reveal ancient secrets hundreds of millions of years old.

"Look here," Pete said enthusiastically. He hurried over and squatted next to a pale green layer of finely stratified sedimentary rock just deposited by the loader. Several pieces of the shale had already split into fragile slabs and the fossil collectors were busily combing through them. Kira spotted the fossilized remains of a bizarre soft-bodied animal. It was one of a group of evolution's first attempts at complex life that for a hundred years had confounded the world's leading paleontologists.

"The exposed layer also contains more complete lower Cambrian trilobites than anywhere else in the world," Pete said. Then he pointed to the gathering layout of soft bodied animals – *Arthropod taxa* including one species of *Canadaspis Novozhilov,*

Perspicaris Briggs, Tuzoia Walcott, and two species of *Anomalocaris Whiteaves.* These strange looking creatures were the ancestors of many of the common phylums today. "Now imagine if we could find the granddaddy of them all. The one we could point to and say this is where all modern life sprang from. That would be something, huh?" Pete's eyes literally twinkled at her.

Pete's enthusiasm was so great, that it was hard for Kira to believe that he was seventy-five years old and a Professor Emeritus at the University of Colorado. Though he no longer taught a full schedule of classes, he still organized expeditions. Kira was the youngest person here, not yet in college, and she was very pleased to be included in this exclusive club. This gathering held the paleontological experts who were the very people who could help her achieve her dream of becoming an evolutionary biologist. Kira wanted to b the first person to answer not only the what, where and when of Earth's evolution, but the most important question of all – the why.

The next morning, Kira was up early. She wore long slacks and tied a bandana around her head, pulling back her long hair into a ponytail. With rock hammer in hand, she descended into the trench cut by the backhoe. At the far end near an old silver smelter, she found a place where mineralization had stained the fossils a deep purple. A two-foot slab of shale hung at a forty-five degree angle near the bottom. It was too big to move, so Kira split it in place. As the slab fell apart, she gasped at the size of the find inside. Twenty-seven circular transparent bodies spread across the rock. She instantly recognized that they were far different from the other soft bodied creatures Pete pointed out the day before.

"Pete!" Kira shouted. "You'd better come see this."

Pete scrambled into the ditch like a youngster after a lost soccer ball. One look and his eyes lit up. Within minutes everyone had gathered around. They all took turns inspecting the slab. None of them touched the actual fossils, but each one nodded and the mood was as if they had just discovered the Holy Grail. But nobody said anything and Kira wondered what they were waiting for.

Then one of the Brits asked, "Where's Derek?"

"Who's Derek?" Kira whispered to Pete.

Pete jutted his chin toward the other end of the trench. "You're about to find out."

The group parted as a man Kira had not seen the day before walked up. He was fair-haired, with blue eyes, in his forties, lean and in shape, and he moved with the effortlessness of an aristocrat. Unlike the others, his hands and face were tanned and he was impeccably dressed. He carried a rock hammer in one hand, jewelers loupe in the other. Kira thought she recognized him but she couldn't place him.

The others hastily made room for him. He carefully studied the find. The silence stretched out until the group's nervousness seemed about to explode.

"Well?" one of the Americans from Yale asked, a little too loudly.

Derek put away his lens. "Extraordinary. What we have here is the precursor to all vertebrates, the oldest form of ourselves – a colony of *salps*."

"I knew it," the American said and pumped his fist in the air. The group began talking excitedly among themselves. All Kira could make out were words like, "brilliant," "revolutionary," and "find of a lifetime."

Derek's voice rose above the babble, though it didn't sound like he was shouting. "Who found this?"

"Pete's friend," the American said, sounding more than a little envious.

Derek eyed her. At sixteen, Kira had already reached her full growth and at five feet six inches, was the shortest person in the group. Derek was nine inches taller than she was. "What's your name?" he asked.

"Kira Taylor."

"Well, damn, young lady, it would be an honor to name this beauty after you. Would that be alright?"

Kira blushed and found herself unable to do anything other than nod her head vigorously.

"I imagine you'll even get a junior author credit on it as well." Derek turned to Dr. Harold Lieber of Kansas, a short, pudgy paleontologist with a growth of beard that stuck out his face in all directions at once. "Harold, will you do the honors and describe these creatures. I'm sure it'll be worthy of an article in *Nature*, eh."

To Kira who was watching what happened, it was like the Pope bestowing New Year's appointments.

Harold nodded and said, "Thanks, Derek." He shouted at the others, "Let's get this slab crated."

Derek crooked a finger at Kira. "Let's walk, young lady. You can pretend to be awed by my accent and I'll pretend not to pay attention." He smiled broadly.

It took Kira a couple of seconds to get that he was joking. "Shouldn't I stay here and help? I mean, after all I did find it."

Derek rubbed a long index finger across his jaw. The corners of his mouth turned up in a mischievous smile. "Finding it is exciting part, the hard part is what comes next. If you're willing to do the hard work, there will be a door open for you at Yale on my team of evolutionary paleontologists."

Kira remembered herself nodding yes.

Derek had been right. The *salp* was something to hang a career on. Unfortunately it wasn't her career. Lieber had taken credit for the find and her name was never even mentioned. Resentment so consumed Kira that she compared herself to Rosalind Franklin, the first person to recognize the DNA double helix, and who later got aced out of her Nobel Prize by the old boys club at Cambridge.

Years wasted, Kira thought bitterly.

Kira shook herself. The scene in Nevada's basin and range faded and she found herself back in Jack's office. Her chest was tight and she was breathing in shallow gasps. "You bastard," she said quietly. "You did this on purpose."

Jack nodded.

"Why?"

"A little angry are you? You're the one that doesn't get angry."

"I don't!" She clenched her fists. "Are you going to apologize?"

Jack said nothing.

"Well, newsflash, Jack, I don't need someone who's going to stab me in the back."

Kira went to the door of his office. "Don't call me. I'll call you if I ever decide we can be friends again."

Jack said completely unperturbed, "You may be angry at me now—"

"You're an asshole, Jack," Kira interrupted. She knew if looks could kill, Jack would be lying dead on the floor this moment. Jack, on the other hand, seemed not to be affected at all.

Kira yanked the door open, trying to get out of the room so that she could tell herself truthfully she hadn't heard Jack. But his voice followed her into the hall. "Derek's actually a great guy."

Kira slammed the door behind her. "You could never see the truth Jack!" she screamed down the hall.

Chapter 8

Derek Simon, the Eighth Baron of Greystoke, had gazed out the rain-stippled windows of his corner office at the sodden streets of Caernarfon many times since he started working for Gentel, but never with a feeling of such uncertainty. It rippled through him and set his nerves on edge. In fact, he couldn't recall being this anxious since his first days at university.

Derek had been one of Oxford's brightest students. He'd had his choice of any career from government service to the aerospace industry. He chose paleontology, disappointing his parents and many of the Oxford dons who had prepared him for what they believed was a greater calling, a greater service to Britain. After finishing his final term, Derek left England for Canada's Rocky Mountains in Alberta. There in the fossil-rich Burgess Shale he helped investigate the 500-million-year-old Cambrian deposits that produced the most bizarre collection of animals the world has ever seen.

For over a hundred years these strange creatures had puzzled paleontologists. But it was here that Derek earned his reputation as a brilliant innovator in the field of evolutionary biology. With uncanny insight, he hypothesized that evolution was functioning differently in the early phases of complex life. He called it the era when life had free reign to experiment with what it was to become.

From that moment on, Derek could have gone anywhere in the world. He deliberately started small at the University of Bristol. By the late eighties he had risen to become head of evolutionary research at Yale's Peabody Museum. More than twenty years later he was back home on Wales' west coast. His wife of thirty-five years couldn't have been happier. Derek couldn't say the same for himself. In the irony of ironies he used to be known for his exhilarating lectures on biological evolution. Now in a very direct way he was putting all his energies into becoming part of it.

Derek rubbed the exhaustion from his face. Exhaling slowly, he muttered, "Am I up to the task of saving humanity?"

Turning from the windows, Derek spotted on the desk the source of his uncertainty – a USB flash drive. A flash-drive left for him by Dr. Ray Howe. *Bloody hell.* Poor Ray is missing, probably dead. Derek had heard the news along with everyone else early this morning. Howe's sailboat was found drifting in the Irish Sea. There was no sign of the geneticist on board – just a bloody smear on the stern. The police were calling it an accident. Derek picked up Ray's flash-drive and twirled it at the end of its cord. He couldn't stop from shuddering. This morning he had plugged the USB device into his computer and watched Ray appear on screen. It was as if the American scientist was speaking from the grave. Ray's message hadn't started with a lot of hope.

"Derek, in case you don't remember me, I'm Dr. Ray Howe and I work in Littleton's Genetics Lab. I'm taking a big chance showing you all this, and for humanity's sake I hope I've chosen correctly. I can't talk to you in person – too much risk. But it's all here. Everything I've been gathering for the last three months, everything that will show the world what Gentel has been working on. But that's only part of it. I've been able to review all the data from all the labs at Gentel, and what I'm about to show you will explain why we have to go public with this. Gentel's approach is *all wrong*. We can't stop the T-gene through genetic manipulation or classic biochemistry solutions. This problem originates much farther back than the origins of DNA. It's a developmental issue straight out of the Cambrian. If Jurgenczak doesn't change Gentel's approach immediately, we'll condemn the human race to extinction just like the Neanderthals." Ray paused in his monologue and Derek could see that the scientist was visibly shaken. "You already know the mathematics. A tipping point is less than two years away. We need to set up a whole new effort, a...a worldwide effort, away from Gentel and their intrusive security. We've gotta do this and I'm counting on you to help me out – to save humankind from extinction."

Ray's face disappeared and streams of data filled the desktop. It had taken Derek most of the morning to sift through it all, and when he finished, he was shocked. He had told his secretary to hold all his calls and had not stirred from his office for the next two hours.

Derek swiveled in his chair and returned to the windows. Mist alternately shrouded and revealed Caernarfon Castle's towers, giving it the mystical quality of a floating palace, and evoking images of a world without humans. *Ray claimed Gentel has been pursuing the wrong approach for more than ten years. Have we wasted all that time and now there's no time left to get back on track?*

Derek shook his head, as much to clear it as to assure himself that Gentel still had time left to stop the Terminator Gene. Ray seemed to think as much – if they changed their approach. *But change it to what?* Ray's last words were unusually cryptic – "a developmental issue straight out of the Cambrian."

Derek pressed his hands against glass and closed his eyes to concentrate. The Cambrian Era contained an explosion of forms. All of life's basic body plans emerged all at once. Then for the next half billion years nothing really new. *Why ?* Derek had asked himself the question many times before. But once again he was drawing a blank.

"Well you can't hold onto this any longer," Derek told himself, picking up the flash drive. "Better tell Jurgenczak and call a meeting of the Inner Circle to see what needs to be done with it."

Chapter 9

Arne Jurgenczak pressed the tips of his fingers together and bowed his head reverently three times, whispering, "Adonay," My Lord, with each nod. He spoke in Aramaic, the ancient language of the Jews, who freed from their bondage in Egypt forged a covenant with Jehovah. It was a covenant that Jurgenczak felt even now three thousand years later deeply in his heart, his bones and most deeply in his soul. A covenant he vowed to keep even though he was a Polish Catholic.

It was not at all hypocritical to him that he prayed twice a day to the Jehovah of the Jews. Jurgenczak was a Fundamental Monotheist, and Jehovah was the one true God, the God of Abraham, the God of Jesus and the God of the Prophet Mohammed.

We're the children of God – your children, Adonay.

Jurgenczak continued kneeling, his head bent in devout prayer. *Thank you, Adonay, for giving me the intelligence and skills to find a cure for the Terminator Gene and allowing me to fulfill Your mission on Earth.*

Jurgenczak pulled his strength from the many others like him – Christian, Muslim, and Jew – all praying for him to succeed. The time of chaos was near. *Just like me all these children of Jehovah feel the time of Revelations is at hand. The End of Days is upon humanity and I swear before all that is holy I will be ready for it.*

Even the pagan idol worshippers sensed something was wrong and the number of the year 2012 signified it. But they did not understand the power of the one true God, nor did they understand the power the one true God poured into Arne Jurgenczak to save humanity from itself.

I am Jehovah's vessel to bring a new heaven on Earth.

Jurgenczak bowed his head once more in humble acceptance that Jehovah had chosen him before all others to carry out His will. Jehovah's plan was not without its consequences, and the knowledge of what he must do to ensure the plan was carried out, filled Jurgenczak with sorrow. He prayed for the souls of those who would sacrifice themselves so that His plan could come to pass.

A soft bell chimed three times in the office outside the small chamber. Three o'clock. The meeting Derek called of the Inner Circle would be starting in fifteen minutes. "*Adonay,*" he whispered a last time and genuflected. Carefully removing the *vestis alba* he was wearing over his suit, he hung the white chasuble by a peg near the room's only door. He paused, eyes drawn to the simple altar of wood that fit against one wall, where moments before he had been kneeling in prayer. He would have liked to have performed his afternoon ritual with candles and a censer, but this room, though well ventilated, would not have permitted it. What none of the other members of the Inner Circle knew was that the room also housed a pair of PPC-8000 mini-tower supercomputers. They filled the opposite wall, leaving enough room in the chamber for a chair and an operator. These computers linked to every lab in Gentel's Caernarfon complex. Cameras recorded every test and procedure, and all work was automatically recorded in the data banks of the computers. The surveillance was necessary so that when a cure to the T-gene was found, Jurgenczak would have immediate access to it.

Then I will have the answer and in that answer lies the power to save humanity and create the Kingdom of Heaven on Earth. He retreated with soft backward steps out of the small closet into his private suite on the top floor of Gentel's complex. He closed the door behind him and heard the lock snick into place. Jurgenczak had the only security card that allowed access to this room.

He strode firmly across the floor, his powerful physique dominating the mostly empty room. At sixty-five he was still stronger and fitter than men half his age. Compared to the closet, the impression of Jurgenczak's office was of immense space.

Only a few chairs, a single coffee table and a desk broke up the vast expanse of carpet as it rolled to the northwest-facing windows overlooking the Menai Straits. Jurgenczak stood in front of the floor to ceiling glass and admired the view of the Isle of Anglesey in the distance. The sun poked through the gray overcast and threw a double rainbow over its lush rolling hills and forest. The omen pleased him.

A knock on the door turned Jurgenczak around. "Come in," he said in a soft voice that carried strongly throughout the room.

The door opened and Frank Littleton stepped in right on time. The geneticist was a kindred follower, a modern evangelical. Though not steeped in the teachings of the original Latin *Bible, The Talmud* and *The Qur'an* like Jurgenczak, Littleton nonetheless believed in his heart that Christ was his savior and that those who did not believe were damned for all eternity. Littleton was the one man Jurgenczak had trusted completely, until the incident with Ray Howe.

Which was why Gentel's founder asked Littleton to meet him before the Inner Circle got together.

Jurgenczak steepled his hands, the index fingers pressed against his lips, as he waited while Littleton crossed the room and sat in the chair opposite the desk. Littleton was shorter than Jurgenczak but broader in the shoulders. His dark eyes seemed to stare everywhere at once, and even the scientists working under him in his division thought he knew their results before they did. But this afternoon, he seemed totally unaware that anything unusual had happened. When he had settled, Jurgenczak said, "I asked you here before the meeting to talk about Ray Howe."

"It's a goddamn shame," Littleton replied, gruffly. "He was the best geneticist on my team and one of my best friends."

Jurgenczak's eyes narrowed. "And you had no idea that he was planning something like this." He tossed Howe's flash-drive onto the desk.

"What is it?" Littleton asked.

"Derek Simon brought it to me an hour ago. Dr. Howe sent it to him last night. It contains an overview of Gentel's research efforts on the Terminator Gene. He somehow got around our security protocols. According to Hawke, your *best friend* was going to send everything to the National Institutes of Health in Washington, D.C. and to *The New York Times*.

Littleton's ruddy face turned pale. "Wh...what?" he stammered. "He...he never said a damned thing to me. That no-good bastard. Why would he betray Gentel?"

"Why indeed?" Jurgenczak eyed Littleton carefully for any clues to his allegiance. *He really thinks Howe's a bastard and a traitor. Good. That's a point in his favor.* "Fortunately Hawke confiscated his phone, and the info he had secretly hidden on it, as Howe was leaving before Howe had a chance to release this information. Unfortunately, it wasn't the only source. Derek found this flash-drive on his desk this morning. I don't need to tell you what would happen if the media got a hold of this. It would shut us down and all would be lost."

Littleton nodded, the shock still plain on his face. "We're at a critical point. A breakthrough could happen any day now. In fact, Ray was working on some very promising genetic splicing."

Jurgenczak stared at the geneticist and wondered if the man was lying and knew what Howe really thought of Gentel's genetic engineering approach to solving the T-gene. *I must test him. It's good to know who the faithful are.*

"Actually Dr. Howe disagreed with you. He was certain that replacing specific genes in a woman's unfertilized egg would never work. In fact, he believed the solution would be found before chromosomal DNA replication began at the end of the Cambrian period."

"I don't believe it for one moment," Littleton said adamantly.

Jurgenczak weighed the man's answer. It was a good and a bad thing. Good that he was one of the faithful and wasn't helping Dr. Howe betray Gentel. But it was bad that the head of

Gentel's genetics division hadn't considered the possibility that gene splicing was going nowhere.

Jurgenczak checked the time. The Inner Circle meeting started in three minutes. "I haven't time to revisit your genetics approach now. Time is running out. If we are to succeed with God's holy plan for saving humanity, I must keep an open mind for any solution – and so must the people working for me. For now, follow my lead in the meeting. I'm hoping Derek can confirm Howe's ideas."

Chapter 10

Derek paused outside Gentel's main conference room and exhaled sharply. The meeting with Jurgenczak had gone the way he'd expected. Gentel's founder never got angry, not like normal people who shouted and slammed doors. In his quiet voice with the power of a volcano behind it, he told Derek to get the Inner Circle together in the main conference room at 3:15. Derek knocked and entered. Gentel's spacious conference room was like an atrium. Two of the walls were windows, and the ceiling was a spiderwork of tempered glass and metal framing. Exotic flowering trees leaned out from tiers of carved marble planters. Cast reproductions of Atlas supporting the world supported a glass oblong table around which bronze-and-leather chairs were arrayed. Two immense smart boards dominated the inside walls.

The atmosphere was soothing – and very misleading. Jurgenczak was the ultimate authority figure. Known as "The Impaler" behind his back, he had reduced more than one Gentel scientist to tears in this room. Jurgenczak acquired his nickname for the way he shredded a colleague's findings with that same powerful quiet voice that left the scientist feeling as if he had been staked to the ground.

Derek took a seat beside Jurgenczak and quickly glanced around the table at the others. The four men seated in that room were among the greatest scientific minds of their generation, and as such, each represented the cutting edge in his field: Frank Littleton was a pioneer in genetics. Yoshi Yamato was Gentel's biochemistry genius. He had the strangest pair of eyes Derek had ever seen in a Japanese. The irises were golden with green flecks in them. Derek's specialty was evolutionary biology and extinction theory.

But the master of them all was Arne Jurgenczak, the world's foremost cellular biologist. His presence was impressive: a mane of long white hair fell to his shoulders. His eyes were the deepest blue Derek had ever seen. Born amid the rubble of Warsaw at the end of World War II, Jurgenczak escaped the Communists with his family ten years later and emigrated to America. His mother brought him up in the Catholic faith and there were rumors he was headed for the priesthood before he turned to genetics. Derek classified him as a fanatic churchman. But his faith never interfered with his science. When it came to the Terminator Gene, no one on Earth was more qualified to talk about it. A member of the Human Genome Project, Jurgenczak had discovered it while looking for point mutations in the chromosomal junk of a woman's fertilized egg. To his amazement a unique group of proteins emerged and produced a *ribozyme* that somehow catalyzed a process leading to de-differentiating embryos and miscarriage.

Dr. Ray Howe's face appeared on both Smart boards. Jurgenczak let them listen to Howe's analysis of Gentel's research efforts before he cut it off. He stared at each man with eyes like ice that made each of them wince. The dull gray light pouring through the skylight and spilling onto the table reflected the dismal mood of the room. No one wanted to be the first to speak.

"Did any of you know about this?" Jurgenczak demanded, his question cutting through the silence.

Yoshi said, "I also received a flash-drive from Dr. Howe. I haven't looked at it yet." They plugged it in and watched: an exact copy of the one sent to Derek.

When it was finished, Jurgenczak spoke. His quiet voice held a great measure of disbelief. "You get a flash-drive from a dead man and you don't bother to listen to what he has to say?"

Yoshi's face flushed but he rallied and said, "My team worked late last night on a synthetic protein we thought might inhibit the expression of the T-gene. I didn't know he had died until Derek told me about the meeting."

Jurgenczak turned his gaze on Littleton, the head of Ray

Howe's lab. "What about you, Frank? You were his friend. Damn, you brought him here and he walked right out of your lab with this information."

Littleton answered smoothly, "I'm sorry, Arne. I had no idea he was planning to go public with the T-gene."

Jurgenczak nodded. "Nothing got out to the media. We dodged a bullet today. We won't be so lucky next time. I want all of you to go over security protocols with Hawke. We can't have anyone knowing what's going on. Especially that Gentel hasn't been able to solve the problem yet."

"We're still on target with the genetic approach," Littleton said. "It's a matter of hitting the right combination."

"As much as we're committed to a genetic breakthrough to remove the T-gene," Jurgenczak said, "the clock is ticking and we don't have an answer."

"We'll get it," Littleton insisted.

"Your top researcher doesn't...didn't agree," Jurgenczak said stiffly. He looked over at Derek. "Derek, you're the evolutionary biologist. What was Howe talking about?"

Derek had spent the last half hour probing his own thoughts and memory banks, trying to come up with an idea of what Howe was hinting at with his puzzling statement: *A developmental issue straight out of the Cambrian*. But his mind kept drawing a blank. Howe was onto something. Cambrian biochemistry and genetics was so little understood. It held secrets paleontologists had been trying to unravel for years. *Something to do with life's early evolutionary development during the Cambrian.*

He was about to shake his head when an idea struck him. He was unable to accept it at first. It was too radical; it felt like the last hope of a drowning man. But the idea wouldn't go away and all he could think was, *Maybe there is a way*.

"Derek!" Jurgenczak's voice cut through his thoughts and brought him back to the conference room. "Was Dr. Howe onto something?"

Baron Derek Simon smiled. "I think so. At least I think we need to give it a go and see what happens."

"Sounds as though you have an idea for an approach," Yoshi Yamato said.

"A little something," Derek answered with typical British understatement.

"Care to share it with us?" Littleton asked. He didn't like the tall Englishman and thought his ideas about evolutionary biology were unfounded. But Jurgenczak was right. Gentel needed to solve the T-gene problem now if the company was going to have any chance at all to save humanity.

"While I was at Yale, I had a grad student working for me who through some extremely hard work came upon a way to extract genetic material from 500-million-year-old fossil *brachiopods*.

"And you think this relates to what Ray was talking about?" Littleton pressed, clearly not buying it.

Derek shrugged. "It's a start. If we could bring my former grad student here to repeat her experiments, perhaps we could get a look at the biochemistry of a creature from the Cambrian Era."

"Why not have my lab do it?" Yoshi Yamato offered. "We can duplicate her research as easily as she can."

"Maybe. But there were, as I recall, some concerns over her process. No one at Yale could duplicate her results."

Littleton laughed. "And you want us to put time and resources into a process that can't be repeated?"

Derek looked at Jurgenczak. The old man held all the power and was the only one Derek really needed to convince. "Like I said, it's a place to start. I for one would love to have a look at some Cambrian genetics."

Jurgenczak drummed his fingers on the table. "Get her," he said at last.

Derek said, "I haven't talked with her in more than ten years and she may not want to see me or even hear from me. Not to worry though, I know someone who's kept up with her."

"Convince her to join us. Give her whatever she needs – money, a lab, even information, but do it quickly."

"Surely she's not to be told everything?" Littleton said.

Jurgenczak fixed the geneticist with a stare. "At the same time our security protocols will be upgraded. Frank, look in on this new employee from time to time. If you find anything out of the ordinary, inform me and Gentel's security chief immediately."

After Jurgenczak left the room, Yoshi reached over and pressed a key on the computer keyboard. Ray Howe's face vanished from the smart boards. The Japanese scientist took out a white tissue and wiped the perspiration from his face. He turned toward Littleton and bowed his head slightly. "I was sorry to hear about your friend. I'm afraid I did not know him."

Littleton shrugged. "Ray was a good guy. I wish I'd known what he was planning," he lied. "I could have brought him back to my place and worked it out."

The Japanese nodded. "I understand."

Derek eyed Littleton. The American said all the right things concerning Ray's death, but his eyes didn't register like those of a man who'd just lost a friend. He watched Littleton leave through the same door as Jurgenczak. *Odd, Jurgenczak pretty much glossed over Frank's security breach concerning Howe. And why didn't Littleton get a USB drive?*

Chapter 11

Oklahoma

Leroy Parker ladled water onto the heated stones. Scalding vapor filled the close, domed chamber. Sweat stung his eyes, and his gray braids hung limp down his back. His breath came in shallow, searing gasps.

But he didn't leave. He endured the discomfort: his granddaughter needed his help.

Lucille lived twenty miles away, in Lawton, where her husband, a Kiowa, was stationed at Fort Sill. The young couple had had three miscarriages. The army doctors could find nothing wrong with either of them. Their Christian priest had prayed on their behalf, but still Lucille was unable to complete a pregnancy. Now she'd embraced her Comanche heritage and sought her grandfather's help.

So Leroy had gone alone into the sweat lodge. The low domed structure had been built in the traditional manner from bent willow branches and buffalo hides. A shallow pit was dug in the earth at the entrance so that participants entered into the lodge as though crawling into the womb of Mother Earth. Inside, the ember glow of the superheated river rocks was the only light. A water bucket with its buffalo-horn dipper rested on the hard packed earth next to the stones.

Leroy had chanted his spirit songs and invoked the spirits of his grandfathers. Now, on the fourth round of steam, his heart opened.

He seemed to float in the Earth's womb. Images materialized on the still surface of the water in the nearby bucket: hundreds of men and women – all races, all colors – waited outside the lodge in the withering Oklahoma heat. Behind them the steeply-sloped ridges of the Wichita Mountains rose darkly against the day, their gabbro peaks of granite and rhyolite gleaming like tonsured heads above dark forests of blackjack oak, hickory and pine.

Leroy floated above the crowd that scattered across the plain. Some sat, some stood. All were naked, and tried to cover their genitals with their hands. Suddenly he realized that none of them cast a shadow. A moan went up from the crowd, and then another, and another, until all the people sobbed and shrieked, and a great howling fear took hold of them. People gathered together in small groups and wept. Someone jostled another person and was pushed back. More shoving, and then they began to fight. The fighting spread like ripples in a pond. Men and women tore at each other with their fingers. Men beat other men with their fists. Women leaped on other women, scratching at their eyes. Some fastened their teeth on the necks of their victims. Leroy flew above them and implored them to stop, but the wailing of the injured and the screams of the dying drowned out his words.

The water pictures vanished, and Leroy cried out, "All my relations!" Instantly the entrance flap was pulled back and hands reached in for him.

He emerged like a newborn into the slanting early morning light. His granddaughter and her husband pulled him to his feet, but when he looked past their eyes, a knife-like pain seared his belly and he fell, clutching himself. They cast no shadows.

Chapter 12

"I just want to have a child," Lucille told her grandfather. "A Comanche child." They sat at a weathered picnic table. The ramada overhead cast a lattice of shadow across them. Beside her, Lucille's husband sipped a beer.

Leroy Parker looked at his granddaughter. She was a modern young woman who was ready to take her place in the white world. It was conceivable that her great-great-grandfather, Quanah Parker, would have been proud of her.

"What do I have to do, Grandfather?" she asked. "What must I do to have a child?"

How could Leroy tell his granddaughter what he had seen? Especially when he was so uncertain of the vision's meaning.

"Come back in one month," he replied, "and ask me your question again. Now come into the house. Your grandmother has gathered herbs to help you relax, to open you, so the Great Spirit can enter and help you."

He stood slowly, grimacing at the pain in his knees, and started toward the house. Suddenly Lucille gripped his arm.

"I don't understand what's wrong." Her voice was filled with anguish. "We just want to have a baby. Why can't we?"

As Leroy reached out to comfort her, a wave of grief swept over him – his granddaughter's agony amplified by that of millions of young women across the world. He would have fallen, but Lucille's husband reached out to steady him.

"It's just my arthritis," he lied. "Go on ahead, I need to rest a little more."

He waved them away, and they continued walking toward the house. As Leroy watched them, he reached out with his being. The grief washed over him in waves. The Great Spirit had chosen him for something. Leroy knew he must find greater clarity. Acquiring the *puha* – the power – to interpret the vision would require a spirit journey, but at Leroy's age, and given his advanced arthritis, such a journey was beyond him. But he would make the sacrifice and travel to the source of all life.

Chapter 13

Omaha, Nebraska

Kira stopped her Highlander in the gravel driveway that led to Jack's home. The Victorian-style house was set well back from the road and overlooked the bluffs of the Missouri River. The front lawn was immaculate – short green grass bordered by the riotous blooms of wild prairie flowers. The house's gray stonewalls, large windows and the immense wrap-around porch invited visitors to come in, but Kira stayed in the SUV, drumming her fingers on the steering wheel. Her anger had gone, and she was once more under control, but the shame and humiliation of losing that control in front of her best friend made her unusually timid. Twice her hands went to the keys in the ignition, intending to drive away. Finally summoning her courage, she got out and went up the wide stone steps to knock on the oak door.

Jack answered almost immediately and Kira wondered if he had been expecting her. He said nothing but enveloped her in one of his mammoth hugs. He motioned her to follow him. Kira kicked off her shoes and strode across the bare wood floors. She noted that for such a big man, Jack made no sound as he crossed the entryway and threaded through the many rooms to the kitchen in the back. It seemed impossible that the floors of such an old building wouldn't respond to his seven-foot frame with squeaks.

The house was as Kira remembered it – sparsely furnished with period pieces from American history. Every room had a different motif and nothing was less than one hundred years old. The only nod Jack made to modern convention was a sixty-inch plasma TV and a Nintendo Wii game console in the living room. She once asked him about it. Jack had shrugged and answered,

"The Dali Lama reads comic books."

They silently passed by the servants' stairs leading to the second and third floors, where the home's seven bedrooms were. Jack slept in a different one each night and his maid had to comb through the house every morning to wake him for work. "She likes the exercise," Jack had once explained to Kira.

The kitchen was spacious with large windows overlooking the Missouri River. A wood stove, ancient ice box and a cast-iron sink lined one wall. A low table occupied a niche in one corner. There were no chairs, only a pair of *zafu* meditation cushions to sit on. A thin ribbon of steam floated upward from two pale blue porcelain cups before each cushion. Still without speaking, Jack took one side and motioned Kira to the other. He lifted his teacup and smelled the aroma before sipping. Kira did likewise and was pleasantly surprised by the gentle fragrance of jasmine.

After several minutes of silence, Kira felt more relaxed than she had all day. She gathered the courage to ask the question she needed to ask. "I am an angry person, aren't I?"

Nodding, Jack said, "Let me speak to anger."

Nonplussed, Kira shook her head.

"Let me speak to anger," Jack repeated.

"I don't understand."

Jack smiled. "Play along. Our ego, our personality is made up of many voices, if you will, each with its own role to play. Anger is one."

Kira didn't want to go back to that dark place. "I don't know about this, Jack."

Jack shifted forward and placed his large hand over hers. "Say, 'I am anger.'"

Swallowing against her fear, Kira said, "I am anger."

"As anger, how does Kira feel about you?"

After a long pause, Kira heard the tiny voice of an eight-year-old girl in her mind and said aloud, "She doesn't like me. She's afraid of me."

"What's your role?"

Kira's little girl voice answered, "If she had let me grow and mature I would be a great partner to her. I could definitely help her see clearly."

Jack nodded and said, "So Kira sort of keeps you locked up in the basement…in the dark."

Anger welled up and the voice answered defiantly, "That makes me mad, but I come out anyhow."

"How?"

"I come out like a two-year-old." The tiny eight-year-old voice laughed. "She's so afraid of me that she goes unconscious, then I can wreak havoc, have my own way."

"Is there another way you surreptitiously come out?"

More laughter and the little voice answered, "Sure. I make Kira overcompensate. She works so hard keeping me in the basement, she'll do anything not to let me come up."

Jack's voice remained gentle. "Can you take us back to the first time Kira felt that way?

The child voice paused for a long time and when it came back, terror laced its tone. "I was eight years old and my parents left me alone in my own tent in the Serengeti. They were ashamed of me and they wanted me to overcome my fear of chimpanzees. They left me alone all night in the tent. I was so frightened, I screamed and yelled. I was so angry that they would hurt me this way. Why would they do this to me? Why would they treat me this way if they loved me?" The little voice broke down in a quiet sob.

Kira looked up at Jack, tears rolling out of her blue eyes. The little voice sobbed, "I was so angry, but not at my parents. I was angry at myself because I thought I must have done something wrong. I was no good so they were punishing me. And I knew if I were perfect, they would never do this again. So all I had to do was be perfect."

A visceral scream poured out of Kira and she collapsed on the floor, quiet sobs of release flowing out of her.

Chapter 14

The sun hung a brilliant gem on the western horizon. Kira and Jack walked hand in hand along the bluffs of the Missouri River. Jack was talking about her past, specifically Derek Simon, and Kira was taking it all in. She couldn't remember if she had ever heard the story before. Quite likely she had but had refused to accept it. Now she listened, shaking her head at her blindness.

"Derek and I have kept in touch over the years. He told me that when you were working on your dissertation and the *salp* paper came out, he had completely forgotten about what he said to you in the Nevada desert about the naming of the *salp* and naming you a junior author on the paper."

"Do you believe him?" Kira asked.

"Yes. He said it was the enthusiasm of the find. There was so much going on that week."

Kira nodded. There had been a lot happening, and while the *salps* had been the highlight of the dig, they were only a small portion of the thousands of fossils that were collected and catalogued.

"The thing that he's truly sorry about is that he didn't do more to help you get a job."

Kira's mouth twisted in a wry grimace. "Yeah, that really made feel like I was back in the tent, waiting for the chimpanzees to come and eat me."

Jack smiled. "I suppose it would."

"Did he say why?"

"It was a combination of things. The beginning of the Human Genome Project and the huge excitement around the role paleontologists were discovering that extinctions played in evolution. Nobody was really interested in some far-out speculative ideas about early Cambrian biogenetics. What he never told you is that he made numerous inquiries about placements for you. But by then you had a reputation of being hard to get along with and he couldn't find anything for you."

Kira bit her lower lip and said, "I've always blamed Derek for the missing credit, and then not getting an appointment anywhere. After my PhD, I really came to hate him." She shook her head and laughed without any mirth in it. "Man, I have been so fucked up."

They walked a little farther up a hill that overlooked Omaha. The city spread out in front of them.

The downtown was not what Kira expected. It was vibrant city of new buildings. "So what happens now?" she asked.

Jack cracked the knuckles of one huge hand. "Once the light of awareness has exposed that little knot of constricted energy, it can never hold you captive again. You'll move on." Pointing to the Omaha skyline, he added, "Just as Omaha did."

Looking at the avant-garde architecture, Kira realized she could have been in any modern American city.

"Impressive, isn't it?" Jack said. "I want you to pay attention to three particular buildings. I'm sure you can pick them out."

Kira peered at the skyline. It took her a moment, but eventually she saw the pattern Jack alluded to. Three of the newest buildings were set roughly in a line running north to south. She pointed them out.

"Good eye. Not everyone recognizes the pattern. What's even more interesting is that seen from the air, they form a perfect equilateral triangle."

Kira's eyes widened. "Something tells me that you don't believe this is a coincidence."

"As my father said, a man who believes in coincidences is destined to travel a very short distance in life."

"So what are they?" Kira asked.

Jack indicated the one forming the southern most point of the triangle. It was a vast expanse of glass and steel with a series of dramatic balconies leading to a pyramid at the top. "Keewatin

Industrial, the largest construction firm in the world. It's owned by George Drake. There isn't a large-scale project anywhere on the globe he doesn't have a finger in. Ultra-wealthy, philanthropic and powerful. Breakfast at the Kremlin, lunch at Buckingham Palace, dinner at the White House all on the same day."

"The next point in the triangle is Bartnum Haggerty." The building was a giant spire of glass that mimicked the Washington Monument, only it was home to a complex of financial institutions from all over the world. "I'm sure I don't have to tell you who owns that one."

"The richest man in the world."

"Of course there's that. But it isn't just the wealth. That building represents the power of the Rockefellers, Guggenheims, Rothschilds and the Toyodas all rolled into one man, the Oracle of Omaha. He sits on the boards of the most influential companies in the world. He controls the economies of billions of people."

"And the third point in the triangle?" Kira asked.

Jack scratched his ear with a blunt finger. "A relative newcomer – Gentel Systems. Gentel's power isn't in construction or finance. It lies in bioengineering. From crops to humans, they're on the cutting edge of the science of the age – genetics. The founder is, Arne Jurgenczak."

"I remember him from my Yale days. He was a big player in the Human Genome Project."

Jack smiled that curious smile of his when his intuition knew more than the facts were presenting. "Three years before the Genome Project was completed Jurgenczak vanished. That same year, Gentel Systems began in Omaha. Since then, depending upon who you talk to, Gentel's either going to turn the planet into a Garden of Eden or send it straight to hell. Impressive city, huh."

"And all these years I thought it was just another of those old industrial Midwestern towns."

Jack didn't smile or laugh like Kira thought he would. He stared at the skyline for a long time and when he spoke again his voice was unusually serious. "Hardly that. Those in the know say that Omaha controls the world but nobody knows it – yet. The big three companies all work together, sit on each other's boards of directors, and from what I can tell, a lot more is happening than scratching each other's backs."

"You seem surprisingly well connected."

"I've met all these guys. They come to my evening charity auctions and fundraisers for the aquarium and write big checks."

"And during the day you go out to lunch with their wives."

Jack grinned. "A guy can learn a lot that way."

"Like what?"

Jack stabbed a finger at Gentel. "Derek works there now. You want answers to the Jacobson's miscarriage and the others like it, talk to Derek." He smiled. "How's that for a bit of karmic irony?"

Chapter 15

Sioux City, Iowa

The tiny bungalow Dr. Kira Taylor rented was quiet, the only sounds coming from outside through the open windows – the chirping of crickets and the haunting hoot of the ubiquitous mourning doves. She listened, her heart beating slowly, loving the early morning, before she returned to her reading. Kira owned only three hardcopy books – a first edition of Darwin's *On the Origin of Species;* a signed copy of paleontologist Jay Gould's *Wonderful Life;* and American philosopher Ken Wilbur's *A Brief History of Everything.* They were dog-eared and battered. Most mornings she read from them before she went to work. She took a great measure of satisfaction as well as comfort that her three most prized possessions were with her always.

Darwin and Gould were stacked together, testaments to her first love of science – evolutionary biology. But this morning she opened *A Brief History of Everything* which Jack had given her five years ago. It had taken Kira nearly all of those five years to get her mind around Wilbur's central idea, an idea startling in its simplicity and yet profound in its ramifications. Wilbur posited a fundamental force that permeated everything since the first nano second after the big bang. He called it the force of ultimate creativity – the evolutionary pulse.

She flipped through the book reading favorite passages, when she remembered a post-it note Jack had placed inside the front cover. She had read it many times before, but after the events of the past couple of days, it took on a special significance. Kira read the quote aloud. "While some may think of equanimity as a dry neutrality of cool aloofness, mature equanimity produces a radiance and warmth of being. A mind filled with equanimity is without hostility and is without ill will. It is a mind that operates from an overflowing abundance, not from scarcity and fear."

A pang of self-doubt shot through Kira that her breakthrough yesterday was momentary and the angry part of her was still there ready to control her once again. Then Jack's words came back to her – "Once the light of awareness has exposed that little knot of constricted energy, it can never hold you captive again. You'll move on."

She'd already called her boss to say she needed to move on. She wouldn't be renewing her contract at St. Luke's. She was now using up her remaining vacation days. Whatever she did next would be a real choice.

Kira's phone pinged. She saw that it was an email from Jack about Derek. The message contained a link and the words, "Click on this link. It's an encrypted line and you'll be able to talk to Derek without anyone overhearing your conversation. FYI, he's at Gentel's research facility in Wales."

Taken aback by the cloak and dagger language, Kira hesitated. *Do I really want to talk to Derek?* But the answer to that question didn't matter. Kira knew she had to make the call. She checked the time and saw that it would be 3:00 p.m. in Wales.

Bluetoothing her phone to her computer, she punched the link. The Skype connection was almost instantaneous, and for the first time in more than a decade, she saw Derek and heard his familiar upper-class British accent. "Who's this?" he asked in his laconic manner of speaking.

Derek was still tanned, fair-haired with blue eyes, though now he was in his early sixties. Kira cleared her throat and said a little louder than she intended, "Derek, it's Kira Taylor."

"I can see that." His mouth turned down in a slight frown. "Very strange."

"Strange weird or strange funny?"

"Funny, I suppose. I was just thinking that it was important that I speak with you and here you ring me up. In fact, I'm surprised that you're even talking to me after..."

"Everything," Kira prompted.

Derek swallowed. "Yeah, everything. I let you down more than once. I should've apologized a long time ago."

His uncharacteristic embarrassment might have pleased Kira before yesterday, but now she leaped above that feeling and said, "Accepted."

Silence again and Kira couldn't tell if her one-time mentor was relieved or chagrined. "Good," Derek said at last. "So you first. Why are you calling me?"

"A mystery I've encountered. I've been puzzled by some early morphogenic anomalies associated with miscarriages. Jack Kelley said you work for Gentel now, and he said you're the only one who can help me find the answers. So you left Yale? I suppose Abigail liked that decision."

"She couldn't be happier, you remember how much she hated New Haven. Are you married?"

"Not yet. I am…was an E.R. doc in Sioux City, Iowa."

"So, you were saying about morphogenic anomalies."

"Women miscarrying in the embryonic stage of development. But it's not as simple as that. These miscarriages are like nothing I've ever seen before. They all occur in the seventh to eighth week, and it's as though the embryo's cells are suddenly triggered to de-differentiate and then are—"

"Reabsorbed by the placenta," Derek interrupted.

Kira blinked in surprise. She hadn't known what to expect when she told Derek about her mystery, but the fact that he seemed to know about it already was somewhat unsettling. "Yes."

"Curiouser and curiouser," Derek said. "That's what I was going to speak with you about." Silence again, then, "How much time do you have…I mean, can we talk more?"

"All the time you need."

"Good, because this is going to take some time. Have you ever heard of something called the Terminator Gene?"

"You're joking?"

"Far from it. The best way to understand the Terminator Gene is from the standpoint of extinction theory."

"Your specialty," Kira said, recalling his lectures on it. Derek had hypothesized that extinctions were not solely the result of meteor impacts, climatic change, and so on, but that the fossil record showed species have finite life spans: species emerge and disappear even when no cause is apparent. He went on to say that Neanderthals had not been wiped out by *homo sapiens* but that their species had reached the end of its designated life span and died.

"Gentel's known for fifteen years now that and least every mammalian species possesses a Terminator Gene. After a given number of generations, a kind of 'off' switch is triggered, and the species dies out."

"And you're implying that the miscarriages are..." Kira couldn't finish her sentence. Suddenly all she could see was Jeanette Jacobson's ultrasound.

She realized Derek was still speaking. His voice sounded hollow and distant and unreal. "Kira, the miscarriages are the Terminator Gene expressing itself in humans. If we don't solve this crisis within two years, maybe much less, it's the end of the human species. We at Gentel have formed a group of the brightest researchers and thinkers in the world to work on a solution. I head up the evolutionary biology section."

Kira could only wonder what her face showed. Derek's was so serious that she almost didn't recognize him. She saw for the first time that he really had aged in the last ten years. Dark circles were under his eyes and his face sagged.

"So why were you going to call me?" was all she could think to say.

"I want to try a new approach and it involves your graduate work at Yale on those inarticulate *brachiopods* from the Cambrian period."

Brachiopods, shelled marine invertebrates of the phylum *Brachiopoda,* fell into two main groups: inarticulates and articulates. Inarticulates originated in the Cambrian period more than 550 million years ago. The earliest forms were no larger than the tip of Kira's little finger. Articulate forms developed fifty million years later. Having evolved a hinge to hold the two halves of their shell together, articulates succeeded so well they became a dominant life form from the Ordovician to the Permian periods. The inarticulates, on the other hand, retreated into a tiny biological niche and had remained virtually unchanged to the present day.

"Yale's a long time gone, Derek. I shredded all my notes, dumped everything when I left to go to med school. I don't know how much I remember."

Derek's eyes narrowed and he said slowly, "I wouldn't be asking this of you if the fate of the human race didn't hang in the balance. Gentel is out of options and you might be it, I'm afraid."

A most unusual tangle of energy surged through Kira's body, bordering on ecstasy. Quieting her emotions, she looked for the source and found it. From the moment she had laid eyes on Jeanette Jacobson's de-differentiated embryo, she intuited it was something much greater than a lone woman's heartbreak. And now that something had brought her and Derek together. *The evolutionary pulse, Wilber called it.*

"What are you proposing?" Kira asked.

"That you come work for Gentel directly under one of the greatest biochemists alive today, Yoshi Yamato. Of course, you'll have your own lab, no interference, and you get to call the shots."

Derek said, "One more thing. Complete secrecy about the project is paramount. Can you do that?"

"You'll have to give me a reason."

"We believe the world can't know about this until we find a

solution. It's a global political problem the world isn't prepared to deal with; just like it can't deal with climate change."

Kira knew this is what she had to do. "When do I start?" she heard herself ask.

"I can send the company jet to Sioux City tomorrow. Yoshi will be on it and can fill you in on the details then."

"I'll be ready," Kira said.

Kira signed off and looked thoughtfully at her computer. *The imminent extinction of the human species...it just doesn't seem possible that evolution would take us from dirt to computers and then nothing. Fuck. Fuck. Fuck.*

Chapter 16

Leroy Parker sat alone on an east-facing outcropping of rock called Medicine Bluff, in the foothills of Oklahoma's Wichita Mountains. The state maintained a buffalo preserve on the grassy plain below. A few of the five hundred animals were dimly visible there under the gibbous moon. A winding stream reflected silver light through the trees along its banks.

Medicine Bluff was a Comancheria power spot. Shamans and warriors had come here for generations to experience visions or to gather power for their quests. His great ancestor, Quanah Parker had made many such visits.

Beside him, Leroy's campfire was reduced to a few glowing embers. He knew what he must do, but he could not yet bring himself to reach for the pipe. Leroy was not a shaman. He was only a simple medicine man who used the sweat lodge to help others purify their spirits, to give them a starting place for healing. Mostly he helped his tribe's young men and women find a path out of adolescence.

But he'd been shown a vision more in keeping with shamanic revelation. The shamans of long ago were powerful men who traveled far into the other world to build up their *puha* – their power. Leroy felt insignificant in comparison. Yet the Great Spirit had chosen him. He prayed for courage to do the Great Spirit's will.

Breathing deeply, sending air to the very center of his body, he emptied his mind. He picked up the sacred pipe of his grandfathers. The bowl was carved from red Minnesota pipestone, the stem from white ash. It had passed to him from the holy men who came before him.

Before leaving his house, he'd filled it with plains tobacco – *kinnikkinnick,* made from the dried leaves and bark of the bearberry bush. To this mixture, Leroy's great grandfather,

Quanah Parker, had added the trumpet-shaped, purple flowers of the jimsonweed, or *Datura inoxia*, a flowering plant related to the deadly nightshade family and was a powerful hallucinogen. When smoked, the plant released great quantities of the alkaloids atropine and hyoscine into the body. With it, his grandfather claimed to have been able to see the future.

Leroy studied the pipe. The stone was carved in the shape of a horse's head. The mane flared back toward the stem and the smoker; the bowl opened between the horse's ears, melding into the long face and flaring nostrils. As he stared at the bowl, Leroy heard the pounding of hooves and felt the rush of wind on his face. The pipe evoked a horse memory in Leroy, a memory so ancient among the Comanche Nation it could well have been forged among ancestral herds on the plains of Asia.

Leroy looked up at the constellations and the waxing moon. He felt good and clear. The time was right. Reverently he pointed the pipe to the four directions, and then to Father Sky and Mother Earth. He asked his grandfathers for help; he beseeched the moon, the sun and the Earth for a smooth trail; he invoked his spirit guide, the red-tailed hawk, to show him the way. He asked for the power of the rapid-filled river. He needed that bit of churn to ride until he learned the meaning of his vision in the sweat lodge.

Using a forked stick, he lifted an ember from the small fire. His hands shook slightly and his arthritic fingers ached. He lit the pipe and inhaled deeply four times, expelling the smoke slowly each time. After he inhaled a fifth time, he held the smoke deep in his lungs for as long as he could, and then let it trickle out slowly. Respectfully, he lay the pipe near the fire and waited.

Chapter 17

There was a flash of brilliant light. Leroy was flying over the prairie from his vision. Another flash swept this away to reveal a shallow sea, covering mossy, grass-like plants. Among the blades he observed jelly-like creatures no bigger than the tip of his finger, adrift in perpetual gloom. He was somehow aware they were the earliest animal ancestors of every living creature.

A third flash of light changed the scene yet again. A river flowed through a landscape of sagebrush and greasewood. He traced its course past falls and rapids to the foot of a snow-topped mountain. When he turned to face the setting sun and get his bearings, something pulled him upward to a plateau where stones were arranged like a large spoked wheel – a medicine wheel, source of power and healing. Leroy hovered there for what felt like hours. At last he heard the rocks singing to him, not those of the wheel, but stones that lay deep within the earth. Their song called forth primordial memories: he became a primitive creature gazing up through a watery heaven toward a wavering, glimmering firmament.

When Leroy had memorized the songs of the stones and emerged from his watery vision, he studied the landscape around him. South and east of the plateau stood a single mountain, uneven patches of summer snow trapped in the shade of snags and overhangs.

There was another flash, and the trance ended. Night was becoming day. He had never seen the landscape of his vision, yet it felt familiar, as though he'd traveled those valleys and hills many times.

He knew he must find that place.

Second Division

The new view of evolution is that the evolution of animal body-plans occurred by a different process than that which controls evolution today. The differences between animal phyla must be explained by a process that operated in the early Cambrian, but not before or since.

-Baron Derek Simon, Oxford Lectures

Chapter 18

Late in the afternoon, Kira Taylor looked out over the bluestem grass of Sioux City's restored prairie as she prepared for her last run here. She was thinking clearly, better than at any time in the past. Ten years after giving up academia in her beloved field of evolutionary biology, Kira was returning to it.

Once she said yes to Derek's proposal for her own lab, a whirlwind of activity followed: packing what she needed, the rest was put into storage, including her car. She cancelled utilities, gave her landlord notice and a post-dated check for the last month's rent, and had her mail forwarded to Jack.

The prairie path turned down toward a small stand of trees and crossed a creek that bisected the park. She splashed through it easily. Once more she was reminded of Tanzania only this time the memory was good. Today, to the surprise of her parents, she Skyped them. After years of estrangement, whatever resentment she once held had all but disappeared. She even talked to them about their latest research on releasing zoo-bred chimpanzees back into the wilds of Africa.

She followed a looping trail back to her car. Her run finished, she texted Jack. *How's this for karma. Boarding Gentel's private corporate jet to join Derek in Wales. I'm going to be duplicating my experiment when I was at Yale.*

Jack wrote back, *Will you be able to pull it off?*

I'm sure I can.

Good luck. Remember karma is only cause and effect.

That night she was too excited to sleep. Instead, she Googled Yoshi Yamato. The list of his accomplishments was Nobel Prize material until seven years ago. Then he seemed to drop off the face of the Earth. But before that the Japanese biochemist had set the world on its ear by figuring out a way to synthesize a hormone that produced a protein in the bone marrow that attached itself to white blood cells. The protein then targeted cancers with massive amounts of white blood cells. What piqued Kira's curiosity was that cancer cells are basically tissue cells that have de-differentiated much the same as Jeanette Jacobson's embryo. Yoshi's treatment was like giving the body's immune system a giant boost.

Kira read on. *This is no coincidence,* she told herself. *Somehow de-differentiated cells are at the heart of what is taking place.*

The Internet was a rich treasure trove of new insights and perspectives on evolutionary theory. What once seemed hard – phylogenic evolution, stochastic calculations of molecular change, molecular clock estimates, and rate-variable methods – all seemed easy now. What was most remarkable was that essentially in the ten years she had been away, new research had thrown into question evolution orthodoxy. Remarkably, her graduate school theories – that the biochemical basis of the Cambrian explosion of complex life varied in some fundamental ways from everything we know about genetics today – now had a strong camp of supporters, including her one-time mentor, Derek Simon.

Chapter 19

Leroy Parker sat in his Dodge Ram truck in the gravel parking lot under a rapidly bronzing sky. On the front seat next to him lay his medicine bundle containing the wing feathers of his spirit guide, the red-tailed hawk, his sacred pipe and a package of kinnikkinnick. In one pocket of his blue denim shirt he carried a drawing of the medicine wheel from his vision. In the other he carried an unopened pack of Camels. He felt guilty about the cigarettes. He had quit smoking twenty-five years ago but had picked up this pack on impulse at his last stop.

The view from the cab was stunning. Far to the north Sheep Mountain speared the underbellies of low clouds. And to the south Bald Mountain stood out like a gray-green thumb. To the west he could just make out the Bearclaw Mountains that edged Yellowstone National Park. He had never traveled this far north before, and sitting here, he felt a little ripple of fear that he had made the long journey all for nothing.

Like the ancient shamans of his tribe, Leroy had left his family, forsaking the rich comforts of Comanche tribal and family life in order to locate the medicine wheel of his vision and find the meaning behind the strange sea with its even stranger creatures.

Finding the medicine wheel had been much easier for him than it would have been for his forbearers. After all, now it was a National Historic Landmark in northern Wyoming. Traveling by interstate took only two days. He drove I-35 through the rain-starved southern plains until he reached I-70 in Kansas. From there he headed west into Denver, where he stayed with a director friend who once used him in a documentary about the Comanche homecoming. From Denver, it was almost a straight shot north, always keeping the Rocky Mountains on his left. In his father's time, the tall peaks were snow-covered, and glaciers filled the cirques throughout the hot summer months. Now they were barren rock. Just outside of Sheridan, he turned onto Highway 14, which wound deep into the Bighorn Mountains.

Late in the evening of the second day, Leroy turned off 14 onto a narrow paved road with no guardrails. Fifteen minutes brought him to the parking lot. Picking up his medicine bundle, Leroy descended from the truck gingerly, the pain in his knee joints withering after two days of driving. Still, he knew he had to make the journey since his granddaughter depended upon him. The quarter mile walk to the medicine wheel took another fifteen minutes, his joints protesting all the way.

A cairn of stones marked the center, from which a web of thirty spokes radiated outward to a rim of more stones. Surrounding everything was a fence. Thousands of small medicine pouches, adorned with feathers and ribbons, hung from the top two wires. The evening breeze made a strange fluted noise when it passed through rattling the small leather bags.

Leroy carefully unfolded the piece of paper with his vision drawing. The medicine wheel and the drawing did not match up, but after walking around it clockwise as though following the path of the sun, Leroy could feel power emanating from the ground. By the time he finished one circuit, the medicine wheel had eased the arthritis in his joints. He knew shamans must be alert for any hints from the other world that indicate places of power and understanding, and he eagerly prepared for another vision quest. Chanting his spirit songs and smoking the sacred pipe, Leroy quested for answers to his disturbing vision of an ocean-flooded land, inhabited by tiny, shelled creatures no bigger than the tip of his little finger.

Though the familiar flash of light followed, nothing happened. The same vision as before returned – the vast shallow sea, the medicine wheel and the urgency of that he must find it in order to fulfill his shamanic quest. Nothing more.

Leroy spent another day and night, moving around the wheel,

sitting in various spots, trying to find the correct conjunction of his body and the wheel's configuration in order to open himself to its power. After two days, he was as ignorant as before he arrived. The only benefit was that his arthritis vanished by the second morning, as yet not to return.

Finally, Leroy gave up. He had failed. Dispirited, he left the site and started the long drive home. He headed west toward Yellowstone National Park. On the way he slowed down to read a sign indicating the Wind River Indian Reservation, home of the Shoshoni Indians, forbearers of the Comanche nation. On the top of the sign sat a red-tailed hawk.

Chapter 20

The Menai Straits were quiet. Even the traffic was subdued with half the normal people for a Friday. *Everything's battened down for the storm building out on the Irish Sea,* thought Baron Derek Simon as he walked along the quay. He liked the silence and preferred the space to a crowded bar. He glanced over at his companion, Yoshi Yamato. The diminutive Japanese scientist had his hands shoved deep into his coat pockets against the chill wind. Derek smiled to himself, knowing the biochemist preferred coffee houses, the more intimate, the better. But what Derek had to tell him about Kira was best said where no one could over hear them. That meant being outside with a storm just a few hours away, bearing down on Caernarfon.

Yoshi inhaled and his nose wrinkled in disgust. "Derek, I would much prefer the aroma of an Americano to this," he said pointing at the slime-covered rocks of the Straits.

Derek smiled. He thought the lowering tide left a pleasant smell of seaweed and tide pools. "Perhaps you're right, Yoshi, but I like the privacy, so bear with me."

The Japanese nodded. "I know you don't buy that DNA is the be-all and end-all…the scientific solution to biology's unsolved questions. There are such mysteries here for me."

"You and I agree on that," Derek said. "Have you ever thought about how through you and me evolution is contemplating itself. Think of it, we're products of the Big Bang, products of the evolutionary process itself here on Earth, and we are investigating the mysteries of evolution. Strange, don't you think?"

"Yes, it is. Do you believe that was what Ray was talking about? That Gentel is lost in a forest of gene babble?"

"Perhaps. The way I look at it, evolution has always been about novelty, and bringing into existence something new, something more complex. Geneticists like Littleton and

Jurgenczak have turned the most powerful force in the universe into the likes of a medieval apothecary. Instead of acknowledging evolution's creative power, they are peddling leeches and practicing bloodletting. Gentel needs to step back and take in a new perspective."

"And you think Dr. Taylor can do this?"

Derek nodded. *My gut says yes.*

The Japanese biochemist stopped and stared out into the gathering storm clouds. He seemed to be lost in something and Derek decided to wait him out instead of pushing to get him to talk.

"Yes, I agree with you, Derek. But I have my own reasons. I haven't told anyone but I've thought for some time now that the T-gene and Hox genes are somehow connected."

Hox genes were a group of genes that were poorly understood. They controlled basic body plans. Small changes in this set of genes could have huge consequences, basically creating a new species, geologically speaking, overnight. They acted with such overwhelming influence there were no intermediate stages. No missing links to be found.

Derek wasn't surprised by Yoshi's idea. He had wondered about it himself. "Why keep it a secret?"

Yoshi shrugged. "Littleton must have seen the connection himself, but he never mentioned it at any of the Inner Circle meetings. I found that odd. Why not mention it? Then you come up with Kira Taylor's graduate work." He smiled and his eyes narrowed. "I read her thesis, her conjectures and the stunning results she had with the cancer cells. Incredible, if true."

Derek waited for Yoshi to get to the point.

"But it went nowhere, Derek. She went nowhere. Her research has been forgotten. What happened?"

"As a PhD. candidate Kira Taylor was a hard worker, persistent. But let me tell you she was a hothead, angry at the world, nearly impossible to get along with."

Derek pulled out of his pocket a buff-colored piece of sandstone covered with tiny white concentric rings of inarticulate *brachiopods*. They were breathtaking patterns of orange, brown, and yellow. Some shells were disk-shaped, others were cones; still others were ellipsoid like tiny footballs. Their delicate beauty was mesmerizing.

He handed the sandstone to Yoshi. "These *brachiopod* shells are over 500 million years old. They're from a site in northwestern Wisconsin, where they literally cover the rocks. Kira had the idea that she was going to extract DNA from these little buggers. She had a couple of amateur fossil collectors send literally a ton of rock to our lab at Yale. To make a long story short, she spent the better part of two years separating the tiny flecks of shell from their rock matrix, separating out the organic compounds from the mineralized part of the shell. The compound she succeeded in synthesizing she called SF-81. Fascinating stuff. A bizarre collection of amino acids and other unidentifiable biochemical stuff. But she didn't have the means at the time to do more than eliminate what it wasn't. With today's technology we can learn so much more, we can learn what it is."

"Did it really cause the cancer HeLa cells to be come normal tissue cells?" Yoshi asked.

HeLa cells were named for Henrietta Lacks, a thirty-one-year-old Black woman from Baltimore, Maryland, who had died of cervical cancer in 1951. Her cancer cells, however, lived on, assuming a life of their own and finding their way into labs across the world. By 2002, the biomass of her cancer cells had become greater than Henrietta had been in real life.

"Yes, that part was well confirmed by her rerunning the tests several times."

"That brings us back to de-differentiated cells – if her SF-81 really exists."

Derek frowned. He knew what Yoshi was hinting at, but he didn't believe it. Kira was nothing if not honest. He didn't believe then, nor now, that she had falsified her data.

Yoshi noted Derek's frown and he said, "I apologize, Derek for distressing you but it has to be said. No one was able to duplicate her work."

"That's true," Derek agreed. "Many tried but they couldn't do it. After her PhD defense, she left evolutionary biology altogether. Now she works as an emergency room doctor in Sioux City, Iowa. She never again worked on the method that isolated SF-81."

"And now?"

"We'll find out, won't we?"

A gust of wind brought the first splatters of rain. The two men turned back toward the town. They walked a few hundred yards in silence and then Derek stopped. "Yoshi, it's important that we tell her everything about Gentel's research."

Creases furrowed the Japanese scientist's forehead. "Jurgenczak was adamant that she learn only what she needs to know to synthesize her SF-81. Why change his orders?"

"We need that fresh perspective on everything. Besides, I hope she will ask questions we haven't thought of."

Chapter 21

Hawke sat at the controls of Gentel Systems' corporate jet, a Gulfstream 650, performing his preflight check. The 650 was the most technologically advanced business aircraft in the sky. It was engineered to withstand a hurricane. With its holographic Heads-Up Display and Enhanced Vision System, it provided pilots a complete range of next-generation technology comparable to the U.S. Air Force's most advanced fighter jets.

Hawke allowed himself a rare smile, thinking about his days at the U.S. Air Force Academy where he learned to fly. At five foot eight and 165 pounds, he was trim and well muscled, like all fighter pilots. But he was also something more. Most fighter pilots were egocentric Type A personalities, boasting about their exploits in the air and on the ground. Hawke let his excellence speak for itself and stayed quiet.

Hawke continued with the preflight, mentally noting every one of the aircraft's systems as the green check lights showed they were operational. As fit with his meticulous nature, if any one system had showed red, he would have grounded the flight until he personally solved the problem.

To someone from the outside, Hawke appeared to be a man engrossed in his task and oblivious to anything else. But Hawke recognized the tiny vibrations echoing through the aircraft before the man boarding even set foot in the cabin.

It was Arne Jurgenczak. Hawke had met Gentel's founder while he was training security personnel for the Air Force Ravens, the elite team guarding the President on Air Force One. Jurgenczak had been one of George W. Bush's science advisors and occasionally flew with the President. From the moment they met, Hawke trusted the great man. Jurgenczak was the only person Hawke met who truly understood that the world was headed into chaos. Hawke had seen it first-hand in Kosovo and later in Iraq and Afghanistan. But while others nodded and agreed that something had to be done, Jurgenczak was the first person Hawke ever met who was passionate about ending destructive conflicts once and for all. After the discovery of the Terminator Gene, Jurgenczak sought out Hawke and put him in charge of keeping word of humanity's impending doom from everybody but an exclusive group of dedicated scientists. Hawke had readily accepted Jurgenczak's warning that knowledge of the Terminator Gene would send the world into panic and chaos as never before.

"Hawke," Jurgenczak said as he entered the plane. He eased forward into the cockpit and shook Hawke's hand. It was a custom the old man employed with Gentel's security chief. The gesture was not lost on Hawke. It made him feel equal to Jurgenczak and wedded him even closer to the great man and his goal of saving humanity. "That's what I like about you, son. You always have humanity's interests at heart," Jurgenczak often told him.

"Yes, sir," Hawke said and waited, knowing the old man would tell him what he wanted without Hawke having to prompt him.

Jurgenczak sat down in the copilot's seat. He could have flown the plane himself, but he never interfered with Hawke's piloting. It was another thing that endeared Jurgenczak to Hawke; he trusted Hawke to do his job and do it perfectly.

"Son, there are rough times ahead and security is more important now than perhaps ever before. I am especially worried since this Howe incident."

"I am certain nothing got out, sir," Hawke said, keeping his face impassive.

"Yes, you saved us on that one. But I'm still worried about Derek, Yamato and this new woman they're bringing on board, Dr. Taylor. I fear they may try to control the Terminator Gene solution for their own purposes. We have to be certain that nothing our processes might achieve gets out beyond the complex."

"Sir?"

Jurgenczak laughed lightly. "Call it a hunch, son. But I think Kira Taylor's the one who's going to lead us to a solution. But nothing of what she does can get out beyond the complex. You understand? I'm the only one that is prepared to deal with the solution."

"I understand, sir."

"I knew you would." Jurgenczak stood and patted Hawke on the shoulder. "Good flying, son. Almost wish I were going with you."

"No Omaha run this time, sir?" Hawke asked.

Jurgenczak eyed Hawke and shook his head. "Remember what I told you. No one here is to know about those private trips."

"No one, sir," Hawke agreed. Still, his mind would not let go of what happened the week before. Hawke had flown Jurgenczak to Omaha. But this assignment was unusual. Instead of accompanying Gentel's founder to the corporate headquarters, as he usually did, Hawke was ordered to stay with the plane while Jurgenczak drove himself. The old man returned four hours later. The only comment he made was for Hawke to tell no one about the trip.

Since first meeting Jurgenczak, doubts about the old man had begun to creep into Hawke's thoughts. He could not stop himself from wondering what Jurgenczak was keeping from him.

Chapter 22

Leroy Parker guided his Dodge Ram pickup down the reservation road toward the Wyoming town of Crowheart, throwing fantails of dust into the early morning haze. He skirted the smaller potholes and occasionally slowed to drive carefully through the large ones. The early morning air was already heating up. A slight breeze kicked dust off the waterless ground in a gray, powdery haze that overwhelmed the truck's air conditioning, coating the inside of his vehicle. His clothes were dirty and stained with dried sweat. Fresh moisture beaded up on his forehead until a pothole knocked a drip loose leaving a fresh, thin track through the dust on his face. The bumpy ride should have aggravated his arthritis, making him grimace with each jolt and dip in the road, but the pain was gone. For the first time in ten years, his hands did not ache to grip the steering wheel, a condition which should have made him smile, but he only stared dismally through the streaked windshield at the bleak landscape on either side of the washboard gravel road.

Most tourists looked beyond the haze and arid land to the beauty of the surrounding mountains. The Earth had been extravagant in the scenic grandeur it had showered on the Wyoming Basin of the Rocky Mountains. The uplifted tableland was endowed with wooded highlands split by deep, waterless canyons and towered over by minarets of colored rock and flying buttresses of granite. In the early morning sun, the mountains and gorges became a palace of flaming beauty.

Geologically, the land held an even greater wealth within its folded and faulted Precambrian, Paleozoic and Mesozoic rock cores. Gold, coal, natural gas, oil shale and uranium lay in vast seams, making Wyoming's human inhabitants even wealthier.

Leroy cared nothing about the area's riches or its panoramic splendor, nor the lack of pain in his hands. He was weary beyond the heat and the dust. After two days of driving and another two days of fasting and drinking no water, he had failed in his vision quest. But his spirit guide was leading him on – hopefully to the answer.

The land around Crowheart was some of the bleakest of the Wind River Reservation land, dry and hot in summer, snow-covered and windy the other two-thirds of the year. Leroy stopped his truck to allow three scrawny cattle to cross the highway. The animals bore no brands or tags and they looked as heavy-hearted as he felt.

When the way was clear Leroy drove to the outskirts of Crowheart and pulled into an ancient green and white Sinclair filling station. The faded green dinosaur emblem hung by its tail over the single garage bay. He stopped next to an old gas pump where a "2" had been penciled in for the dollar figure on the dial. Inside the bay two men worked on a pitted 1970 green Dodge truck. The tailgate was missing and blotches of faded black Rustoleum paint dotted the vehicle. The men looked up as Leroy's new Dodge Ram stopped at the pumps. They stared, neither of them making a move to come out.

A young Indian boy, fourteen, with long black hair sweeping his shoulders and a pockmarked face, came out of the building. A lit cigarette hung indifferently from his mouth. Tinny rock and roll music blared from the headset of an iPod. Leroy stepped out of his truck, his boots rolling slightly on the crushed and cracked pavement of the driveway. The smell of gas and oil was heavy in the air and he was certain that the station's owner had never heard of the EPA guidelines for gasoline storage tanks.

He said to the teenager, "Fill'er up, please, with premium."

The young man pulled the hose free from its bracket, a spatter of gasoline hitting the ground and dripping down the side of his truck. Leroy backed away gingerly, looking for a place to hide in case the boy's cigarette suddenly sparked an explosion. Halfway to the garage he gave up, realizing that no place in all of

Crowheart would be safe if the storage tanks blew.

Inside the service station, the two Indian men, one about Leroy's age, the other much older, had returned to working on their truck and ignored Leroy. The bay was lit by a single bulb hanging from its own frayed black and green wires. Spare parts lay on benches and fan belts hung from the walls next to faded calendars with women in swim suits holding up tools. Everything looked older than the truck the pair of mechanics worked on.

Against one wall next to a workbench littered with tools and crushed packs of cigarettes was an ancient red Coca-Cola vending machine, its compressor humming loudly. Leroy skirted patches of oily grit on the floor and walked to the machine. He lifted the battered lid and the air escaped with a frosty wheeze that felt good against his sweaty face. He stood there half a minute, gazing at beer bottles hanging from their necks in the metal racks, letting the mist from the cooler chill the air. A cold beer would feel good about now and he reached inside but stopped when he felt a cold stinging in the joints of his fingers. Hastily he shut the lid. He flexed his hand, staring at the fingers, and backed away. The tingling sensation stopped.

Behind him, someone cleared his throat. Leroy turned and saw the two men staring at him. The older one of the two men, whose seamed face was heavy with age, beckoned him over.

"Most people think a cold beer would feel good on a hot morning like this one. But it will only make you sick," the man said as Leroy approached.

"You're a long way from Oklahoma."

Leroy nodded. Though the throbbing in his hand was rapidly subsiding, he was afraid that if he spoke, the pain might return. The old man smiled at him and Leroy experienced a sudden jolt as though muscles and tissues, drained by his experience at the medicine wheel, were being revived. The tingling in his hand was gone completely. Leroy concentrated on the old man's face and his words, not wanting to miss anything the man said or did.

"I was in the Fort Sill Stockade for two months," the man continued. "I used to drink. It got me into lots of trouble when I was younger. Kept me out of the Vietnam War, though, so I guess it was good for something at the time." He looked at the other mechanic, who sat inside the engine compartment, tugging at some wires. "I remember Oklahoma was hot and mostly prairie with only a few mountains...none like these, though."

"These mountains are powerful," Leroy said tentatively, feeling for any sensation of arthritis. His body remained strong and this gave him confidence. "They feel like the marrow of the world."

The old man wiped greasy fingers on an oily cloth and extended is hand. "Aaron Walker." Walker was shorter than Leroy by five inches. Tufts of steel-gray hair stuck out from an old John Deere tractor cap. Leroy was suddenly aware of his own hair, which hung in two long, gray braids down his back and were tied off with silver clasps. One of the clasps cost more than these men would make in a week.

Leroy gripped the old man's hand firmly. "Leroy Parker."

The Comanche had taken up the custom of shaking hands from the white man. It used to be when meeting someone from another tribe, a pipe was brought out to welcome him. The smoke tested his spirit and told everyone in the Indian community whether the newcomer could be trusted. In special cases, even an enemy could be sanctified by the pipe's pure white smoke. Nowadays, most people shook hands automatically, most often just a slack grip with no feeling behind it. Leroy could feel the power of the man through his grip and felt instinctively that he could trust him.

"You have a pipe with you."

Leroy nodded, though he did not know how the old man knew.

"You must be looking for something very important to take a

sacred pipe on such a long journey."

Almost in a dream, Leroy undid the pearl snap button on the pocket of his shirt and pulled out the drawing of the medicine wheel he had made after his vigil. Unfolding it he said, "I am looking for this."

Aaron held the picture carefully by the edges so as not to get grease on the paper. Leroy watched as the man turned it slowly until it was oriented to the four directions. Leroy looked at his drawing and realized for the first time that the Medicine Wheel Historic Site had not been like his drawing at all. The differences were major, only the idea of a medicine wheel out of rocks was the same. He shook his head. *How could I have been so blind?* Discouragement welled up in him again.

The other mechanic leaned out from under the hood, looking over the older man's shoulder, and breathed in sharply. "Wey hey," he said softly.

Aaron nodded in agreement.

Leroy's despair seemed to float out of him and he felt in its place an excitement he had not felt for nearly ten years since the arthritis came. "What is it?" he asked.

Aaron and the mechanic exchanged glances. Leroy could feel their unspoken communication, but he could not tell if it was favorable or not. The silence stretched and at last, Aaron said, "It is a medicine wheel but not from around here."

The other mechanic's slightly green eyes bore into Leroy and the Comanche shaman was suddenly afraid to look away. The man's face was the color of buffed charcoal that blended into his faded black T-shirt. His head and neck were supported by wide, heavily muscled shoulders. The man was sitting inside the engine compartment of the truck and looked as though he had grown out of the engine. Then Leroy looked more closely and saw that the mechanic had no legs. They had been amputated above the knee. One thigh rested on the battery case, the other on the brake housing. Leroy didn't say anything, nor did he stare in pity or look away either. He had been a marine corporal in Vietnam and had witnessed many such injuries.

The man's eyes seemed to be asking, "Can you be trusted?" Leroy extended his hand to the mechanic. "Leroy Parker."

"Thomas Firewalker." He held Leroy's grip firmly. After ten seconds the man let go and asked, "Where did you get this drawing?"

"I made it from a vision I had several days ago in the Wichita Mountains of Oklahoma."

Thomas pointed to one of the spokes and said something to Aaron in a language Leroy did not understand but assumed was Shoshoni. When they stopped talking, both of the men stared at him.

Leroy felt they were testing him and he asked, "Can you tell me how I can find the medicine wheel in this drawing?"

The old man shrugged. "It is not around here. This is Shoshoni land."

Thomas Firewalker leaned farther forward, holding onto the hood for balance. "Go to the northwest corner of Comancheria," he said. "Powerful spirits live there and watch over that sacred ground."

"Only your spirit guide can take you to this medicine wheel," the older man added.

"Do you know how I can find this place?" Leroy asked again.

Aaron slowly nodded his head. "If your spirit guide is with you, you will be able to find the way." He handed the drawing back to Leroy, still by the edges. Leroy carefully folded the picture and put it back in his pocket.

Leroy thanked the men. He reached into his other shirt pocket and gave them the pack of cigarettes he carried there. The two men were very pleased. They accepted the gift, shaking his hand.

The legless mechanic stared at Leroy and the Comanche shaman suddenly felt uncomfortable under the light of those green eyes. "Beware," the man warned. "It will be a much longer journey than you imagine."

Leroy kept the disappointment from his face. Though in his heart he had known that the path to understanding of the wheel and the drowned, primordial world of his vision was not going to be easy, he had hoped it would not be lengthy. He no longer possessed the endurance of a young man to see a long hard journey all the way to the end.

Thomas Firewalker chuckled. "Do not be afraid. The Great Spirit chose wisely."

The two men then returned their attention to the truck's engine as if Leroy had never been there.

The young Indian boy was ringing up the bill and called Leroy into the office. He paid and left the station.

Two miles out of Crowheart, Leroy slapped his thigh. He should have asked the mechanic how long the journey would be so that he could prepare himself. Leroy turned his truck around and headed back to the filling station. When he arrived, the garage bay was empty. He went up to the teenager still sitting in the office and asked, "Where are the two men?"

The young boy looked up from the magazine he was reading and pulled down the earbuds of the iPod. He shook his head. "What two men?" he asked.

"In the garage bay only five minutes ago, working on the green pickup truck."

The boy's eyes narrowed and he looked past Leroy into the garage. "Nobody's been here all morning except for you."

Chapter 23

Located just off the runway, Sioux Gateway Airport's corporate air terminal was plush and elegant. The fact that Sioux City had become the center for virtual storage of credit accounts and related data explained the unexpected luxury. For five years now, mid-level bank executives from around the world regularly flew in and out of this otherwise small airport.

This morning, however, Kira didn't relax in the comfort of her surroundings. Pacing the visitor's lounge, she pulled out her smart phone and checked the time. The message from Derek said Gentel's corporate jet would pick her up at 4:15 a.m. Central Daylight. It was now 4:25. The plane was ten minutes late and she had received no word from Derek or anyone about the status of the flight. She began to wonder if something had happened.

She cracked her knuckles, trying to dampen the excitement coursing through her. For the first time since her conversation with Derek, the full reality of the Terminator Gene had sunk in. She was actually witnessing an extinction event of the *genus* homo, a genus which had existed for over 2 million years, of which modern day humans, *homo sapiens sapiens,* were the last surviving descendants.

Kira forced herself to relax. *I'm amazed Derek told me what's going on*. In an odd way, her ego found it very satisfying that she was one of a handful to have this unique perspective of humans' evolutionary dilemma.

Homo neanderthalensis arose 200,000 years ago from our hominid mother species. Neanderthals eventually dominated Ice Age Europe. Sometime around 130,000 years ago another shift in the morphogenic makeup of the mother species gave rise to *homo sapiens sapiens*. And as early as 95,000 years ago yet a third dwarf species, *homo floresiensis,* lived in what is now present-day Indonesia. With the addition of this dwarf hominid, three human species existed on the planet at one time. Such diversity and adaptability had not existed since the Cambrian period.

That the Neanderthals and the Indonesian dwarves both fell to the Terminator Gene so rapidly troubled Kira the most. Her generational calculations painted a picture of an extinction tipping point arriving with the suddenness of an explosion. *Which means the same thing will happen to us...is happening to us.* Yoshi would have to convince Kira that it hadn't already occurred...that there was still time for *homo sapiens sapiens* to find an answer to the T-gene?

"Dr. Taylor," a whispery voice behind her inquired.

Kira turned and stared. She was surprised by the sudden appearance of the African-American man who now stood behind her. He was a few inches taller than she was, well muscled and he stood on the balls of his feet like an athlete. His eyes had a slight slant to them that suggested he was also American Indian. She found it odd that she had not felt him come up behind her, since as an E.R. doctor, she was always aware of the patients, nurses, residents and interns in a crowded emergency room.

"Yes?" she asked.

"Please allow me to introduce myself. I am Hawke, Gentel's head of security. Dr. Yamato is already on the plane. If you'll follow me please." Hawke looked down at the single bag Kira brought along. "Is this your only luggage?"

Kira nodded.

Hawke smiled. "You travel light."

"Yes, I suppose I do. Is Hawke a first or a last name?" she asked.

"It's my name," he answered levelly and picked up the bag, ending any more talk on the subject.

Kira reached for her carryon. "Please don't trouble yourself. I can carry it myself."

"It's no trouble at all, ma'am."

"Please call me Kira. Does Gentel's head of security come to meet all new recruits?"

"I do when I fly the plane. If you will follow me, please."

Normally, Kira didn't like tagging along after anyone she didn't know, least of all someone she wasn't expecting to meet. But such things didn't bother her anymore. Outside dawn was a patch of yellow on the eastern horizon. The air was crisp but the weather channel said the day would be hot and humid. Over in Wales it was supposed to rain the afternoon, about the time they landed.

They crossed the tarmac to a Gulfstream corporate jet and climbed the steps. A figure met them at the top. Kira recognized him as Dr. Yoshi Yamato. He looked exactly like his web pictures. A little grayer, perhaps, but his green-flecked, golden eyes were extremely rare among Japanese and as distinctive as fingerprints. Long black hair was pulled back in a ponytail. His suit was rumpled and a dark necktie with an embroidered red crane was pulled askew from the collar of his blue silk shirt. He looked like he had slept on the plane.

"Dr. Taylor, this is Dr. Yamato," Hawke said, introducing them.

Yoshi bowed and Kira returned the bow. Hawke pushed by and disappeared into the main cabin.

Yoshi studied Kira. The dim light muted the red-gold tones in her hair. "It is a pleasure to meet you," he said, breaking the uncomfortable silence. "Derek regrets that he was unable to make this flight himself, but he sent me along to answer your questions and bring you up to speed. Please strap yourself in. Our pilot is most anxious to take off without delay."

Yoshi led the way into the plane. The main cabin was elegant with six large leather chairs that reclined into sleepers. A steward was placing her bag into an overhead compartment. It closed with the soft snick of perfect workmanship.

To the left was the galley and beyond that the cockpit. The door was open. Hawke was in the cockpit, going through the preflight check. The steward came up and smiled at Kira. He motioned her to take any seat. "We'll be taking off momentarily. Can I get you anything to drink? We have mimosas and Bloody Marys, if you like. Breakfast will be served once we've reached cruising altitude, in about thirty minutes."

He went forward and secured the hatch then rapped on the cockpit doorjamb. "Everything is stowed away and we're ready for takeoff, sir," he told Hawke.

Hawke nodded. The cockpit door closed and the first engine shrieked to life, then the second. Within minutes they had clearance and were taxiing. They reached the end of the runway and barreled into the dawn sky.

Breakfast was as elegant as the plane: Eggs Benedict, English muffins and honeydew melon. It was followed by coffee. Through it all Yoshi remained silent. At last when the steward had cleaned up and returned to the galley, Yoshi beckoned Kira to the back of the plane.

"If you would like to sleep," he said, "we can postpone this talk for a couple of hours."

Kira was too keyed up to sleep. She shook her head and said, "I don't sleep well on airplanes."

"I don't sleep well anywhere since I learned about the Terminator Gene," Yoshi replied.

Kira looked into Dr. Yamato's eyes and saw the tiredness there as well as something else, something she had seen in cancer patients – a person stretched to the limit, empty of hope.

"So what don't I know about the T-gene?" she asked gently.

"I don't mean to sound condescending, but I am more comfortable laying this out step by step."

Kira nodded for him to continue.

"As I'm sure you know, genes are places along one of our cell's forty-six chromosomes. What's fascinating about the T-gene is that it never shows up in the same place twice."

"So gene splicing doesn't work."

"Precisely," Yoshi answered with obvious relief in his voice that he was dealing with someone who could understand what he was talking about.

"How do you explain that?"

"Ah...I can't." Yoshi stopped to wipe the perspiration from his forehead with his breakfast napkin. "I think the Terminator Gene is linked to Hox genes. It's as if the embryo is moving toward speciation and can't make it. The shift is too radical, and of course, the embryo can't go back to a normal developmental sequence. So somehow de-differentiation is triggered at that point."

"You and Derek are hoping the SF-81 will somehow trick it into forgetting it wants to speciate?" Kira asked.

"That's a possibility we need to try. We've prepared a working lab for you. Derek's already gotten buckets of those curious little fossils. They're quite pretty." He patted his forehead dry again and Kira thought he looked a little nervous. What he said next told her why. "What I don't understand is how you were able to extract viable biochemistry with acid. That simply wouldn't work." His voice sounded faintly accusatory.

Kira managed to keep her face clear. She knew why Yoshi was probing her methodology for the SF-81. It was the one part of her PhD work that she had never told anyone about, not even Jack. She hadn't merely bent the rules; she had broken them altogether. Thinking about it now, it was no wonder her PhD committee all but accused her of falsifying data.

At first she had tried different acids. The phosphitic nature of the shells resisted weaker acids and each sample was contaminated by phosphate residues. After many failures, the process came down to the much stronger HCl. But even the weakest strength HCl damaged beyond recovery the organic structure she had hoped to extract.

Kira slowly realized that part of the organic molecules themselves acted as a glue, binding the shell together. If she could "unhinge" the glue, then she could free up the other organic molecules. Years ago this process meant using a new generation of benzene-derived cellular clarifiers – highly toxic substances that were not allowed outside of the Centers for Disease Control in Atlanta or the National Institute for Cancer Research. These dangerous and highly carcinogenic substances were still banned today.

Kira researched the literature and settled on DiBenzylToluSolulene, DBTS, a purified Toluene derivative that was so toxic, a single drop on the skin blinded a person permanently. But none of the labs at Yale had any of these substances and even suggesting their use would have gotten her reprimanded.

Kira contacted a friend at the CDC and called in a favor the young man owed her. He sent a sample of DBTS with the stipulation that she promise never to reveal where she had gotten it.

Three days later, the extraction process worked. Kira kept her promise and in her thesis, she noted that extraction had been achieved by using diluted hydrochloric acid.

Kira took a deep breath. *It's time for the lie to end.*

She told Yoshi all that had happened, leaving out only the part about her friend at the CDC.

The Japanese scientist took it all in and when she finished, all he said was, "I'm amazed you're still alive."

"I was young, not thinking clearly."

"Well getting DBTS won't be a problem. Gentel Systems' resources are virtually unlimited."

Kira eyed him thoughtfully and Yoshi returned her look with a question. "Is there something else you aren't telling me about your extraction methodology with the SF-81?"

"Not that. It's just that with all the resources and power Gentel has, something's bothering me about this whole T-gene crisis. Suppose I...suppose we find a cure or a fix. How's it going to be distributed? Who decides which women will receive it?"

Yoshi waved his hands as if trying to ward off irrelevant questions. "I'm a scientist, I don't concern myself with such matters. And you shouldn't either."

"My T-gene generational calculations suggest we may have already crossed the tipping point. There must be a plan to move quickly. Restore reproductive viability for the human species. How can you not know?" She stated the question with more heat than she intended.

Yoshi's face reddened. "Derek warned me you're some kind of hot head. I never should have agreed to let you help us, not with that kind of attitude."

Kira felt anger and was about to hit him with a sexist remark when an overwhelming sense of compassion for Yoshi filled her. Since her experience at Jack's place, what used to be subjective – caught up in the moods and emotions that ran her life – now became objective. They became objects of her awareness no longer controlling her, no longer clouding her vision of what was actually happening. She could see that not knowing was immeasurably painful for him. He prided himself on knowing and she had exposed him. He had to hide his ignorance at all costs.

Kira let her face soften. "I hear you. I can be like that. I'm sorry. Let's step back a moment."

She saw that all the steam went out of his anger since she wasn't fighting against him and remarkably he released his resistance.

"Okay," he said.

Kira took another deep breath and asked softly, "How fast do I have to work? How fast do you want me to work?"

"We need you to get started right away, if we're going to have any success at all. It's...it's not going to be like administering a vaccine." Yoshi patted his forehead dry. "I have no idea how Gentel's going to organize distributing the cure. I should know that."

Kira shook her head. "No, that wasn't part of your job. Do you think Derek or Jurgenczak have a plan?"

"They must. Like you said, we're right up against that tipping point."

"Let's hope so," Kira mused aloud. Again the sense of an evolutionary pulse arose. She noticed its erotic quality. "It's hard to believe evolution would bring itself to the point where it kills the awareness of itself."

Yoshi looked at her askance and Kira realized that what she said must not have made any sense to someone who had not experienced what she was calling the evolutionary pulse. "It's like one of your famous Zen koan's," she said. "One of us must make a perspective shift. We cannot solve the T-gene mystery with our current way of seeing or reasoning."

"Derek said you would force us to ask questions that we wouldn't think of."

"And the one I want answered most is, 'What's Gentel's plan for administering the solution?'"

Yoshi nodded. "When we return to Caernarfon, I know someone who can help us find out that information."

Chapter 24

Hawke flipped a switch on the plane's console and listened a second time to the soft voice of Dr. Kira Taylor in his headphones saying, "And the one I want answered most is, 'What's Gentel's plan for administering the solution?'"

Who would Dr. Yamato know that could help find that information? Hawke mused. Ultimately, it didn't matter. Hawke would watch Dr. Yamato, and when he made his contact, Hawke would know how to proceed. Until then he would wait. The plane shook slightly. Hawke checked the HUD. The holographic Heads Up Display showed that a storm over Iceland was causing some turbulence. Hawke wasn't worried. Even if Iceland's Eyjafjallajokul volcano erupted without warning, the plane's Mach 1 top speed could get them out of danger quickly.

Pressing the intercom button, Hawke advised his passengers, "We'll have some minor turbulence for the next ten minutes or so. Nothing to worry about. Take your seats until I let you know it's safe to move about the cabin again."

Hawke settled into the routine of flying, his hands and feet automatically adjusting their course and trim, while his eyes checked the Gulfstream's Enhanced Vision System and HUD for any other signs of danger. He felt the plane like an extension of his mind and body and knew he was one of the lucky ones who got to fly with the ease of a bird.

Satisfied that all was under control, Hawke returned to the real question: *What's Dr. Jurgenczak going to do with the solution?* Doubt about Jurgenczak filled Hawke's thoughts, and for a moment he felt adrift.

Hawke forced himself to concentrate on his flying until once more he was part of the Gulfstream. He let out a long breath to clear his thoughts. A part of his mind stayed connected to the plane, but the rest tackled the problem of doubt...doubts about

Jurgenczak. This was the second time Hawke had troubling questions about the old man in less than forty-eight hours. He recognized the source: Dr. Taylor. There was something about her that rattled him. And now she had a question that disturbed him even more. Then with a clarity that would have made his spymaster proud, Hawke zeroed in on the real source of this troubling line of thought. *It's, not Dr. Taylor's question but what it implied. Why don't I know what Jurgenczak is planning?*

Chapter 25

"The name, Comanche, comes from the Ute word, 'Komantica,' meanin' 'enemy' or literally, 'anyone who wants to fight me all the time.' It was given by the Spanish to a band of Shoshoni Indians who split off from the main tribe in the early 1700's, and moved south along the 'Rkansas River to become the Comanche, the most feared warriors of the Southern Plains and lords of all they surveyed. Over the next 150 years, the warriors of the Comanche nation formed the Comancheria, an empire rivalin' in size the Roman Empire and stretchin' from Colorado to south-eastern Texas."

Leroy Parker listened carefully, appreciative of the dramatic storytelling by the Bent's Fort tour guide, who sounded much like the storytellers of his own people. The young man, dressed in the full regalia of a mountain man, used many of the mountain man's colorful idioms as he regaled the group of elderly tourists with the history of the fort. The group was standing outside in the shade of the main building.

"The Comanche empire covered mostly Texas, Oklahoma, New Mexico and southern Kansas. But the northwest corner was here in Colorado. For twenty-five years in the early part of the 19th century, Comanche hunters traded buffalo hides here at Bent's Fort. They were savvy traders too, lemme tell ya. More than one trapper found hisself traded out of his britches 'cause he weren't careful." The mountain man paused. "Sadly, the heyday of Bent's Fort and the Comanche passed all too quickly. The fort was destroyed by fire in 1848 and the Comanche empire fell to white settlers less than a quarter of a century later."

Leroy had come to Bent's Fort following his spirit guide. On I-25 just south of Denver, a red-tailed hawk circled his truck three times and headed east across the Colorado plains. He had followed the bird of prey to Bent's Old Fort National Historic Site.

There, the bird had landed on one of the fort's watchtowers. Leroy could not possibly have passed up such an obvious messenger. He got out and encountered the tour guide addressing a group of seniors.

"Every year bands of Comanche would come through Bent's Fort on their way to a remote area of Comancheria at the Garden of the Gods near Colorado Springs. No one has ever been able to figure out why." The guide's voice dropped to a dramatic whisper. "Another mystery whose answer has been lost to the veil of time."

Chapter 26

Leroy Parker squatted under a late afternoon sun dyeing scarlet the rugged mesas beneath the mountains. He was on a two-lane road that wound through the Garden of the Gods. The landscape was barren. Oddly-shaped orange and reddish rocks pushed through the stony soil right up to the road's shoulder. Slabs of stone sloped away toward surrounding cliffs. Out on the plain of rock, enormous spires, ten feet thick at the base, soared fifty feet above him. There was very little foliage and the day was hot and windless.

The place was unearthly in its beauty but it did not feel right to him. The area was surrounded by houses. Hundreds of young men and women were climbing the pillars and cliff faces, their gaudy clothes matching the eerily-colored rock. The sounds of passing cars and the yells of the climbers drowned out the silence of the land. Leroy tried to think of the right word to describe why the Garden of the Gods wasn't the area he was looking for and then it came to him. *Isolation*. There was no sense of isolation. Even in the 19th century, this place would have been too loud, too busy to the eye and ear. No Comanche shaman would have come here to get in touch with the Great Spirit.

Leroy was disheartened. He had misread what his spirit guide had tried to show him and come to the wrong place. He thought that he might as well go back to Oklahoma because he wasn't cut out for this quest. He was out of his depth, too old and simple a man, nothing like the warrior shamans of his Comanche heritage who had spent their lives fashioning a relationship with the Great Spirit in order to uncover the secrets of power located in the other world.

Leroy stood up and immediately sagged against his truck. The rocks swam before his eyes and he wondered if he was having a heart attack. Then his vision cleared, but in a distorted way as though he were looking through a great lens with the light bending at the edges. He heard no sounds. The sky was a clear blue that hurt his eyes. He stood on a high place looking down upon a valley like in his vision, only the medicine wheel was not present. Behind him were mountains and in front was a great peak, rock at the top and forest below. He realized that he was looking at Pikes Peak and everything became clear to him.

Immediately, light contracted around him and he was drawn swiftly down to the earth. He heard the yelling of the rock climbers as they shouted commands to one another. The air was gritty with smog again.

Leroy was leaning against his truck. To the southwest of him Pikes Peak rose up, a monolith of stone and forest. Leroy trembled knowing that he had to go higher up. He had to find the spot of his vision where Pikes Peak would be beneath the sun and the valley pointed like an arrow to the heart of the mountain. In this configuration had his ancestors placed the Comanche medicine wheel.

Chapter 27

The sun was still well above the horizon as Hawke drove Kira and Dr. Yamato on the short ride from the private airport to Gentel's research facility on the outskirts of Caernarfon. After seeing the corporate headquarters in Omaha, Kira was disappointed in the modest size of the Terminator Gene research facility. Yoshi had explained Gentel's layout on the plane. There were fewer than two dozen of the world's leading scientists from biochemistry and genetics working at the site. Another forty lab assistants, secretaries, and security filled out the remainder of the complex's workforce. Jurgenczak had told Yoshi and the other men of the Inner Circle that a bigger facility and more scientists would have presented too big of a security risk. None except for, himself, Jurgenczak, Derek, and another American, Frank Littleton knew the full range of research underway.

Kira remembered the name Littleton from her days at Yale. He had been a prominent innovator in recombinant DNA therapy. *So this is where he landed,* Kira thought, getting out of the car.

Hawke parked near the entrance. A large security command post barred the way into the building. Beyond it were two sets of double doors with bulletproof glass. Kira recognized their frosty glare from her days working in abortion clinics right after medical school.

The head security guard requested Kira to hand over her purse.

She turned toward Hawke, and frowning asked, "What's with the search?"

"Strict security protocols, Dr. Taylor," Hawke said. "Nothing in; nothing out."

"I'll need my phone if I want to communicate with people; bounce ideas off them without wasting time going to their labs."

Hawke smiled, and Kira saw for the first time something of

the ex-military man whose primary concern was project security. "Gentel has an excellent interoffice communications system. You won't need your phone for any of it," Hawke answered flatly.

"I'll get it back?"

"Whenever you leave the building," Hawke assured her.

The guard handed Kira an ID badge and tapped a buzzer, opening the first of the doors.

Kira was puzzled by the photo ID. The picture was the same as her Iowa driver's license. *Interesting*. It seemed to coincide in an oblique way to the helter-skelter rush of a powerful biotech company moving her from Sioux City to Caernarfon. Coupled with the private plane and the intrigue surrounding the Terminator Gene project, there was something odd. Something wrong about all of it.

"Is everything alright?" Hawke asked, his hand gently touching her elbow.

Kira nodded to Hawke and Yoshi and followed them into the building. They continued along the corridor under soft lights. The complex was set up like a Greek cross. She pointed at the security cameras and asked Hawke, "Who's watching?"

"We have cameras in every part of the facility, including every lab, the cafeteria and as the Brit's say, the loo."

They came to a checkpoint at the center where all four spokes met. The man in charge carefully studied her ID. and then swiped it through a security slot. The device beeped twice and the red light turned green. They let her through and repeated the procedure with Yoshi. None of the guards joked or talked with Hawke.

"Your ID badge also serves as a security card," Hawke said when they were underway again. "The magnetic strip on the back will only allow you access to areas for which you have been cleared, your own lab, the conference rooms and the bathroom." Each lab also requires a retinal scan."

"But you don't have mine on file," Kira said.

"Yes we do, Dr. Taylor," Hawke answered matter-of-factly. Hawke stopped and eyed her. "I must report to Dr. Jurgenczak and let him know you arrived safely. Dr. Yamato will show you to your lab." Pivoting on his heel with an air of dismissal, Hawke took a corridor headed west. But Kira was left with the distinct feeling that the security chief wasn't through with her yet.

Yoshi and Kira continued down the hall. "It's only a few more meters," Yoshi said, "Near the end."

They reached the end of the corridor and the door to her lab was right there. A man was standing beside it. She had half expected to see Derek, but this man was much shorter and balding.

Yoshi stopped. "Dr. Littleton. I'm surprised to see you here."

The American stepped forward. "Wanted to meet our new scientist. Frank Littleton," he said, not offering his hand.

"I know," Kira replied.

Littleton stepped back in surprise and asked guardedly, "You do?"

Kira smiled. "I'm sorry. I'm Dr. Kira Taylor. I recognize you from my days at Yale. I read your textbook on recombinant genetics. Brilliantly clear."

Littleton smiled. "Thank you. Yoshi's giving you the tour of your lab and all, I see. If there's anything I can do to help you during your stay with us, please don't hesitate to call me. My extension's 102." His hand went to his lab coat for a pen. "Perhaps I should write it down."

"Thank you, that won't be necessary," Kira said.

"Please don't misunderstand me, Dr. Taylor, but frankly I'm skeptical that even if you can replicate the bio extraction from the half-billion-year-old *brachiopods*, that it will do anything to bring us closer to preventing miscarriages. I'm convinced that only gene splicing will allow the normal embryonic development."

"We'll just have to see what happens, won't we?" Kira responded easily, consciously deciding to accept the criticism as a legitimate concern rather than a rebuke of her past.

"Indeed, we will. My own skepticism aside, it's nice to have another American working here again, if only for a few weeks." He waved and walked back along the corridor.

Kira and Yoshi stood before a metal door designated Lab 22. Kira noted that her lab was in the south spoke of the complex. Below the number plate was a triple-bladed biohazard sign. The door had no windows and, in fact, no windows anywhere along the wall of the lab. To the left of the door was a rack of Hazmat suits with the characteristic white hoods connected to re-breather units by black flexible hoses. Light glinted off the clear plastic face guards.

Kira eyed them and wondered why they would need Hazmat protection in her lab. But Yoshi ignored them and Kira breathed a silent thanks, glad that after a long flight, she didn't have to negotiate one of the cumbersome suits.

Yoshi pointed to a security slot and an optical scanner to the right of the door. The scanner was a bubble of gray plastic with a thin ribbon of black glass running horizontally through the center.

"Swipe your security card first and then look at the scanner," Yoshi said.

Kira did as she was told. The slot's red LED blinked once and a green light came on. She looked at the scanner and soft amber light bathed her eyes. To her left she heard a loud click.

She looked over and Yoshi was holding the door open. "You have five seconds to open the door or the lock will reset and you have to go through the steps again. If you fail twice in a row, the lock will shut you out permanently until a security officer comes and releases the mechanism."

"Does that happen often?"

"Not more than once," Yoshi said.

Inside, the lab was spacious. A gold foil counter ran down the center of the room. Another counter ran along the far wall with two double stainless steel sinks and white enameled cabinets above and below. A lab freezer and a kitchen refrigerator stood side-by-side next to the sinks. At the far end of the room was a ventilator hood, the wide vertical shaft rising into the ceiling. Near the door she recognized the two-foot tall PPC-8000 mini tower which had replaced the mammoth Cray XMP supercomputers of the 90s. One single mini could have handled every lab service at St. Luke's and have enough computing power left over to run administration and still not max out its capacity. Next to the mini tower was a Yamato automated gene sequencer and a robotic PCR – Polymerase Chain Reaction machine. She heard a low-level hum and saw that computer and machines had green lights glowing. From each corner of the room, she saw the blinking red light of the security camera, just as Hawke promised.

Waiting in the lab was a tall gangly Brit whose nametag read Graham. He pumped her hand vigorously all the while proudly announcing that he had prepared over two thousand shells – *dicellomos politos* – from the Eau Claire formation just like the ones collected more than ten years ago.

"Thanks," Kira said, instantly liking the young man, who reminded her of Dr. Wheeler at St. Luke's.

Yoshi cleared his throat. "Thanks, Graham. We'll see you tomorrow early." He motioned Kira to the door. "I imagine you're tired from the flight and could use a hot bath about now."

Kira nodded,. "You read my mind, Dr. Yamato."

"Please, call me Yoshi. Gentel has rented a flat for you in Caernarfon's Old Town district. It is not so far away and I believe you will find it very pleasant. Now that you've seen your lab and been through security, I will take you there and let you get some rest."

As they walked down the corridor, Kira was struck by the silence. From the moment she entered the building everything seemed a little off, as if something wasn't quite right.

And then there was Hawke, watching at her constantly since they'd met, following her closely, like a shadow. Earlier Kira caught him staring. Locking eyes, consciousness to consciousness, it was he that turned away. Kira knew what that kind of awareness was. It was sexual, pure and simple. *What did he want?*

Chapter 28

Leroy drove deeper into the mountains, passing by the reconstruction of a small Anasazi village. He stayed on the highway through the town of Woodland Park. Pikes Peak's fourteen-thousand-foot summit was behind him now. He moved slowly, looking at the landscape for some clue that would tell him which direction he should go. He caught his breath as he came to a road sign for Rainbow Falls Campground. Stuffed into a crack in the boards were the tail feathers from a red-tailed hawk. He shook his head in amazement at the obviousness of the sign and thanked his spirit guide. Leroy might find what he was looking for, but understanding it would be another matter. He touched the medicine bundle beside him. That was why he had brought the sacred pipe. The smoke from the pipe would help him to understand the connection between the medicine wheel and his vision of vast ocean covered by a blanket of algae and the tiny jellyfish creatures, which swam in it.

Leroy turned onto the forest service road and headed down into a valley. He passed the campground. Rainbows formed in the spray of a small waterfall behind it. The steep sides of the valley were red rock. As he drove, the road turned from gravel to dirt and finally barely recognizable parallel tracks on hard rocky ground. Obviously, people seldom used this road. He rounded a boulder that had shouldered onto the trail and reached a dead end – a padlocked gate. The edges of the road dropped off sharply on either side of the gateposts making it impossible for him to drive around. A small sign warned of private land beyond this point.

Leroy drove up to the gate. When he stepped from his truck, his heart pounded. A feeling swept over him as though he were returning home to some ancestral place of great power. Behind him he could see Pikes Peak looking like the mountain of his vision. Beyond the fence, the road wound upwards for three miles to the top of a plateau.

The padlocked gate, however, stymied him. He was acutely aware that he would be arrested for trespassing. On the other hand, he sensed this was the time he must find his people's medicine wheel and decipher its secrets.

Leroy grabbed his backpack and his medicine bundle from the front seat and left his truck behind.

He started up the steeply sloping mountainside along the winding road. On his left was a five-hundred-foot drop-off to the valley below. Piñon pine anchored rocks and soil on the hillsides. A mile later he came to a log cabin set back in the trees with a wrap-around porch and a huge stone fireplace. Six solar panels were mounted on the roof. Leroy considered stopping to ask permission to be here, but the cabin looked deserted and he went on.

A quarter of a mile past the cabin the road cut deeply through several strata of rock. Spalls lay everywhere and he had to walk carefully to avoid the fragments. Leroy paused to rest and examined one of the larger pieces, which had tiny, reddish-gray shells embedded in its matrix. They were conical and looked something like the shells he had found on the beaches of Vietnam while stationed at Da Nang.

While he rested, Leroy let himself float, gathering energy from the Earth and the sun. After a few minutes he felt refreshed. He tossed the fragment aside and continued upward toward the plateau.

Below him the valley spread out. A small stream ran through it. Sagebrush and greasewood covered the lowland to the rocky cliffs on either side. It was the valley in his vision.

Fifty feet below the top of the plateau, Leroy was forced to stop again. His legs ached from the steady climb. The altitude made his head swim and his lungs burned fiercely. But the sense of being in the right place was palpable and heartened him. After a few minutes he pushed on, through his fatigue.

The top was barren, rugged rock. No medicine wheel. At the rim of the plateau stood a young woman, mid-twenties with short dark hair, glaring at him. "This is private land!" she yelled and pointed a rifle at him.

Dazed from the climb, Leroy stared at the woman, so exhausted he could no longer tell if she was real or a spirit. The rifle looked real, though. He put his hands up.

"My name is Leroy Parker. I'm a Comanche. I am looking for a sacred place of my people. I did not mean to disturb you."

The woman lowered the gun a little. "What kind of sacred place?"

"A medicine wheel that my ancestors made. I thought it would be on the top of this plateau, but it is not," he said, trying to keep the disappointment out of his voice.

"What do you want with it?"

"It is part of the vision quest I am on. May I put my arms down?" The woman grinned and lowered her rifle the rest of the way. Leroy lowered his arms. "Thank you."

The woman came over. She held the gun easily in both hands and was unafraid. "My name is Teresa Lopez." She pronounced the 's' in her name with a soft sibilance. "You're lucky I decided to ask questions first. I can hit a hummingbird's ass at a hundred and fifty yards with this rifle." She swept the rifle in an arc around them. "My family has owned this land for three generations. There are a number of Indian rock structures on my property," She eyed him skeptically. "We've never told anyone about them. How'd you learn about them?"

"I dreamed it in a vision." Leroy answered and pulled the drawing from his pocket.

Teresa studied the picture and then handed it solemnly back to Leroy. "The big circle. It's through those trees another half a mile." She pointed the gun muzzle past him, higher into the mountains. "There's no road and barely a path. But you should find it before dark. You're welcome on our land anytime."

"Thank you," Leroy answered. Dusk was gathering and he was anxious to be at the site in order to be relaxed and calm before night fell. On the other hand, he did not wish to be rude to the land owner. She was not quite finished talking.

"I suppose you're going to perform a ceremony of some kind up there."

"Yes. I thank you for allowing me on your land." Leroy stepped away and began walking into the forest.

By the time Leroy reached the medicine wheel, he was once more out of breath and exhausted. The plateau was at eight thousand feet and the rarefied air made it hard for him to breathe. He set down his pack with the medicine bundle and squatted next to them to get his strength back.

The plateau was wide and flat with views of the valley to the south and west. Tall cliffs rose behind. At one time, the Indians had swept the area clear of loose rocks until the hard packed ground was smooth. Then they had laid out the medicine wheel, orienting the spokes to the four directions. Cairns of rocks at the center and the rim had been piled just like in his vision.

Winds and rain had severely eroded the surrounding red cliffs, but in the dimming light, Leroy could still make out several pictographs on the rock walls. The most prominent one showed a man astride a horse bearing a shield with the waving symbol for a snake on it.

Any remaining doubts that Leroy harbored faded away. Some of the elders in the Comanche Nation of Oklahoma still referred to themselves as the Snake People. At last he felt that he would find the answer to the jellyfish-like creatures he had seen within the sea.

Leroy rested until the sun had set completely, then he began preparations for his vigil. The stars appeared singly in the vast blackness of space, then in clusters and finally, overhead the spiral nebula of the Milky Way lit up the night sky and he could clearly make out the medicine wheel. He picked up the two bundles and went to the center. He sat cross-legged facing Pikes Peak, now a distant shadow of rock and forest. It sat like an ancient warrior, anchoring the family of warriors surrounding it.

Leroy opened his medicine bundle. He removed the pipe and the kinnikkinnick mixture and laid them beside him on the bundle's leather. From his backpack he took out wood, the wing feathers of a red-tailed hawk, and several bunches of sweet sage. Quickly he made a fire. For the next three hours, he chanted his spirit songs, occasionally tossing sprigs of sage onto the flames.

Though the plateau was above eight thousand feet, the night air remained warm as the heat from the valley lifted and rose past him into the clear sky. At midnight, the moon cleared the trees. Much of the darkness vanished. Leroy felt ready for the ceremony. He took the pipe and opened the bag with the kinnikkinnick. He started when he saw that he had only enough of the mixture left for one smoke. He thought about going back to Oklahoma, where he could make more of the special tobacco, but dismissed the idea from his mind. He sensed the urgency of the moment. He had to do the ceremony tonight or it would be too late.

Leroy filled the pipe, carefully tamping the mixture in the horse-head bowl. Then, as before, he offered it to the four directions, to his father the sky, and to his mother the Earth. He asked his ancestors for help; he asked the moon, the sun and Earth for help; he asked the red-tailed hawk for help. He repeated his request several times, reminding his spirit ancestors that he was but an old man, a part-time medicine man who needed their power and guidance.

When he finished his prayers, he swiftly picked up a glowing ember with his thumb and forefinger and placed it on the mixture in his pipe. He inhaled deeply, thinking at the same time how glad he was that his arthritis had been cured. He let the smoke out slowly and repeated the inhalations and exhalations four more times. When the last of the mixture had been smoked, he placed the pipe on the medicine bundle and picked up the wing feathers of the red-tailed hawk. He held the wing in his left hand, singing softly for his brother the hawk to lead him to the answer.

Leroy waited for the familiar flash of light, which followed the smoke, but nothing happened. Slowly the moon arced across the void of space and the night became colder. Soon he was chilled through. He began to fear that he had done something wrong. He reminded himself that, after all, he was not a true shaman. He had not been trained in the art. Mentally, he retraced the steps of the ritual, but he had done everything correctly. Then he feared that he had misinterpreted the signs and was in the wrong place. But even as he thought it, he knew this last thought didn't make sense. When he had first stepped onto the plateau, he felt the sacredness of the medicine wheel drawing power out of the ground from the heart of the planet. Even now, he could sense the power's primordial origin and he became very hot, as though the molten core of the planet were directly beneath him.

A noise to his right, coming from the road. His thoughts froze. He was afraid to look, thinking that Teresa had come to check on him. Her presence would destroy what little hope he had of succeeding. Then a shadow flitted across the clearing and landed by his left hand. Leroy gasped, recognizing his spirit guide.

The red-tailed hawk cocked his head to one side as though studying Leroy with one eye. Leroy held out his arm. The hawk hopped onto his hand. "Why are you here, little brother?" the bird asked in a high-pitched, whistling tone, which Leroy heard inside his head.

Leroy did not think it strange that the hawk should speak to him in this manner. "I am searching for the answer to a vision," he said.

"Listen," the bird said. "Mother Earth is singing to you."

Leroy strained but heard nothing.

"Listen with your heart," the hawk instructed him.

Leroy relaxed and opened his thoughts. Moments later he heard chanting as though it were coming from within him. He recognized the songs and knew he had come to the right place. As he relaxed more, Leroy located the source of the singing. Like before, it was not the stones in the medicine wheel but rocks far below him.

At this point, the red-tailed hawk leapt from his wrist and soared above him. Leroy felt his body float off the Earth and he followed his spirit guide, flying effortlessly. They dropped over the lip of the plateau and plummeted down the cliff face. Leroy should have been scared but he was exhilarated by the steep descent. At the last moment, they pulled out of their dives and came to rest by the winding road a little above the cabin.

Leroy knelt among the fragments and slabs of stone and listened to the songs. They were jumbled together in his mind and hard to pull apart. Slowly he separated the words until he recognized individual songs.

He studied the rocks. Not all of them were singing, just a few. Leroy discovered that each singing stone had odd-shaped shells of gray and white embedded on their surfaces. He began to pile the rocks that were singing to one side of the road. The stack grew steadily, until there were enough to fill most of the bed of his truck. Leroy stepped back.

The hawk flew to his shoulder. "You have done well, little brother, but there is more," the bird said.

Leroy realized that he was no longer alone. A giant bear of a man with a bushy black beard picked up one of the stones and was studying it carefully. Behind the man Leroy saw several Indian men surrounded by a vast circle of Indians and whites. Those inside the circle were dressed in loincloths and moccasins. Wooden skewers pierced the shoulders of some and these men dragged buffalo skulls across the ground from rawhide ropes behind them. Others just danced. All of them had bone whistles and they stared into the sun. Leroy knew he was watching the Sun Dance of the Lakota. By its size it must be the one held at Pipestone, Minnesota.

At one point the giant white man turned to Leroy. His eyes were dark and piercing. An unusual earring hung from his right earlobe. It was a small, prayer wheel with strange writing Leroy had never seen before engraved on it. Holding out the hand with the rock in it, the big man said, "Let me take these."

With a burst of color, Leroy's vision faded.

Chapter 29

As the door clicked shut behind her, Kira unslung her bag and let it fall to the floor. She could have used that long soak in hot Japanese bath, but she settled for a lukewarm shower. Drying her hair, she thought about falling into bed, but it was still early. If she fell asleep now, she would wake up at three in the morning. The key to overcoming jetlag was to fall asleep at your normal time. Putting on a clean pair of shorts, a shirt and sweater, she left the small yet comfortable flat and went out into the night air to walk the Old Town.

Yoshi had given her a brochure about Caernarfon, which she read on the plane to pass the time. The town had been the site of an ancient Roman fort. Its original name was *Caer yn Arfon*, which translated into "the stronghold in the land against the Mon." Mon was the Welsh name for the Isle of Anglesey. Caernarfon dated back to the end of the 13th century when Edward I razed a small settlement on the Menai Straits and erected Caernarfon Castle. A fortified medieval town, also called Caernarfon, grew up around it. Walls circling the town linked to the castle at both ends. Inside the walls became Old Town, where she now found herself.

The street outside her flat was Stryd Twll Yn Wal, which she recognized from the brochure as Hole in the Wall. It was crowded this time of night, and as she walked along unease swept over her, prompted by the narrow street with the black-stained building walls hovering over her. The people she passed spoke only Welsh, and the harsh syllables added to the feeling she was a stranger in a strange land.

Kira's old tried and true patterns of behavior didn't seem to fit. The solidity of herself, of Kira, began to fade. It was if she had become transparent. Then it came to her, the source of her unease. No women, only men at the lab. She had long lived in a world dominated by men, super-achieving men, men who craved power. First at Yale, then in medical school, even at St. Luke's, the E.R. personnel were mostly men. And here it was again. Except this time her need to compete, to be good enough, to be better than all the men, seemed foolish, irrelevant.

Who am I? It was a kind of unknowing Kira had never experienced before. Again rather than resisting, constricting, there was an opening up. Although this unknowing created a background tone of unease, it also felt real, not knowing felt like the only truth.

There was only the feminine. An outpouring of love, love for the old man walking with his cane, love for the teens as they exited the coffee shop, love for the mother with a small baby, love for everyone. Without her usual boundaries she was everything. It was the most real moment in Kira's life.

A strange buzzing noise invaded Kira's space. It was her phone vibrating to get her attention. She watched in amazement as the old structures, the old behaviors, responses, that made up Kira were put back into place. She could see clearly, that the self was an artifice, an illusion. There was no essential Kira that was the source of her personality, her actions, herself. Then back to normality.

The text was from Derek. "Sorry I wasn't there tonight. Let's meet in the morning. Have security escort you to the Extinction Zoo."

Kira blinked and read the message a second time. *What's an Extinction Zoo?* She shrugged and texted back, 'K."

Unexpectedly Kira found herself famished. Across the street was a pub named the Market Hall. According to the brochure, it was the oldest building in Caernarfon. It looked like it would have a good place eat. As she opened the door, she got the sense that someone was looking at her. She turned around, but the narrow street was empty.

Chapter 30

The tremolo of a clarinet drifted between open shoji screens and into the still evening air of the garden. Chosin Yamato paused, his left hand poised above a bonsai cedar, as the notes ascended in the opening glissando of Gershwin's *Rhapsody in Blue*. He knelt alone, his face impassive, eyes half-closed, mind emptied. He awaited the perfect moment.

As the music crescendoed, he snipped a single twig.

He opened his eyes to inspect his work. "Sabe," he said. It meant harmonious, spontaneous, unconstrained. His cut revealed all these attributes, and more. Setting the shears aside, he tenderly replaced the bonsai in its *tokonoma*. This one act had become the pinnacle of his ambition, the only thing he could honestly say he looked forward to. Three years ago he had a profound altered state that lasted for five days, during which his ordinary self-reference was not present. Since this non-dual experience, life had ceased to have any meaning, since life's meaning was dependent upon the illusory self. He knew there was no purpose to anything. Instead, he performed ancient Japanese rituals like this one while waiting to die.

Chosin knelt again and observed his garden in the deepening twilight – the miniature trees, jagged rocks, the patterns raked into the pure, white sand. High above everything, the canopy of clouds was shot through with the fiery hues of twilight. He pulled a packet of Galoises from his shirt pocket and a battered Ronson lighter from the front pocket of his trousers. With great care, he checked the flint and the wick: perfect. His father had taken it off the body of dead American soldier in World War II at Guadalcanal. The action caught the first time and Chosin lit up with the devotion of an addict. He pulled the smoke deep into his lungs, held it there, exhaled slowly, and then eyed the cigarette with gratitude. He wanted another drag – the spots in his left lung ached for it – but instead he placed the cigarette like an incense stick into the sand before the bonsai and bowed deeply. He thanked his father, who had left him this home on Hokkaido, and he thanked the *kami* – the semidivine spirits of trees and rocks and all living and dead things – who watched over the garden.

His smart phone chirped. Chosin should have thrown it away years ago, but force of habit had caused him to carry it around with him. Normally he would have ignored it like always, knowing there was nothing anyone could offer that would interest him. But he sensed something different. A feeling of intrigue passed through him momentarily and then was gone, replaced not by his usual apathy but an expectation he had not felt in years. He activated the phone and looked at the display, knowing full well what he would see.

"Chosin," said the caller.

Even in his state of high indifference, Chosin smiled. The face on the tiny screen was his own – tanned skin, high cheekbones, full lips. The dark curly hair was long and pulled back in a ponytail; the teeth were uneven and crowned. Chosin's own teeth were white and strong, his hair short. But it was their eyes that were most similar – nearly round and slightly golden with green flecks in them.

"Yo-chan," he answered, automatically using the childhood term of endearment for a younger brother. Even though they were twins, Chosin had been born four minutes earlier and was considered the elder brother.

"You are looking well," Yoshi Yamato said.

Chosin eyed his brother, wondering what could be so important that, after five years of silence, the head of Gentel's biochemical division would be calling. But that didn't matter. He sensed the urgency of the phone call as though it had been his own. And in some sense this was true. Like many twins, their lives were intertwined by a melding of thoughts and feelings.

Only their bond was even more powerful, resting upon a shared family tragedy, a tragedy Chosin had abandoned four years ago but still connected him to his brother. Their bond returned just as strong as ever, no distance of time and space between them. Instinctively, his thoughts aligned with his brother's thoughts.

Chosin studied his brother. He'd aged a great deal in five years and he sensed something was wrong, but he knew he shouldn't ask about it. *If I wait, he will tell me what is going on.*

Yoshi switched to Ainu, the language of their mother. Even though Ainu wasn't a language anyone eavesdropping would know, Chosin could hear the caution in his brother's next words. "It's late there in Hokkaido, perhaps too late to be calling."

"It's never too late to hear your voice, Yo-chan."

Yoshi nodded. "But it is getting late here in Caernarfon, late enough that I'm worried about getting enough sleep before work tomorrow. Even so, I wanted to see how you were doing, and I find myself longing for Hokkaido's long summer nights, and I wish I could take time off to see you again."

Chosin's face remained expressionless. He weighed the consequences of helping his brother. It would be extremely hard on him physically. The cancer was nearing its end game and he had only a few months to live, something he no longer cared about. But Chosin knew that on some level the decision to help Yoshi had already been made.

"Yes, it would be good to see you again, brother."

They coalesced as they bowed to each other, each one silently intoning the phrase, "I honor the Spirit in you, which is also in me."

Yoshi's image faded from phone display

Chosin looked around at the silent garden, its colors graying in the fading light. He scratched his chin with the fingers of his left hand. Yoshi needed his help...soon.

Purpose.

He bowed to the garden, turned, and entered his house. The

main room was in shadow this time of day; Chosin enjoyed the semidarkness. But after a moment's hesitation he pressed a wall switch and light sprang up softly. A vast aquarium made up three of the room's walls. Large fronds of kelp drifted in the artificial current. Round, brown Sargassum bladders massed at the water's surface. Scores of rare, brightly-colored butterfly fish darted among vivid spires of living coral.

But the real pride of Chosin's collection lay hidden in the crannies: the *Brachiopoda*. Of the twenty species of this insignificant bivalve that once had flourished in Japan's coastal waters, only three remained. Chosin took the utmost care to maintain optimum conditions for them, but they multiplied slowly. The five he'd collected twenty-five years ago had produced only twenty-three descendants.

Chosin's reflection in the tank's glass startled him. His hair showed streaks of white, his cheeks sagged. After their sister Michiko's death, Chosin and Yoshi had abandoned their father's corporate milieu. Yoshi had become a scientist, Chosin a broker of information and a collector of corporate secrets. These he sold or traded to Japan's *Zaibatsu*, the true wielders of Japanese power. He'd become extremely wealthy.

All of that had become meaningless because of his non-dual experience...an experience that like the cancer had left him in a world without requirement...a world without intention...without ambition. But now he had purpose again.

My brother needs me. Chosin had not been actively engaged in the family company's business in five years. A year later, the cancer revealed itself. He had responded well to the first treatment. And then his experience changed his life. When the cancer returned, he'd lacked any reason to fight it. Chosin sighed. Now his brother was asking him to return to a world he'd left behind. Still, he would do this and he would do it well.

Chosin placed his concerns neatly into their respective mental compartments. Looking past his reflection, he observed the marine life thriving in all its cultivated diversity. He savored the sway of the kelp, the synchrony of the fishes. Then he turned down the lights and left to gather his things.

Chapter 31

The walk to Gentel's complex from Old Town did not take more than fifteen minutes. But through it all, the afterglow of the previous night's experience still resonated through Kira. The complete disappearance of the self had left her heart open. The world was brighter. At first, she tried to analyze what had happened, but a sensation welled up in her so strongly, that she became disoriented and felt as if she were going to die. With great effort Kira was able to snap out of it. For now she decided to just let it be; there was work to do.

At the security command post, the head guard swiped her ID through the slot and asked her to do a retinal scan. He then assigned another guard to escort her to Derek Simon's Extinction's Zoo.

Kira watched the guard walk down to the building's central hub and turn toward the security station. It was strange being surrounded by armed guards who checked IDs entering and leaving a building. It reminded her of a jail.

She waited until the sound of the man's boots clicking against the linoleum floor faded before running her ID card through the security slot. When the LED changed to green, she stared into the retinal scanner. The door buzzed softly and she pulled on it cracking it slightly. She hesitated, not knowing what she would find on the other side. The door's designation was Lab 25, but Derek had called it the Extinction Zoo.

Derek was waiting just inside. When Kira closed the door behind her, he eyed her uncertainly. For Kira, this was a moment she had thought of for years, coming face to face with the man who had betrayed her. But with her experience in Omaha, her old motivation for wanting to meet with Derek had vanished. She saw him now clearly as man who had never meant to harm her, a man who from the deep crow's feet around his eyes was greatly worried, even defeated. Kira did the only thing she could think of to help him at this moment. She put out her arms and embraced him.

Derek held her tightly and Kira's first impressions of his tiredness and anxiety were proved by the intensity of his hug. When they finally disengaged, Derek stood back a little chagrined that his emotions had overcome his dispassionate British upbringing.

"So, here we are," Derek said, breaking the silence.

"Yes, here we are," Kira agreed.

"Time has treated you well."

It was true. At thirty-seven Kira was still in great shape. But that wasn't what was on her mind. "I'm infected," she said flatly.

Derek frowned. "You've had miscarriages."

Kira nodded.

"I'm so sorry. Are you sure?"

"It...it fit the pathology."

Maybe Derek sensed her sadness, because he said gently, "We call it expressing…expressing the T-gene." He smiled then and turned, waving a hand expansively inside the lab. "Welcome to the Extinction Zoo."

There were nine cages that lined two walls leading to the back of the lab. They were large and airy and ultra clean. Each cage held only one animal. From where she stood Kira could see that the animals in the first three cages were females. "This is where we house species that are going extinct."

"Because of the T-gene? All of them?"

"Yes...all of them." Derek picked up a stack of papers with Gentel's logo at the top. "This is a list of animals we know are expressing the T-gene."

Kira read the first page.

Gentel Systems Summary Report on Extinct Mammals

Page 1

Numbat: Australian banded anteater; reddish-brown coat, black and white bars on rump; approximately 2000 remaining.

Kowari: Australian rodent marsupial; reddish-gray fur, white underparts; approximately 5,000 remaining.

Shrew Opossum: Chile; soft dark brown fur, narrow face; approximately 3,000 in 2007.

Moon Rat – Mindanao, Philippines; gray and red coloring; numbers not available.

Chuuk Flying Fox: Micronesia; long soft silky fur, dark brown with silver speckles on rump; numbers not available.

Golden Bamboo Lemur: Madagascar; gray-brown with black face and golden yellow eyes; 1990 population 10,000. 2014 less than 400 remaining.

Indiana Fruit Bat: Eastern U.S.; dull brown coat; population in 1980's was 500,000, in 1999 less than half that. 2015 – none found in the wild.

Prebble Jumping Mouse: Colorado; 8cm, buff, tail longer than body; riparian habitat; numbers unavailable.

Deer Mouse: U.S., East of Rocky Mountains; brown and gray with white feet and underparts and large ears; numbers not available.

"Once we know the female is expressing, we capture the fertilized and unfertilized eggs. We use them to run our tests." Derek sighed and ran his fingers through his hair. Kira noted how gray he was. The boyish energy he had ten years ago seemed all gone now. "I often come here and sit with them." Derek smiled at her. "Am I getting old and sentimental?

Kira shook her head. "Not at all. Everybody else around here...how should I put this? They remind me of heart surgeons, carrying on as if the patient was some sort of mechanical device."

"It's purely defensive, Kira. It happens to everyone. The enormity of the situation has worn us all down."

"So what do we know?"

"Our research has shown that every living mammal has the potential for the T-gene to express itself. A pattern seems to have emerged that since the age of mammals 60 million years ago the lifespan of each succeeding species keeps shrinking. This was particularly pronounced in many of the large megafauna of the last 15 million years. We know that's what did in the Neanderthal."

"And other earlier vertebrates?" Kira asked,

"Probably, we think we found the T-gene in a 40-million-year-old species of freshwater coelacanth living in the Amazon."

"And invertebrates?"

Derek shook is head. "We just can't tell. Morphological development is so different we're not smart enough to pin it down. But from the fossil record there are too many extinctions we can't account for by the usual environmental and competitive factors. Or for that matter the large catastrophic mass extinctions."

Kira looked down at the sheet of paper in her hands. She had crumpled one edge of it. She flattened it out before speaking. "Dr. Yamato hinted that you really have no idea how this all takes place."

"True. It's like evolution doesn't want to give up its secrets. To turn an old adage on its head, 'We're in the trees and cannot see the forest.'" He grinned weakly. "That's where I hope you come in."

Kira returned the smile. "I'm here because of what we used to call your Green Genes theory."

"You remember that?"

"I memorized it." Kira recited, "Evolution, when it was creating all the basic animal body types in the Cambrian period, was operating by a different principle or mechanism. And when it was done, when it moved from the few basic types of animals with lots of variety, evolution shifted to many species with little variation. When it did that, there needed to be some way to assure that eventually every species had a finite lifespan. A way to make room for the new, for ever greater complexity."

"Full marks," Derek said. "And I'm more certain of that now than ever."

"And now the boys over in biochemistry want to get a look at my SF-81."

"Yoshi told me the secret behind your success." Derek chuckled. "I can't believe you used illegal chemicals and didn't tell anybody."

"Well, it was...I was all pretty messed up back then."

"But not now?"

But not now. "So how much time do we have? I mean if Gentel finds some sort of solution there's got to be a huge logistic problem to administer it justly to the world. I asked Dr. Yamato about it and he finally admitted he really didn't know what the plan was. Can you tell me?"

"Jurgenczak, who I'm sure you'll meet shortly, has all the resources of Gentel ready to partner with the UN's World Health Organization to move the solution quickly and equitably to all the nations of the world."

"All nations?"

"It's what he's arranged."

That can't be right, Kira told herself. *Except maybe for third world countries like Ghana and Niger or Bangladesh.* But Kira knew that Europe, South America and Asia relied on internal structures to distribute vaccines. In the U.S. the Centers for Disease control alerted the public and the medical community to a problem. After that it would be up to hospitals, doctors and pharmacies to distribute the cure, the way they did yearly flu shots. But Kira didn't say any of that. She looked at Derek and said, "What's the drop-dead date."

Derek swallowed. "Nobody really likes talking about it. But if my calculations are right, we have less than two years – and more likely this year."

Kira nodded. "So we don't have any time to waste." Her

medical sense of urgency when working a particularly heavy E.R. shift snapped into place. "So let's get busy, get some of that SF-81 and find out if those geniuses in biochemistry and genetics can figure out why those cancer cells re-differentiated."

Kira turned to leave and Derek said, "Drop by for dinner tonight after you're done. Abigail hasn't seen you in ten years...and, well...it would be good to get together in some other setting than a lab."

Kira sensed the difficulty Derek had in extending the invitation. She wondered how much of it was embarrassment of times long past and how much was worry over the future. She decided to put him at ease over the former. "I look forward to it."

Chapter 32

The Extinction Zoo door shut behind Kira, closing with a hiss as if sealing Derek into the room. She wondered if her old mentor knew that he was sliding down the slope into depression. Kira sensed his incapability of dealing with the Terminator Gene, his feelings of powerlessness. She would be lying if she said she wasn't affected by his despair. Her intuition told her she should go back in and check him over, but Derek's own urgency about finding a cure for the T-gene spurred her down the corridor. Kira headed toward her own lab. She was the only one around. Not even technicians were about. So used to the bustling energy of a hospital emergency room, the quiet and absence of humans made Kira feel a little jumpy. It was eerie having no one about.

At the door to her lab, she was surprised to find the Hazmat rack gone. Her security card still worked and the door buzzed open after her retinal scan. The lab like the halls was all but empty. The *brachiopods* that covered the center lab bench were now gone. Kira blinked and pirouetted slowly, carefully looking for some kind of clue as to what was going on. She wondered if Jurgenczak had decided suddenly that Gentel didn't need her anymore and just hadn't sent out the memo yet.

Behind her the security locks clicked loudly. Startled, Kira whirled. Her heart raced and she looked around for some kind of weapon, before realizing she was overreacting. *It's all this cloak and dagger stuff surrounding the T-gene.*

Graham entered. He blinked at the sight of her and then smiled, sheepishly. "Hullo, Dr. Taylor. I see you didn't get the memo."

"Wh...What memo?" Kira asked, wondering if her errant thought about Jurgenczak was true after all.

"We've transferred everything to Dr. Yamato's biochemistry lab. He uncovered some new research on the *brach* fossils. Seems some Swedish geologists have found a new method for the extraction and purification of the associated proteins from organophosphitic shells of inarticulated *brachiopods*. The *brachs* they used were from the Mississippi period, but the methodology is working brilliantly on yours."

Kira's eyes narrowed and she asked, "Is it safe?"

"Like a walk in the park compared to the DBTS solution. It turns out the paper was undergoing peer review over at *Nature's* office. I got to hand it to you though, thinking of using the DBTS was brilliant and awesome. I would have been too scared to use the stuff myself."

"Yeah, thanks." Kira's mind was racing. *Fuck, if they're already doing the extraction process without me, what's left?* "So where do we go from here, Graham?"

"Dr. Yamato sent me down here to get you. He wants to show you something."

"The new method was quite simple," Yoshi explained, as Kira watched his technicians go through the process. "The new protocols involve reduction by a sequence of enzymes in low concentrations of sodium hypochlorite to expose the bio-constituents. It was so simple, it took us only a matter of hours last night and early this morning to create all this." He waved a hand expansively at the center lab bench.

Kira recognized dozens of beakers filled with her SF-81. The lab whirled in a frenzy of controlled analytic action and analysis: pyrolysis gas chromatography...spectrometry (GC/MS)...amino acid residues explored by Principal Component Analysis (PCA) of variance/covariance...epithelial differentiation under a scanning electron microscope.

Yoshi interrupted the clamor. "You'll like this. What's most intriguing is what's not here. No nucleic acids."

Kira stared at him for a moment – the same results she had found ten years earlier. "So, no DNA, no RNA."

"Precisely." Yoshi pursed his lips and blew out a long trail of air. He said with a hint of awe in his voice, "I never thought it possible, but yours and Derek's idea that evolution was operating differently back in the Cambrian just might be true."

"What about the Swedes? What did they find?"

Yoshi smiled and said, "Nothing significant – a read on some proteins and amino acids. Although, compared to our analytical capability, they're in the dark ages."

So what happens now that my usefulness is over? Kira swallowed and kept her face impassive. "So I guess I'm done here."

Yoshi's smile disappeared. "What? No...no. First thing tomorrow we'll test various combinations on the HeLa cells, when we receive them in the morning. I'll need your guidance on the micro-infusion techniques you used."

"Of course. Whatever I can help with."

"By the way, I just received a message from Derek. Apparently he's not feeling well and has to cancel the dinner invitation for this evening."

That was fast. I left him less than twenty minutes ago. On the other hand, he didn't look so good earlier. "Anything serious?" Kira asked. "I could check in on him." She smiled. "After all, I am a doctor."

"His wife texted me and asked that I relay the message to you. She didn't sound as though it was anything bad. At any rate, let's hope he's back on his feet tomorrow. We're so close now."

Kira nodded, glad at least there was something she could contribute to the process. "Guess I'm done until tomorrow."

Yoshi's face took on a strained look. "Might I please offer my humble company as a poor substitute for a dinner companion? I know a little place."

Chapter 33

Pipestone, Minnesota

Jackson Kelley pulled into an immense parking lot, filled almost exclusively with older pickup trucks. His was a brand-new Ford Escape Hybrid. The two female passengers looked a little embarrassed to be in such an expensive SUV surrounded by heaps and junkers. Jack smiled. He knew the Lakota Indians did not think the same way about vehicles as whites. A truck was a truck. A person used it for everything from carrying logs for winter firewood, to hauling manure. They even borrowed each other's truck without asking, returning it to the owner when they were through with it. No, the Lakota had a different way of looking at most everything, but especially material wealth...a communal way that made more sense to Jack than the way Westerners scrambled for things to make their lives easier.

He had come to Pipestone, Minnesota for the Lakota's annual Sun Dance ceremony. The Lakota performed the Sun Dance, as a rite of passage for a few young men so that they could act as wise men for the tribe and not for themselves. By doing so, they could set aside their own needs and desires. At the end of the ceremony each dancer was no longer the same person. From then on they worked not for themselves but for the good of the tribe. It was a transcendence ritual that Jack longed for, but since he was not Lakota, he could never be invited to be one of the dancers.

He pulled into a parking space near the entrance to the large field where the ceremony was taking place. He chuckled to himself at the ease in which he found space so close. He never had trouble finding parking places. Parking karma, his best friend, Kira, called it.

Jack concentrated on his passengers – Emma and Chloe Drake,

the latest ex-wife and daughter of Keewatin Industrial's founder, George Drake. Jack had gone to great lengths to arrange their participation in the Lakota Sun Dance. The Lakota welcomed some whites to participate as watchers. The mother had long been fascinated by American Indian culture and made a very large contribution to the aquarium for the experience. But the daughter, seventeen, blond and bored, could not have cared less. In fact, she seemed indifferent to everything except her smart phone and tweeting her friends every five minutes what she was doing.

"We're here," Jack said amiably.

"It doesn't look like much," the daughter sniffed from the back seat. She was already letting her friends know she had arrived.

Turning with amazing grace and speed, Jack snatched the phone from Chloe's hands.

"Hey! I'm talking to my friends!" she cried.

He cut off her protest with one of his laughs. "I told you earlier, you won't be allowed to take this into the dance." He set her phone on the dash. "Another thing, when we get inside, we'll be separated. The women are escorted to one side of the circle and the men the other. For the rest of the day, you will be concentrating on the dancers, helping them with your thoughts to make it through the test. But it is also a test of your strength of will and character. Once you are committed to this, you can't walk out."

"Whatever," Chloe answered.

Jack led them through the gate onto the grounds where the Sun Dance was already starting up. As always, the dance site filled Jack with excitement. Two days before, five young Lakota men had gone to the banks of the nearby Big Sioux River and cut down a large cottonwood with hand axes, just as it had been done for centuries in the traditional way of the Lakota. The cottonwood was special too, marked by the shaman as the perfect tree for the ceremony. Then the young men stripped its branches, leaving only the bare trunk.

Brought back to the large field, the cottonwood was stuck into the ground forming a central pole. From its top, a latticework of branches fanned out above the dancer's heads and was secured to smaller poles at the circle's edge, creating a large semi-shaded area underneath. Within the circle, three young Lakota men, who had prepared themselves all winter and spring by giving up the pleasures of alcohol and women, would dance for three days. The dance was led by a shaman tribal elder, a man who himself had undergone the Sun Dance ritual, including the painful chest piercing on the third and final day.

Jack remembered watching his first Sun Dance. The men, already exhausted from dancing for two days, were led to the center. Skewers were pierced through the soft skin of the chest above their nipples. Rawhide thongs tied to the cottonwood were attached. The only way the young men could free themselves was to tear the skewers through their flesh. For the next twelve hours they leaned back against the ropes, the skewers wrenching painfully against their skin. All the time they danced, the watchers supported them, dancing and swaying in rhythm to the young men, encouraging them to transcend – to give up their own self-interest and work for the good of the tribe. Only at the end of the day, when the dancing filled them with the strength to surrender all thoughts of personal well being, did they have the power through one final supreme effort to rip themselves free.

A feeling of déjà vu swept through Jack unsettling him. His right hand moved to his own chest and it was as if he could feel the puckered scars of the torn flesh through his shirt. *Impossible. I am not allowed*. He shook himself and the feeling passed. "Come," he said, to Emma and Chloe, his voice strained with the concreteness of the experience.

At the entrance to the site, an old Lakota man stopped them. Jack recognized him. He was Harold Bluestone, the elder who acted as a gatekeeper. The Indian's face was heavily lined and he wore his hair in two long gray braids down his back. He recognized Jack and clasped him by the forearm. When he turned to Jack's companions, he hesitated.

Jack said, "I have prepared them. They know what they are supposed to do."

The old man nodded. "If you vouch for them, then they are welcome."

"He must be a hundred years old," Chloe whispered to her mother.

"I am eighty-eight," Harold said, smiling.

Sweet sage was burned to purify them before they could enter the sacred space. Then, two women escorted Emma and Chloe to the far side of the circle. Jack followed Harold to his place with the male watchers.

"It is good to see you again, *Wakanhca,*" Harold said, using Jack's Lakota name. It literally meant a man who walked in both worlds at the same time – the world of every day life and the world of mystery.

"It is good to be seen by you, old friend," Jack said. Harold glanced sideways at the two women and then back at Jack. He smiled and Jack's senses went on alert. He knew that look. "What?" he asked.

"I think this Sun Dance is not for your two friends," Harold said. "Instead, you will find something you are not looking for, yet it is something you will need."

Jack had no idea what the old Indian meant, but he knew that if he tried to figure it out, then nothing would come of it. Like the dancers, now circling the cottonwood, blowing bone flutes and calling on their spirit guides, he had to wait for what Harold hinted at to manifest itself. He turned his attention to the three young men dancing to deep throbbing of the drum. Special cottonwood drumsticks had been made and the drummers beat out the different tempos. The dancers and the crowd moved in rhythm not only to the beat of the drums but to the each other –

the young men gathering strength from the watchers, and the watchers vitalized by the spirit of the young men. In the months and years to come, the Lakota people would remember this shared moment and it would give strength to the tribe.

Tears rolled down Jack's face and his heart filled with joy and love, not for the spectacle of the dancers, straining beyond the limits of their endurance, but for all the Lakota who shared the experience of this ceremony.

Morning became afternoon, and before Jack knew it, evening arrived. Twilight threw shadows across the dancing ground. With the last rays of sunlight the men fell to the ground and slept where they lay.

It was time to leave, and Jack looking across the circle for Emma and Chloe, saw the teenager on the ground. Emma, uncertain what to do, hovered at the edge of the crowd surrounding her daughter. Several of the Lakota women laid their hands across Chloe's belly and began chanting softly. Jack was forced to squint as Chloe became a bright light with a dark scar in her lower abdomen. The darkness began to shrink as the Lakota women chanted and massaged Chloe's body.

Jack felt himself drawn across the dancing field when a hand touched him on the shoulder.

"You are not needed there," a voice said.

Turning, Jack saw an old Indian dancing. Unlike the Lakota, he was darker skinned and shorter. He also wore a silver bolo tie with a large turquoise clasp. Jack guessed that he was from the southwest, maybe New Mexico or Oklahoma. It wasn't unheard of members of other tribes attending the Lakota Sun Dance. The Sun Dance had become popular among all the American Indian tribes.

In the next moment Jack was dancing in rhythm with the old man, their movements like swimmers in salt water. The beat of the drum pulsed through him. It buoyed him up and he felt lighter than ever, his legs moving effortlessly, matching the old

Indian's movements perfectly. The two men entered the dancing ground and the three Lakota were also there. They were no longer inert but stood surrounding Jack and the old man. The drum throbbed now like the heart of the Earth beating through him. It was the last dance before sunset. A tribal elder handed Jack a deer-horn flute. With the first note he was filled the powerful sense of ecstatic urgency…a readiness…a powerful force that needed nothing.

The dance ended and everyone collapsed but Jack and the old Indian. They clasped forearms. The old Indian said, "You dance well." He let go and disappeared into the crowd.

Jack left the field and met up with Emma and Chloe at the entrance. Emma's face was flushed with excitement. Chloe was silent. Jack put his hand on her shoulder. Chloe's face was tear-stained but gone was the defiance and anger. In its place was sadness and loss that needed to be there...that needed to be recognized. Jack looked down and saw that the scar was gone from Chloe's abdomen.

Looking around for the old man, Jack could not see him. *That's odd. I could have sworn he wanted something from me.*

Jack shrugged and turned back to Emma and Chloe. They were gone. They must have headed for the SUV. But Emma and Chloe were not at the parking spot. A pair of trucks boxed in his car, making it impossible for him to get in. Jack looked around, hoping to spot one of the drivers. He saw no one.

Jack leaned against a Dodge Ram pickup. It was new and stood out among the older pickups that the Lakota usually drove. He glanced in the bed and spotted a pile of red rocks, partially covered by a blue plastic tarp. Picking up one of the rocks, he stared dumbfounded. He recognized the pure white brachiopod shells.

A hand tapped him on the shoulder. Jack whirled around. Standing there was the old Indian from the Sun Dance. He smiled suddenly. "I give these rocks to you for they have no home," he said.

Jack's mouth twisted into a question. But before he could ask it, the old man faded away into darkness.

A knock on wood paneling...a quiet voice – "Señor Jack. It's time to get up." Soft-soled shoes padded away.

Jack stared at the ceiling of his room. Sunlight streamed through a pair of open windows. The quiet rumble of the Missouri River filtered through. He blinked away the sleep from his eyes. *I couldn't have been dreaming. It was too real.* He shook his head in disbelief. He had actually been there felt the texture of the rocks...smelled the burning sweet sage ... heard the throb of the drums.

ack clenched the cotton sheet in his hands. *This is real*...his home in Omaha...the sun...the river. All of it was real. All of it was now.

Jack realized he had just experienced the most incredible dream he had ever had. Chloe was not a bored teenager. She was a twenty-three year old who had just gone through a miscarriage. And the rocks were something he had seen before while doing his undergraduate work at Colorado College. His geology professor had taken the class to the Manitou formation quarries in the Rockies above Colorado Springs.

"Extraordinary," Jack said aloud.

.

Chapter 34

Wichita Mountains, Oklahoma

Leroy Parker sat silently staring out at a stark blue sky. The embers from his fire had burned down to nothing and the cold rocks of Medicine Bluff seeped into his bones. His sacred pipe lay in his hands.

It is morning, he thought, *and there is much left to do.*

Chapter 35

Market Hall was not a favorite pub of the locals in Caernarfon. It catered more to tourists, which was a serendipity not lost on Kira as she sipped her coffee. The aroma of the cinnamon-spiced cappuccino filled her with pleasure. She looked over the rim of the cup at Yoshi. He was sipping an after dinner Bourdeaux. Kira learned that he had earned an M.D. and then had one on to gain two PhDs, finally becoming one of the world's leading biochemists.

"So how did you come to the Terminator project?" Kira asked.

"Like you, I was recruited by Derek. At first, I was incredibly excited to be working on the greatest challenge that has ever faced humanity. But as months turned into years, I felt a higher calling from life. Isn't this really about life? You know, there are many who would say good riddance to the human species. So for me, now, it's about life."

Kira wanted to speak about her own higher calling…that creative urgency she felt on that morning more than a week ago, a morning, which now seemed so distant. Instead she said, "As my friend, Jack, once told me, 'If you get the big picture right, the rest will follow.' So tell me, what's the big picture for you?"

"The project or evolution?"

"Evolution."

Yoshi set down his wine glass and tapped the base with a narrow tapered finger. The green flecks in his golden irises seemed to sparkle for a moment, and Kira had the feeling that the Japanese scientist had given more than a little thought to this.

"Since I started at Gentel Systems, I've written two monographs on epigenetics."

"You're talking about the idea that large morphological changes can take place suddenly, such as when wolves became dogs."

"Exactly. Somehow, Hox genes and the Terminator Gene got all tied together in some way that was set in motion when evolution pointed to us. Isn't it curious that here we are, products of evolution consciously trying to manipulate evolution. Think about it, all the great religions, all the wisdom traditions of the world were founded before the emergence of the evolutionary perspective. What would Christ or Buddha have done or taught if they had known about evolution? The evolutionary perspective changes everything."

"I couldn't agree more with that." Kira smiled. "Remember when Robert Wright's *The Evolution of God*, came out. The claim that God only came into existence when our tool-making ancestors started growing a larger brain."

Yoshi laughed. "It was such heresy."

Kira nodded. "So here's my big picture. Evolution is going somewhere. It has a direction – ever more complexity. Stars crashing into each other produced more complex atoms. Atoms combined to make molecules. Molecules created even more complexity when they joined together and cells arose. Cells became organisms. Organisms produced systems. And now our brain is the most complex thing in the universe. A thing that is aware of the process that created it."

"I agree that we're going somewhere, but where?" Yoshi asked. "Somehow the answer ties into all the discoveries in the last few years – epigenetics microtubules, the discovery that the architecture of neurons is itself a computer with computational powers a billion times more powerful than our neural net. And what really blows my mind is the discovery that consciousness itself is built into the quantum space-time continuum that arose in the first nanosecond after the Big Bang. All that understanding and yet..." Yoshi's frown reappeared. "It'll all come to come to an end when the last human moves from embryo to fetus." His fingers tapped the wine glass stem again, almost like some kind of code. "So, you're the one with the fresh perspective. Tell me, what are we missing?"

Kira's mind was flashing through all the possibilities that Yoshi's words hinted at. It was like a kaleidoscope. Each phrase, each turn of the scope presented a vast new maze of ideas. Then she got what Yoshi was alluding to. "So, in your mind it's not 'simply get over the Terminator Gene problem and go back to business as usual?'"

Yoshi nodded. "My sense is something bigger is going on."

"I get that sense, too. I've been having some non-ordinary experiences, and I have this deep-seated feeling that somehow they relate to that big picture of evolution going someplace."

Yoshi's eyes narrowed. "Like what?"

Kira realized that she couldn't talk about what had happened as some sort of hippy LSD experience. Yoshi needed to know that her experiences were part of the larger evolutionary pulse of humans. "Last night I was walking down Hole in the Wall Street here in Old Town when I entered a state that's hard to describe. But it was a state where my self-reference disappeared. There was just stuff happening. No watcher. No hearer. No thinker. Just seeing, hearing...actually no thinking. Once you have this experience, it's perfectly clear that the self, the me, is an artificial construct."

Yoshi's golden eyes narrowed even further and Kira's heart sank. *He thinks I'm an idiot.*

Then Yoshi smiled. "Four years ago my brother had just such an experience."

"And?"

Yoshi shrugged and Kira thought he was going to drop the matter. But Yoshi added, "He now lives on Hokkaido and has withdrawn completely from life."

"How is he now?"

Yoshi abruptly stood and looked around as if he expected to see someone. He pulled out a wad of English money from his pocket, selected a few bills and dropped them on the table. "Let's go," he said tersely and led them out of the pub.

Kira craned her head from side to side wondering who the Japanese scientist was looking for. She saw no one. But she recalled her feelings from the night before of being followed.

Outside the Market Hall, Kira tugged on Yoshi's suit coat and made him stop. "Do you get the sense someone's following us?"

"Not us. I suspect you are being followed, since you're an unknown."

"Okay, I'll buy that. So what's next?"

"We take a little walk, where we can talk freely."

Yoshi led them in silence along the wall of Old Town. To their left, late evening sunlight skipped off the placid waters of the Menai Straits. Kira, surprised by the depth and breadth of Yoshi's philosophical understanding, felt embarrassed by her outburst on the plane. Clearly he was feigning ignorance about the ultimate goal of the project.

Finally, Yoshi broke the silence. "Would you like to see Caernarfon Castle in a unique way?" Before Kira could answer, he walked out onto a dock and stood beside a small dory floating among the large sailing vessels at the local marina. As he pulled back the tarp covering the narrow, flat-bottomed rowboat, Kira spotted fishing gear neatly stored in racks along both sides. With surprising agility, the Japanese scientist leapt lightly onto the craft. He pointed to the rope mooring the boat's high prow to the slip.

"Untie us," Yoshi said.

Kira unlooped the line and let herself easily into the boat, glad she had worn her running shoes to dinner. As Kira put on her life jacket, Yoshi deftly unshipped the oars and maneuvered the boat into the Straits.

Neither of them noticed a shadowy figure on shore following their movements with a pair of high-powered binoculars.

As the dory swung easily into the calm waters of the Straits, the man cursed silently. The conversation in the Market Hall had been fascinating and easily picked up with a microwave transmitter. But out on the waters, there was too much white noise to make heads or tails of what the two were saying. Still he followed them.

The sun-lit castle cast long shadows across the last tourists lingering among the stony battlements.

Yoshi kept rowing, pulling the oars easily. "When I'm not working in the lab, I come out here to fish and think."

"It's calm and peaceful." Kira said, waiting for Yoshi to get at what he really meant to say.

"More than a week ago," the Japanese continued, "A high-level researcher in Littleton's division, went for an evening sail, just like we're doing. Only he never came back. The day before died, he sent Derek and myself flash-drives. On them he stated that all of Gentel's work is basically useless. No conventional approach was going to unlock the secrets of the Terminator Gene. Anyhow that's why you're here. Dr. Howe, that was his name, said the problem was developmental. To my surprise Jurgenczak agreed, and even more to my surprise, he agreed to bring you here when Derek brought up your thesis work."

Kira frowned. "Derek told me none of this."

"I'm sure he didn't. There's more to Dr. Howe's story. His plea for a different approach was underscored by a belief he held that the time had come to inform the world about its potential fate. I think he tried to do just this."

"He tried to tell the world about the Terminator Gene?"

"And he paid the price. I don't believe his death was an accident." He paused in his rowing while he let this information sink in.

Kira wasn't able to hide her shock. *What has Derek gotten me into?*

Yoshi pulled in the oars. He unsnapped a long ocean fishing rod with a casting reel from its clips and handed it to Kira. "Do you know how to use one of these?"

Kira nodded dumbly as she watched him take another one for himself and cast the line sixty feet out across the water. She couldn't help but wonder at Yoshi's strange behavior. In fact, now that she thought about it, he had been acting strangely ever since she met him. She knew this judgment didn't make sense, since she didn't have anything to compare his behavior to. Now that she thought about it, his unstoical behavior on the plane should have tipped her off.

Kira managed a decent cast without fouling the line.

"That's why I had to play dumb on the plane," Yoshi said, answering her unspoken question.

"You mean we were being bugged." Kira said.

"I suspected so. Now that we're just a couple of colleagues fishing, let's talk about Derek. I presume you asked him about Gentel's plan to disseminate the cure?"

"Uh-huh," Kira answered, thinking that this was an entirely different Yoshi than the man she had met forty-eight hours earlier. "The distribution plan he laid out using the World Health Organization, to put it bluntly, was a bunch of crap."

"I suspected as much."

"What's interesting is that I don't think he was lying."

"I'm sure you're right," Yoshi agreed. "Remember that I said I knew somebody on the outside who can help us find out what's going on."

"Yes."

"I contacted my brother. Before he withdrew from life he was one of the best at a rather unique occupation."

Kira normally liked fishing, but Yoshi's strange conversation had her on edge. Yet his demeanor was anything but threatening so she calmly said, "Fascinating coincidence. And what did he find out?"

"I'm still waiting to hear from him. In the meantime my plan is to keep you as valuable as I can for as long as I can."

"I'm in danger?"

Yoshi's face assumed an unreadable mask. "We'll find out soon enough, won't we."

Chapter 36

Jackson Kelley sat in his office at the Scott Aquarium. The curtains for the floor-to-ceiling windows were open and the panorama of Omaha spread out before him. He stared at the conspicuous spires of Keewatin Industrial, Bartnum Haggerty and Gentel Systems. Jack still could feel the ecstatic urgency that infused his dream body during the Lakota Sun Dance.

Jack thought of himself as a seeker of the path. Raised in the Tibetan Buddhist tradition of his Rinpoche father, by the time he was sixteen Jack rebelled against everything the monks taught him. It became all about science. Science had all the answers. Anything else was merely alchemy. In time Jack found that science with injunctive methodology had answers but not to the ultimate questions about life. That's when he started sampling various spiritual practices: Hindu's Vedanta Yoga, Aikido and Western psychology's voice dialogue and clearing. All had something to offer but Jack was never totally satisfied. He wanted that mind blowing experience – the big awakening. But he never thought it would come in the form of a dream.

He reflected: *This isn't about me; it's about something bigger, way bigger.*

Turning away from the Omaha skyline, his gaze fell upon a pinkish-red chunk of dolomite that occupied that central part of his desk, where pictures of his family would be, if he had a partner and children. The dolomite held a pristine trilobite about the size of a silver dollar that he had found on a field trip in his college days. The *leiostegium* was his most-prized possession, an example of the mystery behind the Manitou – was it upper Cambrian or lower Ordovician? Jack asked his computer to find "Manitou formation field trip." The result splashed across his Smart Board – a link to *Fossil Field Trip Manitou Formation 1999*. The article was written by Dr. William Reed, his geology professor at Colorado College in Colorado Springs.

Jack scrolled through a myriad of pictures, all trilobites. The last image, however, was a small cream-colored brachiopod. The caption read, *lingula,* named for the typical tongue-shaped shell, hence the name *lingulata,* from the Latin word for tongue. It was the very same fossil he saw in his dream.

He couldn't remember exactly, but these appeared to be the same kind of fossils Kira had used to extract her ancient SF-81. The field trip mentioned three locations where significant fossil collections had been made – the Air Force Academy in Colorado Springs and two farther west. One was called Mount Deception at Rainbow Falls.

That's where we went, that's where I found my trilobite. Jack wirelessly downloaded the *lingulata* picture to his smart phone. He was about to send it to Kira along with a link to the field guide, but then he hesitated. It was one thing to intuit the unlikely synchronicity of Kira, Gentel and the *brachiopods.* It was another to follow through with what seemed obvious. He didn't want to do anything that might be suspicious where Kira was concerned. If Derek's pronouncements about Gentel's security protocols were even slightly true, they most likely had tapped Kira's phone by now. It would be beyond coincidence to Gentel's Security that files containing information on *brachiopods* – the very thing Kira was working on in Caernarfon – would suddenly show up. Certainly they would copy anything he sent her.

Jack's mind quietly went through the alternatives and then the simplicity of the solution made him smile. *Kira loves games,* he chuckled to himself. He deftly made a few keystrokes, subtly altering the *brach* image and embedding a cipher in it. Kira would see it immediately, but anyone else would think it was an anomaly in the picture. He pressed 'send' and the image went to Kira's phone. Next he uploaded the files on the Manitou formation into the cloud, where no one without the password could find or trace it back to the source.

Chapter 37

Yoshi walked Kira to her flat and said goodbye at the door, disappearing into the night even before she had her keys out. Once inside she walked to the window, pondering the day's revelations. Since her non-dual experience the night before, her former fear-based reactions had all but disappeared. She recognized danger. The Terminator Gene project had become a great unknown, a partial source of that danger. But its possible impending peril arose just as a fact to be dealt with. Kira tried to get a sense of how she was holding the events of the last few days. The closest she could come to an overall feeling was fascination. Everything was new and fascinating.

Absentmindedly, she checked her phone for messages. There weren't many. Something from her dad and an email from Jack about a strange dream he had.

No friendly tweets or texts. *It's amazing. I've gone through life and except for Jack no close friends.* Since Kira could remember, she had never let people get close to her. Particularly men. She enjoyed sex and the excitement of courtship, but when it started to get emotionally intimate, she recoiled. It was as if anyone got too close, they would suck the life force out of her. *Is that still true?* She thought back over her evening with Yoshi. *Hard to tell.*

She looked outside the window again. The sun had set, but in June this far north she could still see clearly. Without thinking she slipped out of the skirt she wore to dinner and donned her running clothes. She stuffed clothes into a runner's pack and took off for the lab.

She set the pace at an easy lope, intending to run several miles in a loop through the city before ending up at Gentel's complex. But she had hardly taken more than a dozen steps when an idea flashed through her mind. She took several breaths, calming her mind. She didn't know how to explain what she was thinking, but the only way to figure it out was to go to the lab.

At Gentel's main security gate, the guards balked at letting her in so late. "It's most unusual, Dr. Taylor," said a young man with a black beret. He wore green fatigues, and an Uzi machine pistol hung by its strap off his right shoulder. "I'll need Hawke to authorize this."

Gentel's security chief arrived within minutes from inside the building. After making Kira leave her fanny pack at the gate, he allowed her to enter.

Kira and Hawke walked down the long hall without speaking. When they reached the junction of the cross, Hawke stopped. "I did not think you would be returning this evening, Dr. Taylor."

"I had an idea I wanted to test."

Hawke eyed her and his lips pulled down in a slight frown. "Secrets, Dr. Taylor are my bailiwick, as the English like to say."

"What you're getting at, Hawke?"

"I know what you and Yoshi are up to."

"And what's that?"

Hawke's brow furrowed and his eyes locked on Kira's. He had often practiced a look that was intended to intimidate even frighten. But what Kira saw was something else – the radiance of the human potential. It filled her with awe, almost reverence. Puzzled by her reaction, Hawke took a step backward. He had never felt anything like this before. Unaccountably tears welled up. His own emotional response nearly overwhelmed him and he was forced to turn and walk away.

Inside Yoshi's lab a number of technicians were still running tests and entering the results into the Mini-tower super computer. Kira's assistant, Graham, was preparing a large group of shells for chemical processing. Behind him a machine that looked like a miniature sewage treatment plant was macerating other shells. Graham spotted Kira and motioned her to come over. If he noticed she was wearing running shorts and a T-shirt, he didn't say anything.

Probably he's used to seeing scientists come in here in all manner of dress to check on an experiment, Kira told herself.

"What brings you here so late?" Graham asked.

"Has anyone thought to run a test for any signs of antigens in the SF-81?"

"What are you thinking?"

Kira shook her head. "Don't know yet. Just a hunch."

Graham walked over to two technicians and talked to them for a few minutes. "Sure," she heard one of the men say. Graham gave her a thumbs-up.

Suddenly, the excitement of the day, the dinner with Yoshi and the unexpected encounter with Hawke caught up with Kira. She found a large chair and curled up in it. She fell asleep immediately.

Chapter 38

Standing in the shadows of Caernarfon Castle's Black Tower, Yoshi Yamato shivered and peered anxiously through the silent gloom for signs of his brother. Irritable at being up so late, he uncharitably thought Chosin too clandestine keeping to shadows and insisting that they conduct this meeting so late and in a so out-of-the-way place. Abruptly, Yoshi shook his head and smiled ruefully. *Chosin is right. Things at Gentel are uncertain at best.* And even though he was standing in the darkness of the Tower's doorway, Yoshi found himself pressed against the stone.

He stamped his feet to stay warm. In spite of the long days, at this latitude, once the sun set the night turned chilly and the cold seemed to radiate out of the serrated battlements of the castle's towers. Below him, the town of Caernarfon spread out in a muted beauty of old and new. A few cars moved along the road by the Menai Straits, and from the castle's seaward side, the only sounds came from boats creaking at anchor.

Using the light from his phone, Yoshi reread the piece of paper he had found taped to the underside of his car's steering wheel when he left work this evening. It would have been easier to send a text message, but Chosin sometimes refused to trust the new technology. "Anything in cyberspace can be cracked," he had said many times. The note, in Chosin's hand, was written in Ainu and read, "Meet me at the Black Tower at the hour of the monkey."

Yoshi checked the time. Chosin was now twenty minutes late and despite his earlier cavalier attitude toward his brother's profession, Yoshi was beginning to worry that something had delayed Chosin. *I'll wait ten more minutes and leave.*

Then he felt it, like a slight pressure in his mind. It was a familiar feeling that had been there all through childhood and adolescence when he and Chosin would finish each other's thoughts or an entire conversation could pass between them through a simple glance. When Yoshi heard the cough in the darkness behind him, he turned slowly. His brother was standing there, shaking his head. Yoshi could feel the disappointment in the gesture.

"Every time you use your phone light, I can see your face as plainly as if you were at home reading a book," Chosin said.

Chagrined, Yoshi answered apologetically, "I was worried about you. I was afraid you weren't going to show up."

Chosin leaned against the stone. His lungs ached with the cancer and the effort of slipping into the castle and climbing the steps had tired him more than he thought it would. "I'm getting old, Yo-chan."

Concerned, Yoshi put his hand on his brother's shoulder. He studied Chosin in the gloom. Intelligent, capable, single-minded, but he looked older than he was. A flash of insight told him his brother was hiding something, and he worried he was asking too much.

Chosin waved his doubts away. "I'm strong enough for this, Yo-chan. So here I am."

"I'll be brief," Yoshi began. "Behind the work I'm doing is a secret so profound no one could even imagine it twelve years ago." Yoshi laid out the science first, explaining about the Terminator Gene discovered by Arne Jurgenczak and Gentel's role in finding a solution. "Everything changed ten days ago when one of our high-level recombinant genetic researchers, Dr. Ray Howe, died under suspicious circumstances. It happened after he threatened to reveal the existence of the T-gene to the world. He wanted to openly involve many more scientists. Curiously, his reasoning was that Gentel was taking the wrong approach at the time and he thought we needed a new infusion of ideas to get us back on track."

"New Ideas?"

"Howe wanted us to take an evolutionary or developmental approach. Everybody here knows he was right. We are running out of time."

"How much time is left?" Chosin asked.

"We can't know for certain, but if our calculations are correct, it could be less than a year."

"Do you know why this is happening at this time?"

"It's part of the natural process of evolution."

Chosin raised his eyebrows and Yoshi hurried on to answer his brother's unasked question. "Events led to bringing in an American doctor, a former student of Derek Simon, Kira Taylor. She's a paleontological expert as well as an M.D."

Chosin eyed his brother carefully. He could see in his brother's body language that Yoshi liked the doctor. But more than that, he sensed they were kindred spirits. "This American is special?"

"I trust her. She has had experiences close to your own. She has a rare gift to be present. Doesn't talk a lot. But in her presence my ability to think clearly is greatly increased. Like with you there is an unspoken, felt communication."

Chosin knew what Yoshi meant. Whatever either of them was in touch with, the other was there too. "I would like to meet her."

"You will, I promise," Yoshi said. "She's the one who speculated that the T-gene emerged at the end of the Cambrian period as a mechanism to hasten evolution. It forces new species to emerge by guaranteeing that extinctions occur, consequently always opening the door to ever greater complexity."

Chosin's non-dual experience had left him with a unique capacity for clear seeing – to look at an idea or a thing without the distortion of emotion or past history. *If you wanted evolution to become aware evolution itself, what better way than to evolve a brain capable of supporting consciousness*. "How ironic," he said.

"Yes, a true paradox," Yoshi agreed, sensing his brother's thoughts. "We as a product and a part of this process have grown to the point where we can direct the process that has produced us while at the same time never escaping the process."

The brother twins stood silently, each sensing the other's

thoughts, a game they had played since childhood. *Yet at the same time, evolution has condemned that species to death by the very same mechanism.*

Chosin breathed in slowly, felt the rales deep in his chest. Life had chosen a different form of death for him. "But you didn't ask me to come to Caernarfon just to tell me the human race may soon disappear from the planet."

Yoshi shook his head. "Kira and I believe we have a found a means to circumvent the T-gene mechanism and allow the human race to continue. If I'm right, eliminating the Terminator Gene will force us to make a quantum leap in consciousness."

"But you see a problem with this."

"I'm convinced that Jurgenczak is sincere in wanting to find a solution, but he has lied about how he would disseminate the cure."

"And that's why you need me to play my old game again." Chosin smiled. In spite of the profound indifference that had arisen after his non-dual experience, he knew he should do what his brother asked. He would treat it like a game.

Yoshi shrugged. "Yes. That's why we need your special skills, Chosin. We need you to find out what's going to happen if a solution is found."

"Is there any information you can give me that would point me in the right direction?"

"Start with Gentel Systems. The corporate headquarters are not here but in Omaha, Nebraska. Jurgenczak takes frequent trips there."

Chosin kept his face impassive. Omaha was home to Keewatin Industrial and Bartnum Haggerty, two firms he had done business with in the past. He chuckled to himself. Business was a euphemism for stealing corporate secrets for them.

Yoshi smiled and thanked the *kami* for his brother. "One more thing. If I want to get data out of Gentel, do you have anything that could help me?"

Chosin hesitated. He didn't want to alarm his twin, but his sixth sense warned him that his brother must not try anything so foolish. "No Yo-chan, you must rely on your memory."

"It would be easier if I used my lab's computer and uploaded everything to your phone."

"Easier but not possible. Gentel has some kind of jamming field around their complex. Nothing can penetrate – in or out."

"You're sensing something bad is going to happen."

"Perhaps it is nothing, but I think you should take this precaution. Write nothing down that is critically important to the solution. Store it all in your memory. And be ready to leave at a moment's notice."

"When will we meet again?"

"I will contact you." He looked around, uneasy staying in an exposed place so long. "We should go now," Chosin said.

Yoshi bowed deeply. "Thank you, brother." When he looked up, he was alone.

Chapter 39

Hawke looked out the window of his office at the empty Gentel System parking lot. The glass was electrically charged. He liked the seclusion and the fact that he could see who came and went no matter the time of day and night with no one able to see him. The anonymity gave him a sense of security, and now he needed that more than ever. His earlier encounter with Dr. Kira Taylor had unsettled him. She should have been nothing more than a security issue, but the look she had given him this evening brought up feelings he had thought safely tucked away…feelings never to be brought up again. It was a look he had seen in the eyes of his first and only girlfriend – his first and only time in love.

Unable to stop himself, Hawke envisioned Caitlin Yee. She was an inch shorter than Hawke; long chestnut hair, slightly almond eyes that gave away her Chinese ancestry. A state high-school gymnastics champion, she had chosen the Air Force Academy over a tryout for training to make the 1992 Olympic team. Like Hawke, Caitlin was of bi-racial parentage with a foot in both worlds. In her case she was Eurasian.

Hawke grimaced thinking about his own parents – Black and American Indian. He had never known either of them. They had been killed by a drunk driver on the Crow Indian reservation in Montana, when the family had gone to visit his mother's grand-parents. Life after that was a series of foster homes in Detroit, never knowing who he really was, what world he fit into. Taunted by blacks and whites alike. He might have been lost in the Projects forever, except for a math teacher, Mr. Finzen, who got him an appointment to the Air Force Academy.

But the unfairness of his mixed race heritage followed him there. And it landed on Caitlin Yee as well. In the 1990s, the U.S. military had a 'don't ask, don't tell' policy for gays. It gave them a way to remain private. But for men and women like Hawke and Caitlin, there was no way to hide their genetic heritage. And everyone who looked at them saw them as outsiders.

Their similarities brought them together at the academy. Their academic excellence and athletic performances gave them something to talk about. Their feelings as outsiders made them fall in love, looking for that someone they could confide in, talk to…that someone who would watch your back. For six months it had been wonderful. They hiked through the foothills above the academy. Shared views on everything from math, to politics, military history. Caitlin came from old money, and on their days off, she and Hawke spent glorious nights in the best hotels in Denver.

Then one day in the middle of their second year she was gone, Caitlin left the Air Force Academy without a word. When Hawke asked the academy commander what had happened, he was told only that her case was sealed and she would not be returning.

Two months later, Hawke overheard two upperclassmen talking in the library. One of them bragged about how he had forced the Chinese half-breed to leave the academy by raping her.

It had taken Hawke two years to even the score. But that upperclassman never flew again, never walked again, and never fed himself again.

Hawke had tried to get in touch with Caitlin to tell her he knew what had happened. But she secluded herself behind her family's fortune. Over the years bits and pieces of her life came out – married, mother of three, divorced and now head of the family's philanthropic foundation for foster children. He had come to think of it as her way of remembering him.

Hawke forced himself to stop reliving the past and concentrate on what he was going to tell Jurgenczak. Over the last few days a sense of uncertainty had befallen him. Hawke hadn't felt this way since that the day Caitlin had left the academy. He knew the source of his uncertainty – the project was nearing its end.

He swallowed in a dry throat. *What's next?* For ten years he hadn't had to ask that question.

His phone chirped. Hawke knew without looking that it was Dr. Jurgenczak. No one else would call him on this line. It was a simple text message, "Come."

"I'll be right up," Hawke typed.

Jurgenczak's office was the only second floor room in the complex. It sat like a turret overlooking the Menai Straits. Hawke never tired of the view and liked meeting the old man here. But tonight, uncertainty crept into his muscles and left him tense, like a cat who didn't know friend from foe.

Jurgenczak beamed at him from the windows. His face was more animated than Hawke could remember. His handshake was firm and held a feeling of euphoria that Hawke hadn't felt in years. It was as if the pall of failure over the Terminator Gene project had been lifted.

Jurgenczak turned back to the windows. Moonlight splashed across the Menai Straits. "Where are they now?"

"Dr. Yamato is at his house and Dr. Taylor is downstairs sleeping in his lab, sir." Jurgenczak's bushy eyebrows lifted in surprise and Hawke continued, "She has an idea."

"My, my. So, have you been able to follow their movements, determine what they think?"

Hawke thought of Dr. Taylor and forced himself to remain impassive. "They've been quite secretive."

Jurgenczak nodded. "That's to be expected. Still, it's very good that they're working together. I was worried. It seems Dr. Taylor has quite a reputation for impulsive behavior and anger. But from all accounts of the people she has interacted with here, Dr. Taylor is nothing like her reputation."

Hawke watched Jurgenczak stare out into the darkening night. The sun was completely set and still a bright band of light edged the northwest horizon. He wondered what the old man saw out there.

"I haven't met her yet. What do you think of her? Do you think she's a Christian?"

"I could ask, sir."

"No, no, it's not important now. What's their assessment of the biochemistry that everyone's been analyzing? Can you tell?"

It was then that Hawke realized that he had seen Jurgenczak's joy and excitement in Yamato and Taylor. *Something big must be happening and no one's talking. Why am I being left out of this?*

Jurgenczak misinterpreted his silence. "Come my boy, your days running security for Air Force One must have given you some profiling abilities. How are Taylor and Yamato reacting to all of this?"

"They appear to be very encouraged, sir," Hawke said carefully.

"Very, you say?" Jurgenczak asked.

"Very."

"So the day we've been hoping for is near," Jurgenczak mused aloud.

Hawke felt his mouth go dry and he was unable to keep the uncertainty out of his next words. "Do you believe it is near, sir?"

Jurgenczak, as if reading the cause of Hawke's anxiety, smiled benignly. "No need to worry, my son. There's plenty more to be done, and I'd say your real job is just beginning."

Hawke managed to hide his relief. "Thank you, sir. You can count on me for whatever needs to be done."

Jurgenczak lost his smile. "How do you think the news about Dr. Simon will be received?"

Hawke took a few moments to arrange his thoughts. "Though Simon recruited Dr. Taylor, they've been estranged for ten years. I don't believe she will be adversely affected. Dr. Yamato, on the other hand, was close to him, and following on the heels of Howe's death, this may rattle him somewhat at first. In the end, however, I believe it should bring them together."

Jurgenczak nodded his approval. "Good. Make sure all

outside communications are carefully monitored and controlled. You've done well, Hawke. Go home and get some sleep. The next couple of days are going to be crucial and I'm going to need you at your best."

"Yes, sir. Good night, sir," Hawke said and left the room, silently closing the door after him.

Jurgenczak, watching the younger man leave, gauged him for any sign that he was hesitant. He knew Hawke was completely devoted to him. His loyalty was what had led Jurgenczak to offer him the post of chief security officer at Gentel's Caernarfon Complex. But the next few days were going to be the greatest test of devotion Hawke ever faced. Satisfied he saw nothing that would keep Hawke from carrying out his orders, Jurgenczak put that part of the plan out of his mind. But his own part in the plan was not so easy to dismiss.

Jurgenczak lifted his eyes upward as if staring into the heavens and looking Jehovah in the face. *It will be the greatest test of my devotion as well, Adonay. Now that we are close, your children can be saved.* Jurgenczak steeled himself for the trial that must come in a few days. *I will not fail you, Adonay. 'Thou hast created all things, and for thy pleasure they are and were created.'*

But the burden of carrying out Jehovah's will fell heavy upon Jurgenczak, especially when he thought of the many fine men and women working at Gentel's Caernarfon Complex. They filled a vital role in Jehovah's plan. But now that role was coming to an end. Jurgenczak often thought of them as soldiers...Jehovah's warriors in the fight to create an Eden on Earth. *Their time in this fight is coming to an end. I must be certain that their sacrifice will not be in vain. Including Dr. Kira Taylor.* Jurgenczak sighed. *And now there is another soul to pray for.* He thought of his own soul then and the black deed he must carry out to insure Jehovah's plan worked. *Surely, Adonay, you will forgive me for the deaths of so many in order to create Your Earthly paradise.*

The door to Jurgenczak's private alcove opened and Jurgenczak turned, putting his thoughts about the upcoming trial away. Dr. Frank Littleton stood in the entryway, hands clasped as if praying.

"You overheard our conversation?" Jurgenczak asked the American.

Littleton nodded.

"And do you now agree that Yamato and Taylor are on the right track and have found the answer?"

"I had my doubts, but after following their work, I can't see any other way to explain it. They're going to do it."

Pleased by Littleton's response, Jurgenczak let a beatific smile fill his face. He could feel the perfect happiness and inner peace flow out into the room. "Praise the Lord," he whispered.

"Amen," answered Littleton.

Chapter 40

Comfortably resting in that wonderful place between the dream world and wakefulness, Kira couldn't recall sleeping so deeply since Derek Simon first told her about the Terminator Gene. She could feel the effects of sleep in her bones and muscle tissue. It was a cleansing and left her feeling not only refreshed but so powerful she could accomplish anything. Then all at once she was fully awake. Yoshi's lab assistants were high-fiving each other. Graham looked over and noticed she was awake.

"Sorry about waking you, Dr. Taylor, but Jurgenczak has called all the teams together for an important announcement." As Kira joined others in the complex headed toward the large conference room in the south end, Kira thought Jurgenczak was going to talk about the lab's breakthrough, like Graham suggested. But as she walked along, she sensed the mood of the others was more somber.

The conference room was shaped like the nave of a church, with the plain wooden seats descending in ten rows toward the chancel, separated by a simple wooden railing. The chancel rose like a stage above the nearest row, and at the far end of it was a low table that Kira was convinced could double as an altar.

She looked around for Derek and Yoshi, but neither man was here. Graham and the other techs from Yoshi's lab joined a group of younger lab assistants to one side, so she had no one she could ask about what was going on. A hush fell over the crowd and Kira saw Yoshi and Littleton come out on the stage followed by Jurgenczak.

None of the men smiled and Kira could feel that the announcement was something grave. She discovered she was holding her breath and let it out slowly.

"Dear colleagues, dear friends," Jurgenczak began, "I am sorry to have to convey to you that Derek Simon passed away last night. I just spoke with his wife, Abigail. God bless her. He had gone to bed early last night after telling her he wasn't feeling well. She found him this morning. He died in his sleep and did not suffer. God rest his soul.

"Dr. Simon was dear to many of you. We will, of course, arrange a memorial service for him in a day or two, and for those of you who wish, please take time off and mourn or pray in your own way." The crowd, silent and shaken by the news, did not move. Gentel's founder cleared his throat and added, "I feel I must speak as Derek would wish on this day. He recruited most of you, and like you, he was totally committed to the project. And, now on the eve of finding a solution, he will not be here to share in our glory. But we would not be so close without him and he would want you to put aside your grief and move forward. I know he would say to you now if he were here, that humanity is counting on us to move forward. I think we should honor Dr. Simon by redoubling our efforts to end this threat to our children and grandchildren as quickly as possible. Thank you."

Jurgenczak led Littleton and Yoshi off the stage. Kira tried to catch the Japanese scientist's eye, but his head was down.

Looking around her, she saw the Complex's personnel moving up the aisles toward the two sets of double doors leading out of the conference room. Everyone seemed to have someone to talk to and their muffled voices fled past Kira in the emptying room. Kira found that she couldn't talk. She stood there numbly, staring at the empty stage. *I should have gone over last night. I saw him that morning. The signs were all there. I should have seen them. I was too excited about what we were doing – and I forgot my oath as a physician to heal.*

Kira ignored the tears in her eyes. She dwelled on how she and Derek had just been reunited after ten years of her anger keeping them apart. And now when she had so much left to say to him, time had run out. Kira shook herself. She knew that dying from a heart attack was never peaceful. The image of Derek alone, in great pain tore at her. Her chest tightened and her breathing came in searing gasps as though she were also suffering his final moments..

This is silly, she admonished herself. She had seen death many times in the ER. She should have been able to detach herself. Instead, Derek passing washed away all the confidence she had gained since her non-dual experience. Unworthiness replaced it and she fell into despair. *How could I have believed I could solve the Terminator Gene problem. I've just been pretending. The whole project sucks.*

Kira took one last look at the empty stage and stormed up the aisle. *Humanity can go to hell.*

She reached the double doors and was ready to run out of the complex, when fingers gently touched her shoulder. Shrugging them off, Kira snapped, "Let me go!"

"I can't do that," a familiar voice answered.

Kira turned and saw Yoshi. His puffy eyes were evidence that he too had been crying and shared the loss of Derek as deeply as she did. He embraced her and Kira recalled the desperate hug from Derek just the day before. "I am such a fraud," she said, voice tear-choked. "I should have seen this coming. I could have stopped it."

"Perhaps," Yoshi said.

Kira shook her head. "No perhaps. This shouldn't have happened."

Yoshi blew out a stream of air as if counting to ten. Then, "All right. It shouldn't have happened and now you want to quit. Perhaps punish yourself."

"Next you'll tell me Derek would want me to stay and solve the T-gene."

Yoshi shrugged. "I don't know what Derek would say. But I am pretty sure I know what you would say to a patient's family in this case."

Kira felt her face flush. She tried to look away, but Yoshi held her with his eyes.

"Whether you like it or not, you and I together need to solve this Terminator Gene right here, right now. Can we go to work?"

Kira felt herself nod, knowing it was what she had to do, however reluctant her heart was.

Chapter 41

Yoshi and Kira followed the corridor to the complex's main biochemistry lab. "So, why were you looking for antigens?" the Japanese scientist asked. "That's very unusual."

"It was just a silly idea," Kira said. "I don't know that I expected to discover anything. It just seemed as if it should be the next step. A kind of leap of faith, I guess."

"I understand," Yoshi said. "Derek was my best friend here at Caernarfon. Over the past seven years whenever the project seemed to be going nowhere he was the one that pushed us forward. He never wavered from the belief that life was preparing for a leap. A transformation into greater complexity."

Kira nodded. "It was something he talked about often while I was at Yale. He called it his Green Genes theory. He was very enthusiastic about it back then." She frowned. "I had almost forgotten."

Yoshi put his hand gently on her shoulder. "He never lost that enthusiasm. He always reminded us that life was using our little group to take the first step in this transformation. He once told me that any evolutionary transformation had to have a physiological component."

"I don't understand."

"You will. Over the last months he had become, how should I say it, mystical. He told me only a few days ago that the time had come for him to make way. I now believe he was making way for you."

Kira stopped, unsettled by the news that she could step into Derek's role. "But...but that's a mistake. I've been a fake, a phony all my life. I've just been pretending that I knew something."

The lines on Yoshi's brow furrowed and he stared at her for a few moments. "It's good that you can see the truth about yourself. It will give you clarity. The time will come, when we will scream and mourn Derek's death. But not at this time. Now is the time for us to see what that SF-81 of yours can do for old Henrietta."

He resumed walking down the hall. Kira let his words sink in. She knew he was right. Now was the time to prove that Derek's theories were right. In spite of her misgivings about herself, she was as curious as Yoshi to see what the biochemistry extracted from her old SF-81 would do to the immortal cancer cells of Henrietta Lacks. Kira hurried to catch up.

Yoshi and Kira entered the biochemistry lab. All the lab assistants except Graham had cleared out.

Graham looked up and said, "Everything's ready." He ran his hand through his hair and breathed out slowly. "Dr. Yamato, I hope you don't mind, but I need to go out for a long walk. Derek and all."

"Take your time."

"I'll be back. If you need me, beep."

Yoshi waited for the door to close behind Graham. He turned to Kira and said, "What procedures did you use? How did you get the HeLa cells and the SF-81 to interact?"

Kira couldn't stop from blushing. "This is going to sound really stupid, but it was an accident. It happened when we were goofing around in the medical lab of one of my friends. I should have told you and Derek right away. I never really needed to come here."

"I figured as much," Yoshi said thoughtfully. "We'll just have to keep going. A lot has happened since your *accidental* re-differentiation of cancer cells. In the last decade, we've been able to use a variety of chemical agents, and re-differentiation of cancer cells is pretty common now."

Kira could only nod, amazed by how much science had progressed in the decade since she had accidentally spilled some of her SF-81 on Henrietta.

Yoshi went over to the gold-leaf lab bench. "Here's what we're going to do. We've isolated eleven potential substances from the shells biochemistry that might have played a role in the re-differentiation of your HeLa cells. We'll test these eleven on the HeLa cells and *neuroblastoma* cells simultaneously. We were also able to synthesize two of the polymer groups from the shells, and we'll use them as controls."

"Why *neuroblastoma* cells?" Kira asked, knowing that *neuroblastomas* made up that part of the sympathetic nervous system that sends danger signals to the conscious and unconscious mind.

"Like you, I had a hunch. We're going to use two procedures with each agent. Micro-fusion directly into the cells and something like your technique." He laughed. "We integrated each agent into an *invitro*-growing medium for the cell cultures. But I want you to see clearly how we do each of these procedures."

Kira shook her head. "Why me? This is something a lab assistant could do." *And do it much better since he would be more familiar with the technical procedures.*

"Call it another hunch, but I'd rather there were two of us with knowledge of everything we're doing."

They worked for nearly two hours with Yoshi carefully explaining the steps. It had been years since Kira studied biochemistry, but the intricacies of the eleven agents extracted from the SF-81 were easy to understand now. She readily mastered the micro-fusion technique. And the procedure for integrating the agents into the growing medium for the cells she committed to memory by using her system of copying everything down. When Yoshi asked her about the notes, she laughed and explained the textual mnemonic.

"Make certain you destroy these notes before you leave here today," Yoshi cautioned in a whisper.

"Another hunch?"

"A precaution from a friend," he said and ended the matter by glancing at the camera that was in his lab recording their procedures.

Kira completed the last of the micro-fusion tests and pushed back from the lab bench. Her shoulders and neck ached from being hunched over for such a long stretch. But Yoshi had insisted she perform the last five micro-infusions by herself explaining to him the procedure as if he were a new tech,

See one...do one...teach one, Kira thought. It was an old learning method that was used in ERs across the country. She glanced at the notes she had written, but she knew she had left nothing out.

Yoshi bowed to her. "You look like an old pro at this."

"I had a good teacher."

"So, any questions about the procedures?"

Kira shook her head. "I'm a bit surprised at how easy it is since I used to have problems with these kinds of things."

"Really? You looked so confident and clear."

Kira shrugged. "It seems silly now that I think of it. But I used to agonize about learning all the steps. That's why I developed my habit of writing everything down. But now I...I don't know why it matters, but yes, I feel perfectly clear."

She rubbed the back of her neck, trying to massage away the stiffness there. "I could use a break though." Kira remembered then that she had run to the complex the night before and had slept in a chair in the lab. Here it was late afternoon of the next day. She hadn't showered in more than twenty-four hours and her muscles ached as though she had worked a double shift in the E.R.

Allowing a rare smile, Yoshi said, "We could both use a rest and I know just the place."

"I hope it's nearby," Kira said.

She followed him out of the lab and down the hall to the complex's cafeteria. Kira looked askance at her colleague. "Here?"

"I made friends with the cafeteria manager. She stocks a

special tea for me – Kiko-cha. It will revitalize you."

They took a table by one of the windows that overlooked the Menai Straits. It was late afternoon and the boats were returning to their mooring spots. Yoshi sat with his back to the nearest security camera. He pulled a pad of paper and a pencil out of his lab coat and began writing in it, shielding his words. In a world dominated by SDs, iPads and Blackberrys, the sight of an old-fashioned pad of paper and pencil made Kira grin in spite of the surveillance.

She saw that he was writing upside-down for her benefit. "My brother is here. He's eager to meet you, to talk about your non-dual experience."

A cough behind them made both Kira and Yoshi jump. They turned and saw Arne Jurgenczak eying them. Kira noticed Yoshi deftly slide the pad with his message into his coat pocket, before standing. "Dr. Jurgenczak, I believe you haven't had a chance to meet Dr. Kira Taylor yet."

Arne Jurgenczak took Kira's hand and bowed, his back straight, like a military officer. Kira noticed his hands were large, yet soft, the cuticles well manicured. His long white hair was tied back with a black ribbon. "I'm sorry we have to meet under such tragic circumstances," he said.

Kira frowned, feeling the sadness well up in her. All of her doctor training could not prepare her for the loss she was feeling, so she decided in the spirit of her new found understanding to follow it through. "I was just getting to know him again. We had been estranged for a number of years and now he's gone. I don't really know quite how to deal with it yet."

Jurgenczak sat down without letting go of her hand. "I'm sorry for your loss. You should know that Derek admired you. It was on his recommendation we brought you on board. You should keep that in your heart."

"Thank you," Kira said, meaning it. In spite of her misgivings about Jurgenczak, his sincerity warmed her.

Jurgenczak patted her hand once and let it go, turning to Yoshi. "You knew him well. Do you think he would want a Christian memorial? I believe he was a Christian."

"He was fascinated by the history of Christianity. I would ask Abigail what she wants."

"Of course." Jurgenczak's right index finger traced a cross on the table top. "And how were you raised?"

"I was raised Buddhist, then I studied and practiced Zen for a number of years."

"Buddhism has no God."

"Buddhists believe in the 'eightfold' path of ethical conduct, wisdom, and mental discipline."

Jurgenczak turned his attention back to Kira. "What about you, Dr. Taylor?"

Kira couldn't help but feel that he was testing her, but to what purpose, she couldn't say. "I used to say, I'm spiritual but not religious. Now I don't know anymore."

"So you have doubt, that's good. Doubt can be good."

For a moment Jurgenczak seemed to forget Kira and Yoshi were there. His eyes drifted to look at the late afternoon scene unfolding outside the complex and his voice became downcast sounding like someone carrying a heavy burden. "I'm often filled with doubt," Jurgenczak said at last.

Kira had often seen this kind of sadness in patients who were given bad news about loved ones. "I'm sorry for your loss, too, sir," she said.

Jurgenczak sighed. "It's too bad Derek didn't live to see this day."

"What day is that?" Yoshi asked.

"Why the glorious day we've all been working toward is almost here. The reason Derek brought Dr. Taylor here. It heralds a real breakthrough in our search for the cure."

"Yes it does. But then what?" Kira asked.

Jurgenczak pushed away from the table, his mood once more

ebullient. "We'll celebrate of course." With that he turned away. "Let me know the moment you get results."

Kira watched him leave through the room's double doors. "Strange man...not what I expected."

"He avoided the question about what happens after."

Chapter 42

Back in Yoshi's lab all twenty-six of the test results were playing out live on a giant smart board, the images of the cultures provided by video feeds from powerful endoscopes at each of the test stations.

Yoshi studied the first of the tests. After only a moment he shook his head, puzzled. Quickly he went from one culture to the next. At each stop his face grew more concerned. By the last one he was muttering to himself.

Kira didn't hear him. She was watching the security cameras follow Yoshi as he went from one image to another. *Someone's guiding the video feed.*

"Kira!" Yoshi's voice broke through her thoughts. He was clearly shaken and bewildered.

Looking away from the cameras, Kira said, "What?"

"Come look at these. I don't understand it. All of the cultures appear to be dying."

Kira peered at the image of the first culture, which Yoshi had prepared. Then she studied the last one she prepared. "It seems to me that the simplest of chromosomal separation cannot occur."

"Exactly. Except over here – the controls. Their cell division is robust. Then look at this one. Something's happening, or at least trying to happen." He shook is head. "It's all very curious."

The lab door swung open and Graham entered. His face was haggard and it was clear that he had been crying. When he saw Kira and Yoshi, he straightened. "I see you've started running the cultures."

Yoshi nodded. "But we're not getting anything like what we expected." His voice took on a stern quality and Kira wondered for a moment if the diminutive Japanese scientist blamed his lab assistant.

Graham studied the images and whistled tonelessly. "Dr.

Taylor, when you were doing your work at Yale, how did you deal with the shells radioactivity?"

Kira blinked. "There was never any radioactivity."

Graham raised his eyebrows. "The sandstone matrix containing the shells was highly radioactive. They were giving off a toxic level of radon gas and I had to wear protective gear while I removed shells from the rock."

Kira recalled the Hazmat suits at the lab entrance on the first day she arrived. "I never encountered radioactivity ten years ago when my collectors gathered specimens in Wisconsin." She tapped her fingers against the bench. "I wonder..." She started toward the computer but abandoned that tack. It was a dead end. Gentel allowed no contact with the outside world via the web on the lab's computers. Kira needed her phone, but she had been forced to leave it at the guard station when she arrived last night. Silently she cursed the strict security.

She turned to Yoshi and Graham. "Look, I can't be certain of this, but I think we're looking at the Exxon Factor here."

Yoshi and Graham looked at each other. "What's that?" Yoshi asked.

"The Exxon Valdeez. remember?" Kira asked. "In the 80s, the oil tanker spilled over 11 million gallons of crude oil into Prince William Sound. Even though it was cleaned up, twenty years later the beaches are still contaminated with PCBs. They leach into the rocks and soil and stay there forever.

"If I'm recalling my news correctly, sometime around 2004, a similar thing happened around Eau Claire. Exxon was eying the area where my collectors gathered the original specimens. They were looking to mine copper and other metals. Some environmental types sued at the time, claiming that tailings from the mining process would be radioactive and contaminate the area. Their arguments didn't matter; Exxon won. Now Graham finds residual radiation in all the samples you got for me."

Graham shook his head. "Is it really possible that small

amounts of radioactive contamination could be affecting these cell cultures?"

Arne Jurgenczak's voice startled everybody. "Dr. Taylor's assessment is correct about the radioactive contamination. As the radon breaks down, small amounts of radioactive energy are released. When the radiation passes through a cell, it releases its energy along its path. In short, it donates energy to atoms or molecules inside the cell. The result, highly unstable atoms called radicals. Radicals are chemically very reactive and can damage the chromosomes. In most cases the cell can repair the damage, but that's in normal healthy cells, not these cancer cells.

"This isn't good."

Yoshi pulled himself away from one of the *neuroblastoma* cell images he had been studying intently. "Perhaps not. Something is going on here. Not re-differentiation but something very interesting."

Jurgenczak and Kira crowded around him. Jurgenczak spotted it first. "Yes, I get it. We need to test all the different isolated chemical agents from the shells in all possible combinations."

"Of course, we'll have to find a new source for the shells," Yoshi said.

Jurgenczak looked at Kira expectantly. "Do you know where we can find Cambrian *brachiopods*?"

Kira shook her head. "The Eau Claire formation is the only place that has *dicellomos politos* in any quantity. In fact it was unique. Inarticulate *brachiopods* have always been a very minor part of the oceanic ecosystem. Even today."

Jurgenczak nodded. "We'll find some, the resources of Gentel are searching as we speak."

Kira glanced at the great man. *Of course. The cameras. He knew what was going on before he came down here. It doesn't matter though. Now that they have the steps for the cure, I'm not needed here any more.*

"And I guess that's my cue to be going. I mean, you really

don't need my expertise any longer."

Jurgenczak shook his head. "I believe you underestimate your contribution, Dr. Taylor."

"Maybe, but you guys can handle it from here and I'm ready to leave."

"You forget tomorrow's Derek's memorial service."

Kira thought about it. After ten years she and her one-time mentor had at last reconciled. She owed him at least to show up to the service and say a few words. "I would like to speak tomorrow."

"Everyone needs to be there," Jurgenczak said.

Chapter 43

Kira closed the door to her flat behind her. It was early evening and the lowering sun sent streamers of light across the bare floor. She shook herself, trying to will energy into exhausted muscles. But it seemed to take all her effort to keep from collapsing. Her mind and body were overwhelmed from the events of the last two days. Derek's death and the radioactive specimens had taken their toll.

Gathering her energy, Kira shuffled forward and grabbed her travel bag to pack for the journey back to Sioux City tomorrow. Jurgenczak had arranged for the Gentel corporate jet to take her home after the memorial service. She was surprised that Gentel's founder had so readily agreed to allow her to leave, especially with her intimate knowledge of the T-gene. On the other hand, he was certain they were close to finding the solution, so perhaps he didn't think of her as any kind of threat to security anymore.

Or would she disappear like Dr. Howe? *Don't go there,* she berated herself. *No one knows what really happened to Howe.*

Perfunctorily she started gathering her things. She had never really had time to unpack, except for her running clothes and an evening skirt.

She glanced at the mirror and was shocked to discover she was still dressed in shorts and a T-shirt from the night before. *I'm so tired I forgot I ran to work.* Shaking her head, Kira muttered, "It's not my work, not anymore." She sighed and peeled off her sweat-stained clothes, stuffing them into the pack. *I'll sort everything out in the morning.*

Kira wandered into the bathroom. She could have used a long hot soak in a tub, but the water was tepid, so she had to settle for a quick shower. Returning to the bedroom, she flopped down on the bed, still too tired to do more than think.

A part of her wanted to get back home, to be free of the

emotional rollercoaster that had been the Terminator Gene project. She felt buffeted by events way out of her control. It was a microcosm of her life, maybe all life, magnified by a power of a thousand. But another voice insisted on being heard.

Stay, the job is not done.

Unable to summon the energy to fight this new voice, Kira let herself listen to it. She was surprised to find the source was her own doubt. *Do I really want Gentel to find a solution to the Terminator Gene?*

She recognized where the question came from – self-doubt spilling over into qualms about humanity's right to exist on Earth. With a population of nearly seven billion, humans were an enormous biological success. Yet throughout the world there was massive poverty and suffering and no obvious means to set it right. Human-induced climate change was producing one catastrophic event after another, each greater than the former. Resources were dwindling. Whole ecosystems were being wiped out by an economic model of ever-increasing growth. And then there was never-ending war. For the first time Kira was seeing the condition of humanity in a different light. *Yes, human beings are a great success story, but it's all based on fear, an ever-present fear.*

Even now, lying here exhausted, she could sense her own background of inexplicable fear. Always fear, fear out of her control. *If I had to choose, would I let humanity pass into cosmic oblivion?* Kira knew she could, but would she?

I don't know.

Then there it was again. That feeling of urgency Kira had experienced the day of Jeanette Jacobsen's miscarriage. An overwhelming force, coming not from fear but some unspoken need. She strained her mind, trying to find what the need represented. It was like the feeling of having to make, at all costs, the most important appointment of her life. But the answer to what the *need* was eluded her.

Chapter 44

Kira woke up, her mind groggy. She expected to see night through the window of her bedroom but it was full day instead. Startled, she grabbed her phone to check the time. It was nearly eleven in the morning. She had slept for over twelve hours. *I haven't slept twelve hours since junior high school.* It took her a few minutes to clear her mind and recall where she was. And then she remembered – Derek's memorial. There was nothing in her travel bag appropriate to wear. Cursing herself for not thinking of it last night, she dressed hurriedly and rushed out to buy something appropriate for the service.

As she walked out onto Hole in the Wall Street, she spotted Hawke standing next to a Gentel Systems car as though waiting for her. He nodded to her without smiling and his mirrored sunglasses revealed nothing of his eyes. Intrigued by his surprise appearance, Kira stopped. Her mind raced through possibilities. *Why does Gentel need me now? The project's all but over and I'm of no use them.*

As if answering her thoughts, Hawke said, "I was concerned that you didn't have anything appropriate to wear to the memorial service."

"Thanks. As a matter-of-fact, I'm on the way to the store now."

"May I drive you?" Hawke asked politely.

"Do I have a choice?"

"Of course."

"Ok, let's go."

Hawke drove like he was part of the machine – silent and mechanical. The only time he spoke was when they arrived at the store. "I'll wait here for you."

Inside she debated over a dress or a simple pair of dark slacks and a matching blouse. She decided on the latter. As the cashier rang up her purchase she found herself checking text messages from the past few days. One caught her attention – a low-resolution picture of an inarticulate brachiopod sent by Jack. *What the hell is that about?*

As Kira exited the store, she had the strangest feeling as though being on display. She looked at Hawke, but he was already moving to open the car door for her. Recalling Yoshi's concerns that she was being followed, Kira looked around but saw no one. She laughed at herself. *You're just feeling edgy because you really don't know what's going on anymore.*

Hawke had the door open for Kira as she approached but did not step aside. He said, "The other night in the hall."

"What?" Kira asked, taken aback by his manner and question.

"At Gentel, when you arrived late."

Kira's eyes narrowed as she studied Hawke's features. He was on edge, but he wasn't hiding anything nor was he angry. She forced herself to relax and be open. "Yes, I remember."

"What were you doing?"

Kira could sense the hesitancy in Hawke's voice. She would have called it fear in another person, but she realized he was searching for an answer to a question that puzzled him. She knew the question because she had felt it in herself that night in the complex: *I have been afraid of relationships. Am I attracted to this person?*

"I don't know what you mean," she said.

"Something happened between us...some kind of exchange."

"I wasn't doing anything; I was just really open." Kira didn't want to add that at that moment she had felt the kind of love a mother must have for her newborn child. "Sometimes it gives people a sense of not being judged, of being understood and accepted for who they are. What did you feel?"

For a moment Hawke's security expert mask fell away and he focused on her, one human being to another. Kira sensed the attraction between them even more intensely. Then the mask slipped back into place.

"I'd rather not say," Hawke answered and moved toward the driver's door.

Kira placed a hand gently on his coat sleeve. "I understand."

Refusing to look her in the eye, Hawke continued around the car.

Once inside, Hawke was again silent, a part of his machine.

Outside her flat, Hawke glanced at the car's chronometer. "It's just after noon," he said. "The service is at seven-thirty. You should have plenty of time to get ready."

"So, is this good-bye?" Kira asked.

"Yes. I won't be at the service this evening."

She watched Hawke drive off and then entered her rooms. *Another very strange man,* she thought, shaking her head. Then a completely different response came into her mind: *Will I ever see him again? Do I want to?*

After a shower, she changed into the new clothes. They felt a little stiff but they would have to do. Grabbing a small hip pack, she stuffed her passport and smart phone into it. She still had plenty of time before the service began. Time for coffee and a scone and to coordinate her thoughts on what she would say about Derek. *So much water under the bridge.* The cliché seemed to say it all.

Chapter 45

Outside the lab complex Kira waved at Yoshi, standing by himself. He looked uncomfortable in his dark suit. She noticed again the red crane tie he wore and thought there must be a story behind it. *Now is not the time to ask.*

"How are you doing?" Yoshi said as Kira approached.

"Surprisingly well. I can't believe I slept for over twelve hours. Guess I needed it."

Yoshi nodded. "Are you still leaving us?"

Kira thought about the strange meeting with Hawke and her face twisted into a grimace. "Last night it seemed the only thing to do. This morning, I'm not so sure."

Yoshi said, "Maybe this will change your mind. I was unable to sleep last night, so I spoke with my Swedish contact. I was able to secure a large sample of their brachiopod biochemistry. The sample was very illuminating."

"DNA and RNA?"

"Exactly. Remember your sample came from a species related to the Eau Claire *brachiopods*. However, theirs is a much younger, now extinct species from the Pennsylvania. So your and Derek's hunch was correct."

"His Green Genes theory. Everything goes back to the Cambrian."

"Speaking of hunches, tell me yours relating to the testing for antigens."

"It seemed important at the time, but now I'm not so sure. I had this idea that some global event occurred across the Earth's oceans during the end of the Cambrian that affected every living micro-cellular organism. I thought it might be some invading bacteria. A bacterium that found its way into the free-floating eggs of all Cambrian organisms."

Yoshi made another one of his rare smiles. "Of course, if the chromosomal material in the cell was originally symbiotic bacteria, then the absence of any antigens might suggest this invasion had not yet taken place."

"And with all that happened yesterday, I never did ask Graham about the results." She glanced at her phone. It was nearly time for the ceremony. More people were arriving. She recognized only a few of the techs from Yoshi's lab. Oddly, security wasn't stopping anyone and asking them to surrender their smart devices. *It must be the service. Everyone's a little bit numb right now.*

"There's no time to check on the results," Yoshi said. "We can do it after the ceremony. But..." He pulled her out of the stream of people heading into the complex. "For some time now, some people, myself included, have come to believe there is evidence for a major evolutionary shift that took place in humans around the time that they moved from roaming families to a more sophisticated clan type or tribal type of social structure. The Hox genes suggest there was a sudden change in the anatomy of the sympathetic nervous system. It created a more effective social group. But for the first time, it also saw members of their own species as *the enemy*."

The significance wasn't lost on Kira. "Since the cancer of the *neuroblastoma* cells occurs only in children. It all comes back to the early period of development, doesn't it? The human embryo dedifferentiating...miscarriages?"

"Yes it does, the time of becoming what you will be."

The two of them rejoined the line. Kira filed past security not even bothering to hand over her phone. At the door to the large conference hall, she saw Jurgenczak standing with Derek's wife, Abigail. On impulse, Kira went over and embraced her.

"Abby, I'm so sorry. I..." her voice trailed off.

Abby squeezed her and whispered in her ear. "He never stopped admiring you. You were his favorite student...through everything."

Tears formed in Kira's eyes. *I should be comforting her.*

Jurgenczak touched Kira's shoulder. "You'll speak after Frank Littleton. In the meantime, could you please escort Lady Simon to her seat."

"Of course."

Kira walked with Abby down the sloping aisle to the front of the room. The chancel was plain and the simple table was clothed in black. "I hear you're leaving," Abby said.

"I was but after speaking with Dr. Yamato, I might stay."

Abby squeezed her hand and Kira could feel the gratitude in the soft fingers of the older woman's hand. "That would be good, dear. It will give us time to have that dinner."

Returning the squeeze, Kira said, "I'd like that."

Kira joined Yoshi near the doors. People whispered among themselves but not loud enough to overawe the gentle strains of Mozart's *Requiem*. Kira recalled that he always listened to Mozart.

Yoshi checked his watch. "It's nearly eight. I wonder what's taking so long to get started."

Kira shrugged. "Jurgenczak probably wants to be certain everyone is here."

As if her words were a cue, the lights in the hall dimmed. At the back of the low stage a screen flickered to life. Derek's smiling face looked out upon the crowd. He was directing people who overturned slabs of rock looking for fossils.

Chuckles through the room and even Kira smiled. *That's Derek all right...just as I would like to remember him.*

Behind Kira, the doors to the hall closed and she heard the snick of a lock plunging home.

The short movie ended and lights came back up. Kira looked around for Jurgenczak to begin the service, but the man was not in the room.

Fear welled up in her. "Yoshi, where's Jurgenczak?"

She felt the pressure wave before she heard the terrifying

sound of the explosion. Kira dragged Yoshi down to the floor behind the seats.

It's already too late, Kira's mind shouted at her.

A heavy object struck her head. Blackness followed.

Third Division

There is a debate today whether biology has evolved to embrace consciousness or if evolution of biology has produced consciousness, consciousness that is aware of evolution itself. What is not debatable is that consciousness is evolving faster than anything else in the universe.

-Baron Derek Simon, Oxford Lectures

Chapter 46

Yoshi was choking. Dust clogged his nose and mouth. Darkness surrounded him and he could see nothing. Nearby a broken pipe was spraying water and he felt it trickle beneath him. He struggled to move but his legs were trapped. Panic threatened to overwhelm him, when he heard his phone buzz and felt the vibration. He fumbled for it in his suit coat pocket. The dim light of the display revealed the rubble and twisted wreckage of what had once been Gentel's main conference hall. Disbelief gripped him, not knowing what had happened, only that he was somehow caught in a monstrous pile of debris.

His phone buzzed again. It was a message was from Chosin. How could his brother's phone signal penetrate Gentel's security jamming field? Then he realized that the field, like the building, must not exist anymore. The text was in Ainu. *Brother, I know you survived the explosion.*

He swallowed his pain and concentrated on Chosin's message.

Do everything I say if you want to live. Under no circumstances contact anyone but me with your phone. Do not call out to anyone or answer anybody's call. Your life depends on it. Some of the first responders could be there to make certain there are no survivors. I have pinpointed your location using your phone's GPS signal, and I believe you can work your way free, but you will have to wait until darkness falls. I will be waiting for you at the Castle's Black Tower. Chosin.

His brother waited nearby! Yoshi was suddenly filled with hope. Using the phone's lighted display, he renewed his efforts to free himself. He pulled away some drywall and bricks. His spirit sank as he saw his legs were trapped under tons of concrete.

He heard a moan, and craned his neck. He gasped as the light showed Kira in a fetal position a foot away. Blood trickled from her nose. Her eyes fluttered once and then she didn't move. Twisting his torso, Yoshi could just reach her. His fingers found the pulse at her throat. It was strong and steady. He breathed a sigh of relief. Her chest rose and fell rhythmically. None of her limbs were bent at awkward angles.

Yoshi texted Chosin, *Brother, I'm pinned and can't get out. Kira is here with me. She's unconscious but looks unhurt. I'll contact you when she wakes up.*

Chosin's reply was quick. *She can help free you.*

Yoshi leaned his phone against a broken brick. Strangely, the dim light made him feel safer. *Jurgenczak's behind this! He must want the solution for himself.* His eyes went to his trapped legs and he grimaced. *That means Kira's the only hope to get the solution to whole world.* Pulling a handkerchief out of his coat, he moistened it with trickle of water and laid it across Kira's forehead. "You have to wake up," he muttered.

The wreckage shrieked and shifted then, sending a shower of dust into the small cavity that protected them.

"Quickly," he urged.

Chapter 47

Arne Jurgenczak entered Gentel's private hangar at Caernarfon, careful not to be seen. Silently he crossed the concrete floor to the Gulfstream 650's boarding stairs. Once there he paused and eyed the fifteen steps. All at once they seemed like a mountain too steep to climb. In all his sixty-five years, he had never felt such a burden. Every step carried the weight of his final decision concerning the Caernarfon complex. Sixty-two scientists . Technicians, guests, gone. Sacrificed in the name of God. Sacrificed for His plan – God's Kingdom on Earth. He let out a breath and squared his shoulders. *I have done God's will.* But no peace followed this thought.

At the top of the stairs, Jurgenczak raised his eyes toward heaven, as if he could see God through the hangar roof's spider-work of rafter supports and metal sheathing. *I know it was time, Adonay, just as you told me it would arrive, but tears stain my heart even so.*

Hawke emerged from the pilot's cabin. "We're ready to leave when you give the order, sir."

Jurgenczak noticed that the security chief's voice was calm and his hands steady and he wished he could feel that too. "Everything is arranged as planned?"

"Yes, sir. The plane's transponder has been changed. We are now Keewatin Industrial, Two Alpha."

"No one saw you board?"

"No, sir."

Gentel's founder took a deep breath to steady himself. *It will all work out.* He made himself comfortable in his customary chair on the right side of the plane. The steward came out of the galley and placed a glass of white wine on the table beside him. "Dinner will be served in thirty-five minutes, sir."

"Nothing for me this evening, but make certain Hawke gets

whatever you have prepared."

"Very good, sir." The steward hesitated.

"There's something else?" Jurgenczak asked.

"Yes sir." The steward reached into his vest pocket and pulled out a smart phone. "I was told to make certain you got this, sir." He left it on the table beside the wine.

As soon as the steward closed the door to the galley, the phone buzzed. The display faced Jurgenczak and he bit back a gasp. It read George Drake, Keewatin's CEO. Hastily he gulped the wine and wiped his palms on his pants. *I have nothing to be afraid of. I have done what Jehovah commanded.*

He answered the phone.

"I see it is done," a grating baritone voice said.

"Yes, the building is gone," Jurgenczak said, wondering how Drake had found out so quickly.

"You must have the solution to the T-gene then."

Jurgenczak swallowed in a dry throat. "Not yet, but only I know where the solution will be found."

The silence was deafening and it took all of Jurgenczak's will not to tremble. At last Drake said in a sharp voice, "You have acted prematurely, endangered the plan."

Jurgenczak forced himself to be calm. "I do not believe so."

"Enlighten me then on why you have destroyed a 150-million-dollar complex and taken the lives of the researchers who could find the solution. Not to mention, put Keewatin Industrial at terrible risk if it's discovered I had anything to do with this."

Jurgenczak had anticipated this moment and he ticked off the reasons quickly. "We have everything we will ever get from this facility, for one. Second, the timing was fortuitous with Derek Simon's death. And finally, there were too many people who knew about the Cambrian *brachiopods*. Someone was bound to leak the solution. There was no other choice."

"Perhaps you were right," Drake said. He paused and

Jurgenczak waited, hoping this was the end. "Meet me at the Omaha facility after you land," Drake said.

The phone went dead.

Jurgenczak would never tell Drake the truth that the destruction of the Caernarfon complex was God's will. He was a nonbeliever, a tool whose money financed God's vision for an Eden on Earth.

He's another of God's soldiers that will have to be sacrificed.

Chapter 48

The blackness ebbed. A dim gray light swirled at the edge of Kira's vision and then was gone. She could hear the sound of a soft voice whispering her name. Someone patted her forehead with a damp cloth. She wanted the voice to go away and stop bothering her. She batted at the hand and winced in pain. Her right shoulder throbbed and her head felt as if she had gone through the windshield of a car.

"Kira. Kira. You have to wake up," the voice insisted. "An explosion has knocked you out."

An explosion? Bits and pieces of what happened came back then. Derek's service…Jurgenczak not there…an explosion of some kind. *Yoshi*!

Kira's doctor training took over. She had to stay awake. *Sleep is the worst thing for a concussion*. She could slip easily into shock otherwise. She forced her eyes open. Everywhere was black.

Before she could say anything, a finger lay across her lips. "Speak softly. Do not yell," Yoshi ordered. "Stay still, I have a light." She heard him fumbling in the darkness. Dust motes spiraled around a square shaft of light that suddenly lit up the area. She recognized his smart phone. It took Kira's eyes a few seconds to adjust.

She studied the layout. They were in an area the size of a small tomb. A large I-beam rested on the rows of chairs and formed a ceiling above them. *It must have sheltered us from the worst of the falling debris*. Walls of broken concrete, wood and metal fragments surrounded them on three sides. Beyond Yoshi, darkness seemed to extend into infinity.

Yoshi was lying on his side facing her. His legs disappeared beneath a wall of rubble. A dark stain oozed underneath him. Kira's immediate instinct was to help him. But she knew she had to take a few moments to check herself. Slowly she eased her muscles back and forth. She breathed a silent thanks of relief. Unlike Yoshi she could move. No broken bones just some bruised muscles. She felt her scalp where she'd been hit. Her hand came away wet, but the bleeding wasn't heavy. *Assuming there're no internal injuries, I'm doing fine.* In fact, she thought she was doing better than fine. In spite of being knocked unconscious, Kira felt clear-headed. It was as if the veil of confusion and unease that had surrounded her ever since she arrived in Caernarfon was lifted.

She heard Yoshi grunt in pain and the light wavered. She squirmed around until she could look at his legs. A quick survey revealed that only a rescue team could free him. She placed a finger on his femoral pulse. It was weak. Her hands moved gently up his abdomen and she stopped. The belly was distended and hard, which meant he was also bleeding internally. Even if the rescue teams got here in the next twenty minutes, the chances of his survival were very low.

She examined Yoshi's face. The skin was chalky but his eyes were bright, the green flecks twinkling in the display's light. "Is there pain?" Kira asked softly.

"It is tolerable," Yoshi answered.

Kira picked up his hand. Acutely aware that the Japanese scientist had only a few moments left, she waited for him to speak.

"Wait until it is dark before you try and escape," Yoshi said. He went on to explain what Chosin had told him. "My brother will be waiting for you at Caernarfon Castle, near the Black Tower." Yoshi pressed his phone into her hand. "Take this. He will know it is mine."

Kira nodded. "I have never met anyone like you."

"I feel the same." Silence passed and Kira could feel Yoshi's hand growing colder.

"Do you ever think about death?" he asked.

"Every day."

"When my father died, he died horribly. He had pancreatic cancer. He fought his death to the very end. He was in total denial about the fact that he would die someday. So much so that just an hour before he died he got up from his bed and tried to walk out of the room. It was terrible for our mother."

"After that, I vowed I would die differently. I would be fully awake, fully aware in that moment just as I am in every moment that preceded it. Life and death are the same, no preference."

"And the afterlife?"

Yoshi smiled. "Terra incognita."

"And what should I do?"

"You have all the science that you need."

"Not as well as others."

"That's no matter. You are unique. It's like miso soup, and you are the scallions. Too many and the dish is ruined, too little of you and it's also ruined. The dish will tell you what's right if you can see clearly. You will get it, what's correct for you is correct by being correct for everyone."

He smiled and closed his eyes. Kira sensed that her presence was all that Yoshi needed and she sat quietly.

Yoshi's eyes opened suddenly. "Tell Chosin I've had a wonderful life." He took a final breath and whispered, "Terra incognita."

Gently, Kira closed his eyes.

Chapter 49

Chosin sat in shadow, eyes partially closed, breathing even. If a passerby had happened to see him, he would have appeared asleep or even dead. But he was far from it. Though his mind and body were completely at rest, Chosin's senses remained hyper alert. He sensed Caernarfon Castle's Black Tower soaring above him, its stone sheltering him in an embrace of seclusion. Far to his left a cricket chirred softly, waiting for sunset. He smelled the lowering tide of the Menai Straits and with it the tang of storm far out in the Irish Sea. He smiled, loving storms.

Chosin was completely at peace, mind open, body relaxed. It had been years since he had waited like this. In his old life as a broker of corporate secrets, waiting had been different. Then he waited tensely, ready to spring into action, to move, to make a contact or simply to vanish, leaving no trace.

Unexpectedly, thoughts flickered to life. Chosin sensed his brother approaching. His first notion was that Yoshi must not have been trapped as he first reported. When he opened his eyes, he saw nothing. When he closed them again, Yoshi was a luminous sphere of light walking in the shadows of his mind.

Yoshi stopped ten feet in front of Chosin. He beckoned him to follow. His mouth opened but no sound came out. Yoshi's figure began to fade. In its place appeared an old American Indian man. His eyes glittered like black diamonds. Long silver hair held together in two braids framed a well-lived face. His lips curled up in a warm smile. He held out one hand and spread upon the ground tiny, oval, white shells. *I give you these,* the old Indian said.

The scene shifted. The old Indian now stood in Chosin's house in Hokkaido in front of the aquarium. *Metamorphosis,* the Indian said. Then he disappeared. *My brother is dead,* Chosin thought. He could no longer feel him in his heart or mind, and for the first time Chosin knew he was truly alone.

Chapter 50

Kira pulled herself forward until at last she could see clearly. Just beyond a tangled web of girders and twisted rebar was the street that passed in front of the complex. *Another fifteen feet and I'm free.*

She sighed and rested. She checked her hip pack with the two smart devices and her passport. *At least I'll be able to leave the country once I get away from here.*

It had taken Kira nearly an hour to reach this spot. There were a couple of wrong turns and backtracking. All the time the wreckage settled and groaned around her. But at last she was close to freedom. She studied the situation. Her knees and elbows ached from scrabbling on all fours across broken concrete and around piles of rubble. Her shoulder still hurt, but her legs were fine and she would be able to make the mile and a half to Caernarfon Castle and Chosin easily. But for now she had to wait until the way was clear.

Rescue workers were combing through this part of the wreckage. *Trust no one except Chosin,* Yoshi had warned her. Fortunately, no one had found this passageway yet.

Kira checked the surroundings again from her spider hole. Emergency lights lit up the area like day. *How am I going to get past these people without being seen?*

The wreckage began to settle again. A shriek of tearing metal sounded nearby. "Get out of there!" a voice shouted. People scrambled away. Above Kira a girder shifted. Her escape route began to close. *Now or never!*

She scrambled on her hands and knees. Behind her the building collapsed and she rolled out of the makeshift tunnel amid a cloud of dust and fragments of concrete. Kira gasped and knew she was lucky to be alive.

She didn't hang around. She picked herself up and ran into

the night, shielded by the dust. Crossing the road, she went down a short embankment into a row of buildings. She didn't stop until she came out onto the road fronting the Menai Straits. The lights of Caernarfon Castle were a mile away. She began to jog when the sight of a distant car slowed her to a walk.

Need to appear normal, she told herself. For a moment she wondered why she was thinking and acting so calmly, especially after barely escaping with her life and watching Yoshi lose his. But this state of being was her now.

She made it to the castle without anyone stopping her. And as far as she knew, no one followed. Kira ran up the castle's ramp, her breathing hardly labored, and entered through the King's Gate entrance, stopping at the top of the ramp to peer into the gloom of the interior. Where do I go from here? She had no idea where the Black Tower was. She would just have to wander around and hope that Yoshi's brother would care enough to find her.

Chapter 51

The young Black woman activated her laptop computer and brought up the tracking program. Within seconds the screen was a blaze of tiny blinking lights, all clustered together in a tight area. She counted them. Frowning, she checked her numbers again. Quickly and efficiently, she expanded the search field out to one kilometer and then two kilometers. Jerking in surprise, she double-checked what she saw. She noted the time in her log. Looking up from the image she scanned the wreckage of Gentel's Caernarfon complex. Figures roamed through it. She pressed the button on her throat mike and said in a strong southern accent, "Sir, you'll want to see what I've got on the screen here."

A figure detached itself from a group probing around a mangled set of girders where the complex's main conference hall should have been. He easily made his way through the rubble and within a minute was at the woman's side. He was compact, well-muscled with short graying hair and the bearing of a U.S. Navy Seal. "What have you got?" he asked.

She showed him the first screen and the cluster of lights. "I counted only sixty locator chips, sir. So I expanded the view." Two lights blinked far away from the complex.

"How far are they?"

"About two kliks to the north and east."

The man stared off toward the Menai Straits at Caernarfon Castle. "What's the time stamp on this image?"

"This is real time running, sir." The woman said.

The man checked his watch and noted the time: 10:47. Then as he watched, the two lights winked out. His eyes narrowed and he said sharply, "Could this be a glitch of some kind in the tracking chips?"

The black woman looked up at her superior. "No sir. There's only one way this would happen. Someone deactivated them."

The man thought a moment. He punched a number into his phone. "I'm calling the plane. Find out who those chips belong to, stat. Dr. Jurgenczak isn't going to like this."

Chapter 52

Kira kept close to the wall, hiding in the shadows as much as possible. She was sure no one had followed her but she thought it best to be careful. In spite of the trauma of being nearly buried alive, her mind felt clear and she was at ease. If a patient walked into her E.R. like this, she would have diagnosed her in shock. But Kira knew this was not the case for herself. She seemed to have reached another level of consciousness where events flowed around her in a seamless calm. At the edge of background quiet waited a dominating sense of excited anticipation.

Entering the castle's Lower Ward, she came upon a large expanse of ground. *Good. I should be able to see Chosin coming.*

The ground seemed to grow in front of her taking the shape of a man. She stepped back in surprise. *Where did he come from?*

"I know my brother has passed," the man said.

Kira relaxed. *It must be Chosin.* She sensed no violence in him, just a calm waiting, so she did the same. She studied him. It took her only a moment to realize that she was looking at Yoshi – the same face, the same body build, and especially the same green-flecked, golden eyes. *Christ, Yoshi never told me they were twins.* She smelled the musk of his body, and listening carefully, she heard something ominous, which she could distinguish even without a stethoscope – rales. *The man has stage-four lung cancer.*

Clearing her throat, she said softly, "Yoshi didn't tell me you were ill."

Chosin shrugged. "He didn't know. How was he at the last?"

"He said to tell you he had a wonderful life."

"He died without fear then?"

"Yes."

Chosin nodded. His eyes darted around the area, but to Kira, it was like a reflex action. The set of his face told her he was thinking about something else. "Did he say anything else?"

Kira said, "His last words were 'terra incognita.'"

Chosin's eyes widened and Kira could see something click in his mind. "I have many questions but we need to leave now," he said urgently.

"I don't think I was followed."

Chosin led her out of the castle. "On the contrary, a man shadowed you from the complex." Kira looked around but didn't see anyone. "He's no longer here," Chosin said. "Nonetheless, this is not a safe place. We must go."

They came to a dark van. A sleeping bag was spread out on the floor and a laptop computer was open. On the screen was video feed of the destroyed complex. With all the emergency lighting she could easily see rescuers combing the wreckage. Every once in a while a figure would stop, nod his head and move on. She realized sadly that they were counting the dead. As she watched, a figure detached from the others and walked out of frame. In the corner, Kira noted the time stamp. She checked her phone and saw that the image on the laptop was in real time.

"May I see your phone?" Chosin asked.

Kira handed it to him. "I have Yoshi's too." She pulled it from her hip pack and handed it over.

Chosin stripped the back, revealing the circuitry. His fingers were blunt and powerful-looking, yet they easily manipulated the tiny battery and the SIM card.

"What're you looking for?" Kira asked.

Chosin motioned for silence.

Slowly, he held up a tiny microchip piggybacked to the SIM card. "Military grade," he muttered. He set it aside. Quickly he stripped Yoshi's and found the same bug. He crushed them and threw them out of the van.

"What were those things?" Kira asked, after the window hissed shut.

"Miniature transmitters. They will know very soon, if not

already, that you are alive."

"Who are they?"

"First things first," Chosin said as if answering her thoughts. "We need to put as much distance between you and this place as possible."

Starting the van, he punched a sequence into the onboard GPS navigation.

Kira recognized the name – Gatwick. "We're heading to London," she said. "Isn't that a little overexposed?"

"It's a private hangar for Yamato Communications. We'll be able to keep a low profile." He paused. "Do you have your passport?"

Kira held it up.

"Good. That will make things easier and give you time to disappear."

Kira shook her head.

"Whoever is following you will know you're headed out of the country. They'll do the obvious checks first – airlines ships, even the Chunnel train to Paris. It will take them a while to think of private jets and go through those registers. By that time, you should be in America."

Chapter 53

Hawke settled back in the cockpit. The plane was on automatic pilot, but Hawke watched the dials and the radarscope. He swallowed in a dry throat, unaccustomed to the feelings racing through his body and mind. Not since he had been bullied as a kid, had the uncertainty of the future filled him with such fear. *Why was I kept in the dark about the annihilation of the complex? Does Dr. Jurgenczak no longer trust me? Oh my God, what's happening? Will it soon be my turn to die? Should I make a plan to disappear the moment we land in Omaha?*

Jurgenczak knocked softly on the cockpit door and let himself in. He slowly lowered himself into the copilot's seat and said nothing, staring out into the twilight sky with a sad little smile on his face.

Hawke remained silent. *He's aged in the last twenty-four hours.*

Jurgenczak let his breath out slowly and at last said, "I couldn't tell you, son. I couldn't put the burden of all those innocent souls on your shoulders."

Hawke digested this information. A part of him was grateful that the old man had protected him, but not knowing what the plans were put his own life in jeopardy. "I see. So, what do we do next?"

"It appears that Dr. Taylor might have escaped."

Hawke couldn't stop the fleeting smile across his face.

Jurgenczak nodded slowly. "You're pleased with this news?"

"No. I'm amazed. The explosion appeared quite thorough from the newscast images. Do you know for certain she got out?"

"The transmitter signals from hers and Dr. Yamato's phones were picked up outside of the old castle."

"Dr. Yamato also survived."

Jurgenczak shook his head. "His body was found a short time ago in a small pocket inside the rubble. He died from internal bleeding. The presumption for now is that Dr. Taylor was trapped in the same place."

"But they found no body?

"No body."

"So you don't know for certain that she's alive."

"Not for certain."

"How do you know all this?" Hawke asked.

Jurgenczak ignored the question. "You got to know her, didn't you?"

"A little."

"What do you think she'll do?"

"Without any friends or resources in Britain, she'll try and hide until she can find a way to get back home."

"Who will she try to contact?"

"Aside from her parents, the only other person she received messages from was a Jackson Kelley in Omaha."

Jurgenczak smiled. "Praise the Lord, I know him. Did he send her anything interesting?"

Hawke remembered the text picture of the brachiopod shell Jackson had sent her. He had stored the image on his own smart phone, but instead of showing it to Jurgenczak he shook his head.

Jurgenczak eyed him thoughtfully and Hawke held his breath, wondering if the old man saw through his lie.

But the old man said, "Could you kill her?"

"Of course," Hawke answered automatically.

"Good. After we land, you will turn the plane around. Find her."

"If she's alive."

Jurgenczak nodded. "Others may be looking too. Report only to me when you find her."

Jurgenczak got up to leave, but stopped at the door. "My son, be careful and may God guide your steps."

Hawke watched the door close softly behind the old man. He

was more confused than ever. It was as if he and Jurgenczak were talking in different languages.

What game is the old man playing?

Chapter 54

Kira glanced at the figure next to her. The muted glow of the van's dash lights highlighted the face she knew so well. It was confusing for her to accept that Yoshi had died amid the rubble of Gentel's Caernarfon complex, already 123 kilometers behind them. But even as she had trouble acknowledging this, she noted tiny differences between Chosin and Yoshi. Chosin's face was more ascetic, and his eyes lacked the animation of Yoshi's. He was quieter. Whatever caused Chosin's ennui, Kira knew it went beyond the cancer.

Gingerly, she touched her head and the two-inch laceration left by a piece of rebar. The wound had stopped bleeding but her hair and scalp felt gritty. She had wanted to stop by her place or at least a chemist's shop to get the supplies necessary to clean it. But Chosin vetoed the idea.

"It's too dangerous. There will be plenty of time to take care of your wound when we reach London," he had explained and then said nothing more, concentrating on his driving.

It seemed a lifetime ago that Kira would have blown up at such controlling behavior, but now she sat back and accepted the wisdom of his words. *We're both in uncharted territory. Right now he's doing what he thinks is best, which is to get us out of England. Then what?* She hoped she would know what to do once they made it that far. *Is it possible I can find the cure to the Terminator Gene*? In her body she felt she could. She shivered at the thought of Graham and so many others dying horribly in the explosion.

"We are in a most peculiar situation," Chosin said, breaking his silence.

Kira nodded. "We are perhaps the only two people in the world who know about the Terminator Gene."

"No," he said flatly. "Jurgenczak is alive and, more than likely there are others in Omaha."

"How can you be so certain?"

"Jurgenczak's only experience before founding Gentel was running a small genetics lab for animal testing."

"You're saying he had help?"

Chosin nodded. "Lots of it."

Kira recalled the picture of the Omaha skyline from Jack's office at the Scott Aquarium. "Keewatin Industrial and Bergstrom-Haggerty," she said matter-of-factly.

Chosin's eyes narrowed. "How do you know this?" he asked.

"Two weeks ago I was in Omaha. A friend pointed out the connection to me. It didn't mean anything at the time."

Chosin watched the road for a few moments. "It is good that you already know this. It will make what else I have to say easier for you to accept. A few days ago, Yoshi asked me to investigate Gentel and Jurgenczak. I was able to find out that the plan all along has been to do something unusual with the cure for the Terminator Gene."

"What does *unusual* mean?"

"I had to call in a lot of favors to find the information Yoshi asked me to get for him. Unfortunately, much of what I heard was nothing more than conflicting rumors."

What kind of favors?. The realization struck Kira that though Chosin looked like Yoshi, he was in reality nothing like the friend she had just lost. "Who are you?" she asked.

Chosin pursed his lips and blew out air slowly in the same way Yoshi did when surprised or thinking on a problem.

"All right," Chosin began carefully. He turned to look Kira full in the face, surprised again at what he saw – the uncanny resemblance to Michiko, his and Yoshi's sister. *Ah Yo-chan, you could have told me*. Chosin, for the first time concentrated on the emptiness, the void left by the death of Yoshi. *Terra Incognita*.

"It is a long story, but the essence of it is, that my brother and I took different paths to end up where you and I are now headed, but we both started from the same place, a place of anger, a place of frustration, a place of disappointment with our father. He was a very successful man by Japanese standards, a brilliant businessman and very wealthy. Yet as a human being, he was corrupt."

Chosin passed a car going slowly. He peered at it. Then satisfied that it was just a young lady driving, he sped on.

"How much do you know about the *Zaibatsu*?" he asked.

"Only that it's the name Japanese give to their largest business conglomerates, such as Sony and Toyota."

"Yes, that's true, and it's much more than that. The *Zaibatsu* of today are basically an extension of the clans that have warred for control of Japan for twelve centuries. Only in the 21st century, they no longer use Samurai. Instead, they use men like our...my father – information brokers – to gain a technological edge over their competitors.

"I am sure you have never heard of Inoue Yamato. Yet he founded Yamato Communications and everything you use from your smart phone to DVD players to high-resolution TV screens to super-fast microchips are the result of technology my father found in the West and brought to Japan, where he brokered deals among the most powerful of the Japanese *Zaibatsu*. He never cared who he hurt with his deals, never cared about what the outcome would be. He only cared for his share, for the wealth and power that it brought him. That is until he got cancer and then he only cared about living."

Kira said, "Yoshi told me he died badly."

A smile flitted across Chosin's face and was gone. "Before our father became ill, both Yoshi and I renounced his way of life. Yoshi was always the smarter of the two of us. He had a higher calling to serve humanity. I didn't.

"Like my father I became a trader of secrets, of industrial information. Only the information I traded was the new product development my father was brokering. Eventually, I began trading my own information, always maneuvering to stay one step ahead of my father. I suppose in many ways, I was like him."

"Yoshi spoke of you with the highest respect."

"Let me finish. One evening I was staring up at the emptiness of the pale blue sky. For a moment there was nothing, then everything. Everything was radiantly alive with divine energy. There was no me. It was totally impersonal. This state lasted for nearly five hours. When it was over I knew the truth."

Kira could feel the excitement growing inside her, a powerful understanding of her own experience in Caernarfon. "Which was?"

"Life in all its meaning is based on an illusion. There is nothing to do, nowhere to go, nothing to know.

"But it's not the whole truth, is it?"

Chosin looked at her, his golden eyes like a raptor, studying her every movement.

"There's something else, beyond. I felt it," Kira said. "A pull toward something. An energy, a feeling of intense urgency."

"Is it there now?"

Kira shook her head. "But it always comes back."

Chosin coughed and Kira heard the cancer in his lungs.

They drove on in silence for a while, the kilometers going by smoothly. Kira noted that Chosin drove like Hawke as though he were part of the machine. But Chosin's movements were more fluid.

"Okay, what I want to know is what will the elimination of the Terminator Gene do?"

"Your brother thought that something happened biologically when humans were becoming highly social, like a stage that led to all our technology, and most importantly the emergence of consciousness. I think he believed the elimination of the Terminator Gene will put an end to the old rules or mechanisms of evolution, and in its place new capacities will emerge."

Chosin nodded and in that discreet motion, Kira found another similarity between the two brothers. They both shared an intuitive understanding of the rightness of things. It made discussions much more facile. "And that means?" Chosin asked simply.

"The embryo will continue to develop and there will be something new. Something new will evolve in a single leap."

"A super human?"

Kira shrugged. She didn't have Yoshi's assured manner of making conclusions. "Maybe. Genes, all our morphological development, is really an incredibly complex process. Geneticists and biologists really have only been pretending they understand what's really going on. Did Yoshi mention Derek Simon?"

"I know who he was, the emotional leader of the project."

"That was well put," Kira said. "While he didn't have the hard science background of your brother or the other scientists on the project, he nevertheless believed that removal of the T-gene would result in a physiological changes in the nervous system. A change that would support the rapid evolution of consciousness."

"Which leads to the most important question of all. Do you know how to eliminate the T-gene?"

"Maybe. Yoshi and his team were working with proteins and polymers derived from the shells of 500 million year old *brachiopods*."

Kira quickly laid out the progress made at Yoshi's lab over the past few days, as well as the stumbling block they encountered when they discovered that the shells had been contaminated by radiation. "So, while results look promising, nothing is known for certain at this time. In order to go any farther, we need to find another source of Cambrian brachiopod shells."

"Was such a source identified?

"I don't know. Gentel certainly has the resources to make an exhaustive search."

Chosin nodded. "Then I suppose you will have to make an

exhaustive search as well." Chosin eased into the high speed lanes of the M1, heading directly toward London. "We'll be at Gatwick very soon. It won't be long before you can be safe – at least temporarily."

You won't be coming with me, Kira told herself, hiding the disappointment from her face.

"If we find another source of *brachiopods,* what would it take for you—"

Kira's mouth turned up in a smile. "You said 'we.'"

"There are others like me, like you," Chosin said, "who share the same experiences."

"Right now I feel a little like a chess piece being moved by forces I don't understand. Am I to trust you?"

"Haven't you noticed that nothing really turns out as we thought it would, not even a simple walk down the street. We're always trusting."

They drove on. Kira noticed that thoughts weren't coming as they once had. It was as if exhaustion had finally turned off a switch in her mind. *What the hell? Is any of this for real?* Then almost out of nowhere she heard herself say, "Can I turn on my phone? I want to check something."

Chosin frowned. "They undoubtedly have your phone's GPS signal."

"It's important."

"Alright. But be quick or they'll be able to determine our position."

Kira went directly to the text picture that Jack sent. She stared at it for a few moments before a broad smile split her face. She chuckled, *Good old Jack. He remembered.*

Turning off her phone, she tapped her fingers against the dashboard of the van. "Do you have access to the net?"

Chosin stared at her questioningly.

"My best friend, Jackson Kelley, is the director of the Scott Aquarium in Omaha. He sent me a picture of a fossil brachiopod and a cryptogram...a private code we made up for the fun of it during our college days. He's letting me know that he put something in the Cloud for me. I need to get it."

"Once we reach Gatwick, you can have access to the plane's on board computer. It's encrypted and will be safer to use than your phone."

Chapter 55

Under the muted golden lights of the laboratory, Dr. Arne Jurgenczak stood beside the stainless-steel table and waited for the other man to speak. If Hawke had seen him at this moment, he would have thought his boss was facing death. Less than an hour earlier, Gentel's founder had flown into Omaha from Caernarfon.

He arrived at night. Below stretched a sea of lights, and as Hawke circled the airport preparing to land, Jurgenczak wondered what waited for him in the darkness. *Yea, though I walk through the valley of death, I shall fear no evil.*

After landing, Hawke guided the craft to Keewatin Industrial's private hangar. As the engines whined down to nothing, a young woman entered the cabin and spoke only to say, "Mr. Drake is waiting at the facility as requested."

"Do you wish me to come along, sir?" Hawke asked, knowing he already had his orders.

"This is a private meeting," the woman objected.

"Of course it is," Jurgenczak said, mustering all the calm he could. Even with God's help, he recognized how uncertain the days ahead were going to be. He would have liked to have Hawke's help, but his security chief knew nothing about the special lab he was going to. Jurgenczak said to Hawke, "Go with God, my son."

Hawke nodded and returned to the Gulfstream's cockpit.

Before Jurgenczak entered the waiting limousine, he heard the first engine shriek to life. It sounded as though the last tether to security and normalcy was being cut.

The limo reached its destination in less than thirty minutes. It was a strip mall. The car stopped in front of a building with a sign on the front that read Gentel Pharmaceuticals. The guard at the front desk recognized Jurgenczak and ushered him into the building with a "Good evening, sir."

He walked down a long hall toward a set of double doors, the clicking of his shoes against the spotlessly clean linoleum the only sound. It was here, at this small lab, that Jurgenczak had started Gentel in 2001, while working on the Human Genome Project. It began as a small provider of gene therapy delivery systems for domesticated animals, mostly pets. Then came Jurgenczak's astounding discovery of the Terminator Gene. *It was a most fortuitous day, Adonay, a day when you spoke to me for the first time.* Jurgenczak recalled the strong, sure voice commanding him to be the Lord's servant. Jurgenczak had obeyed, and since that time, had carried out every one of Jehovah's wishes to prepare the Earth for Jesus's Second Coming.

But the way had been difficult and the only means to achieve God's directive was to find a partner with enough money to covertly fund an expansion of Gentel. Jehovah had pointed the way to George Drake of Keewatin Industrial. Drake agreed but only for a majority share of the restructured company. A year later Jurgenczak trusted him with the information about the Terminator Gene. Drake instantly recognized the importance of maintaining secrecy until the cure was found. But Jurgenczak had easily seen through the man's sin of avarice, his desire to use a cure as the ultimate way to increase his status and wealth.

From that moment on, Keewatin's head directed Gentel on everything except on the Terminator Gene research. He personally chose the location for the lab in Caernarfon and supervised the construction. He even turned Gentel into a phenomenally successful company, creating a cover business by developing a suite of medical, chemical and genetic products. By 2010, Gentel's annual sales topped 50 billion dollars.

Now, Drake had called Jurgenczak to meet him here at the Omaha facility. And even though this pet laboratory was Jurgenczak's home ground, the ways of the Lord were mysterious, and he could not help but feel anxious. *Adonay, have you led me here to my death?*

Jurgenczak pushed through the double doors into a huge lab. Benches loaded with equipment spread through the room. Cages for domestic pets lined one wall. A large bench occupied the center of the room. "Good evening, George," Jurgenczak said.

George Drake nodded. He was forty-seven years old, sandy-haired and broad shouldered. At six foot four and a half inches, he towered over the shorter Jurgenczak. His narrow ascetic face and ice-blue eyes carried the hard lines of his life: born into poverty in Fargo, North Dakota; abusive father; his only way out of small town obscurity was a hockey scholarship to Harvard; a five thousand dollar loan from a wealthy college friend started his first construction company; his first marriage to Esther, a wealthy English widow, was the closest thing to friendship Drake had ever known; her son Graham was like a young brother; when Esther died in a gang incident, killed by a stray bullet, Drake used her fortune to found Keewatin Industrial.

Now twenty years, three more wives, three divorces and three children later, George Drake was an angry alpha male, overachiever, a man who was often described as a sociopath, a man who used the resources of Keewatin Industrial to create the largest construction conglomerate on the planet.

Drake stared at Jurgenczak, his face an unreadable mask. *What am I going to do about Graham, you smug religious son of a bitch?* he asked himself. Graham had informed Drake of every step that occurred at the lab. Drake had had big plans for his stepson, a young man only ten years younger than Drake himself. *And now he's gone because this son of a bitch acted too soon.* The rescuers hadn't found Graham's body yet. It would likely be days before everyone was accounted for. Drake let a cold smile flit across his features. *I can wait until then to decide your fate.*

Jurgenczak stopped beside the bench, his eyes locked on Drake. *No mercy there,* he thought.

"I'm not a happy man," Drake said.

"I understand your feelings, but allow me to show you the next room." Jurgenczak walked past him to the single door at the far end of the room. It could be opened only by a retinal scanner.

Drake's smile was brittle. "You've killed more than sixty people, jeopardized the entire project, and you've put me and Keewatin Industrial at too great a risk with your ill-timed destruction the Caernarfon complex. Give me a good reason why I shouldn't abandon everything right now, tell the whole world about the Terminator Gene, and hang your ass out to dry?"

Ignoring Drake's indictment, Jurgenczak put his eye to the optical scanner. The door swung open automatically and the two men gazed upon a separate processing facility – a secret lab within a lab.

Drake looked around. The room was pristine. Benches lined the two long walls. Plastic covered some of the equipment. Others were fully operational. Smart boards filled the space above the benches. The blinking lights of a two-foot-tall PPC-8000 mini tower supercomputer showed they were the only live machines. "What the hell is this?"

"It is a duplicate of the essential facilities at Caernarfon."

He beckoned Drake to follow. At the other end of the lab stood what looked like a large industrial refrigerator. "Here."

Peering inside the sealed glass doors, Drake saw racks of vials. Each one looked like a tiny glass straw. Sweat beaded up on his forehead, and with an effort he kept his composure. "Is this what I think it is?"

"That depends on what you think it is?" Jurgenczak answered softly.

"Human embryos."

Jurgenczak nodded.

"There must be thousands," Drake marveled.

"Tens of thousands...25,000 thousand to be exact."

Drake tapped the glass and quickly pulled his fingers away from the intense cold. "This a cryogenic container?"

Jurgenczak nodded again. "It is unique, an ark for protection against extinction. It houses 25,000 embryos of a very distinctive nature. Each one of these embryos is only one day old. They have been mixed with a cryoprotectant, which prevents ice from forming in between the cells and preserves them up to fifteen years. For the last year, my technicians have been collecting these embryos."

Drake, stunned by the presence of all the frozen embryos, said nothing.

A beatific smile lit up Jurgenczak's face and he seemed oblivious to Drake standing next to him as he continued with his explanation. "When the time comes for the frozen embryo transfer, the embryos will be taken in groups of four from the freezer and allowed to thaw naturally until they reach room temperature. They are steeped to remove the cryoprotectant, then warmed to body temperature, where they are mixed with a special culture medium before being implanted into a suitable host."

"Why four at a time?"

"To insure a viable pregnancy, four embryos need to be implanted."

Drake wiped the perspiration off his forehead. He had approved the expenditure for a second secret lab to carry on the research of the Caernarfon complex. But this was not what he expected. He was about to ask Jurgenczak what all of it meant, when a revelation struck him. *He said it's an ark. He' planning on repopulating the Earth. Christ, the old bastard thinks he's Noah.*

Drake mastered the chill sweeping through him. "So, here's where you'll be testing your solution to the T-gene?" he asked, careful not to let Jurgenczak believe he knew what was really going on.

Jurgenczak nodded, happy that Drake hadn't guessed his real purpose yet. *Let him think that he'll become Earth's hero-savior and first trillionaire. Adonay has other plans.*

"Of course, you'll need help to pull this off, more research, a new supplier of brachiopod shells. Who's going to assist you?"

"Any well-trained technicians can help me with the necessary research."

"So this huge investment...all this risk depends only on you."

Jurgenczak was glad that Drake accepted the fact that he and he alone could find the solution.

But Drake was far from satisfied with everything he had heard so far. *Christ, something happens to this old bastard and everything's screwed.* Drake cleared his throat and glared at the scientist. "Like I said before I'm not happy."

"It's going to work," Jurgenczak insisted. "We've already rounded up enough Cambrian brachiopod samples to complete the testing. Eventually we'll need more if we cannot synthesize the critical biochemistry."

"Why can't you just find more like at the Eau Claire site in Wisconsin?"

"Mass die-offs like that of an already-rare species are very rare. Usually, inarticulate Cambrian brachiopod fossils with the original biochemistry still intact, are very few and far between."

"In other words, you're telling me we might be screwed no matter what." Drake's eyes locked on Jurgenczak. His voice grated, "This is turning into a very bad business proposition. I should shut all this down, and like I said, 'let the world take care of the Terminator Gene.'"

The old man swallowed in a dry throat. *Adonay, do not let me fail when we're so close.* "No! I can get this done. Give me a week."

"A week?" Drake made a fist, cracking the knuckles of his hand. *So much riding on the efforts of one old man,* he fumed.

Drake turned toward the door, all but decided to end this debacle when a new thought struck him. *Or does everything depend on this old fool?* "You seem very sure of yourself, considering this is an idea that wasn't yours to begin with."

"That's not true," Jurgenczak protested. "We've been investigating this line for a number of months now."

That isn't what Graham *told me.* "Kira Taylor. Wasn't this whole Cambrian biochemistry thing her idea in the first place?"

With a great effort Jurgenczak kept his surprise under control. *How does he know? Did I mention Taylor on my last trip to Omaha.* "We, that is Derek Simon, asked that we bring her in to help him with some theoretical ideas he had. After he died we were ready to send her home. Besides, it doesn't matter any more; she died with the others," he lied.

Drake nodded but he wasn't buying any of it. Mentally, he brought up the text messages he'd received from Caernarfon informing him of the destruction of the Gentel complex. It was money well spent to pay one of the Welsh police inspectors to report on the lab's security activities for him, though the second text message sent a little over two hours after the explosion had been disturbing: "The woman, Kira Taylor, you asked me to run a background on is alive. She met up at the castle with an old contractor of yours – Chosin Yamato. They've since driven off. Destination at present unknown. At your service, S. Ross."

Christ! Yamato! Drake's heart hammered in his chest just thinking about all the arrogant Japanese bastard had done for him. *If he's with the Kira woman, that's an unexpected complication.*

Drake watched the old scientist. "You have your week, doctor. Then I'm pulling the plug." Drake gestured to the room. "On all of this."

Jurgenczak nodded, unable to speak from the fear that coursed through him.

Drake smiled, glad to see the old man rattled. "One week," he repeated and left without a backward glance.

"One week," Jurgenczak echoed hoarsely.

The time is near, Adonay. In three days I have a meeting with the Interregnum Catholic Mission. The ICM was a small splinter group from the ultra-conservative Opus Dei organization of the Catholic Church. They believed that the ultimate end of humanity, the end of days prophesized in Revelations was coming true in 2012. *When they hear about my divine mission, they will know what to do,*

Chapter 56

Hawke waited until Jurgenczak and the woman left the hangar, then he shut down the Gulfstream's engines a second time. He took several deep breaths, trying to reconcile the emotions pouring into his body. *Does the extinction of the human race rest somehow in my hands?* He could barely control the shaking of his limbs.

After the destruction of the Caernarfon complex, Hawke knew he could no longer work for Jurgenczak. Sadness wracked him as he accepted this. Upon their first meeting, Hawke had met a man whose vision and word he trusted without question. But now, that trust was shattered. Thoughts about Dr. Ray Howe, the man he killed on Jurgenczak's orders filled him with remorse. *I am no longer serving the greater good, preventing the world from falling into chaos by protecting against the revelation of the Terminator Gene's existence.* For the first time Hawke admitted to himself that he had been played all along.

Now there was Dr. Taylor. Jurgenczak had ordered him to locate Kira, and that he would do. What he would do with that knowledge was another thing altogether.

It was simple enough to use his top-secret clearance to access the military satellite in geo-synchronous orbit over England. He quickly downloaded her smart phone's GPS record. At the same time, he downloaded the GPS signal of a vehicle that correlated perfectly with time and place with Kira's phone. It was then a simple matter of overlaying the two GPS signals with a map of England to determine where they were heading. Within seconds he pinpointed the vehicle's last known location – Gatwick Airport in London. But what was even more curious was the satellite's reception of a plane's transponder signal taking off from that airfield within fifteen minutes of the van's arrival. It was a plane registered to Yamato Communications. Everyone in the intelligence community knew about Yamato. The company had siphoned American technology, albeit legally, for fifty years.

There had to be a link to Yoshi Yamato. The coincidence was too great to ignore. Was Yoshi working for his family all along? If this was true, then finding Kira could be a bigger problem than he imagined. The Yamato resources were vast.

Hawke sat at the controls of the Gulfstream, his mind going over the possibilities this new information provided. *One step at a time,* he cautioned himself. He carefully laid in a course for London. The travel time would put him behind the other plane, if indeed it was carrying Kira Taylor, but he had to make certain first if she was alive – and if she was, who was helping her?

Chapter 57

Kira Taylor followed Chosin Yamato onto the jet. She had worried that Jurgenczak's people had cast a wide net for her, and once she flashed her passport at the private terminal, security would arrest her. But the agents waved her through. She noted the plane was the same model as Gentel's corporate jet – a Gulfstream 650. "You can fly this?" she asked.

"I used to love flying," Chosin said matter-of-factly.

"I meant with your cancer."

He nodded and pointed aft. "You'll find a bathroom, shower and robe behind that door."

"First-aid kit?"

"It's there too." Chosin disappeared into the cockpit.

Kira had the shower running before they were airborne.

Sitting in front of the large mirror in the plane's lavish bathroom, She hardly recognized the face staring back at her. The gash just above the right temple was worse than she had imagined. It would need stitches. Fortunately, the medical supplies like the plane were lavish, even down to the lidocaine syringes and suture kits. She was finished in ten minutes. But her questions about the destruction of the complex were endless. Her mind seemed caught in a loop of questions. The last time she was on a plane like this, the enigmatic Hawke was the pilot. She wondered if he had been the one to trigger the explosion – and murder innocent people.

As Kira stared into the mirror, slowly her consciousness shifted into her body. Unlike Kira's mind, it was ready, primed to move. She had felt this way before when making love, the moment just before an orgasm. This was a feeling she could trust. It was clear and decisive. In a flash, the oneness of everything filled her awareness. The plane, her body, her inner turmoil, the cosmos, her observation of it all was all the same, was all one thing.

Kira left the bathroom, crossed the cabin and entered the cockpit. She slid into the copilot's chair as if she had sat there a thousand times before.

Chosin glanced over at her. Instantly he recognized her altered state of consciousness. "You're different."

"I know who you are. For a moment I was you and you were me. Our natures are the same."

"I know."

Then Kira watched herself slide back into normalcy. Like her other experiences of altered consciousness, a residual afterglow stayed with her. Everything was lighter, brighter, more present.

Kira looked away from Chosin. "I need to see what Jack has waiting for me."

"On the black lacquered table is a silver laptop computer. You can use it to download the information you need."

"Is it safe to use?"

"It's a secure machine."

Kira quickly accessed the Cloud. There she found what Jack had left for her – *Fossil Field Trip Manitou Formation 1999*. After scanning it quickly, she returned to the cockpit and strapped herself into the copilot's chair again.

"What was it?"

"Basically Jack sent me a report of a field trip to an early Ordovician formation called the Manitou. Among the other fossils described in the report is the abundance of inarticulate *brachiopods* with the original shell material preserved. Probably enough to begin work again."

"That raises some interesting possibilities," Chosin mused. "Think about it. Something very exciting is happening here, this could all be a fortuitous coincidence. Fate. Or something entirely new."

"And that means?"

Chosin sat silently for a moment. Kira recognized that he was gathering his thoughts and she waited patiently with him for those thoughts to express themselves.

At last Chosin said, "Right now there is a feeling, a feeling I haven't felt in years, that there is something to do, the desire to experience exactly what's happening."

"I think I know what you mean. Almost ever since you raised those questions about the Terminator Gene, I've been thinking about what I should do: tell the world or step back and let it all play out as intended." Her eyes narrowed and she added, "Here's the impossible one, try to find out if there is a fix, follow through on what Yoshi and I were doing at the lab."

"Why is that impossible?"

"There are so many resources needed, it's beyond hope. Yet, I'm drawn to trying. Even stranger, I feel pulled toward it, as though evolution itself is expressing itself through me."

"Then let's do it."

"You say that as though it's going to be easy."

Chosin made another of his rare smiles. "As I said earlier, there are others like us, others who will help. Where is the Manitou Formation?"

"The closest city is Colorado Springs, Colorado."

"I know it well. It's a center of your military-industrial complex. In particular, a center for developing laser technology for military purposes. Something Yamato Communications specializes in. What's next?"

"You understand I'll need a sophisticated biochemistry lab where I can duplicate the work we were doing at Yoshi's lab in Caernarfon. This includes a supply of HeLa cells...cancer cells."

"Will mine do?"

"You made a joke." There was another long pause, and then Kira said, "Eventually I'll need embryos where the Terminator Gene is expressing itself. It's all just too impossible." She slumped in the chair.

Chosin adjusted the plane's course. When next he looked over at Kira she was asleep. Gently he nudged her awake.

Opening one eye, Kira said, "I know where the bed is."

Chapter 58

Chosin watched the cockpit door close behind Kira, heard her footsteps dwindle away. Checking the Heads Up Display, he saw that the trip would be unaffected by any major weather systems. He let the autopilot take over. With Kira sleeping, he had time to reflect.

For some time Chosin had been able to observe his inner milieu as easily as the outside world, and he knew a fundamental change was occurring. After his non-dual experience four years ago he had entered what was called in spiritual literature a state of "high indifference." It contained neither joy and bliss nor sadness and suffering. Normal opposites – good and bad, right and wrong – naturally complemented each other. There was neither love nor hate. In the months that followed his experience, Chosin had learned, that while he had entered this high indifference state in what Zen Buddhists call a sudden *kensho,* most others had walked a long purposeful path to arrive at the same place. A path of not choosing and picking, not having any preferences. A way so simple, yet so difficult.

Within Chosin everything was solid and calm. To others, he appeared as a man without agency, a person wasting away his life. In his research into this state, Chosin had discovered there was a community of people like himself spread throughout the world. Many, who had had similar experiences, reentered life fully energized. Others had glided gracefully toward oblivion as he had. But oblivion no longer held his interest.

Is it the presence of this woman? Chosin asked himself. He had no answer for this. What was becoming clear to him was that a shift was occurring. Faced with doubt, the unknown – *terra incognita* – a disruption in his balanced equilibrium was occurring. Something new was forcing its way to the surface of his illuminated consciousness. All he could do for now was watch.

Now, Chosin thought, the word forming an agenda of action within his body. *Now I must use the community.*

Chapter 59

Kira Taylor walked along the tree-lined sidewalks of the Colorado College Campus. She breathed deeply, taking in the rich scent of pine and new mown grass, glad to be on American soil again. While the real world changed almost daily, Colorado College appeared to be trapped in the late 90s. Here, the summer session was in full swing. Young students she passed talked eagerly about almost everything. Filled with hope and promise, the future was new and exciting to them. Kira knew there was another aspect to life, not so idyllic. War, famine, environmental catastrophes, terrorism, crime, political crises – the Terminator Gene also defined the real world.

Checking the campus map on her smart phone, she saw the building where she needed to go.

Upon landing Kira and Chosin agreed she would contact the author of the field guide Jack had provided. Professor Emeritus of geology Dr. William Reed had an office on the second floor of the Russell T. Tutt Science Center. *It'll be good to discuss the T-gene with someone,* she told herself.

Inside the center the smells and sounds of academia filled her with nostalgia for her own student days at Yale. The memories were bittersweet, but she found herself easily focusing on the joy of it.

She opened the door to the second floor office and saw an elderly man sitting behind a desk piled with books and the manila folders of dissertations. "Dr. Reed," she said.

The man looked up at her from behind narrow reading glasses. Though semi-retired, he was lean and fit. A well-chewed Meerschaum pipe hung from the corner of his mouth. He reminded Kira of Pete Englund, the geologist who introduced her to fossil collecting when she was sixteen.

"You must be Kira Taylor, the woman who called my secretary

for an appointment," Reed boomed, his voice filled with enthusiasm. He motioned her to a chair, while taking out a match and relighting his pipe. "Always glad to speak with a student of Derek Simon. How is the old bugger?"

"I'm sorry to bring bad news, sir. Derek passed away a few days ago."

Reed frowned. "That is bad news. A great loss for paleontology. I didn't know him personally but I read everything he wrote. You know, I was one of the few that accepted his so-called 'Green Genes' theory."

"It's what I'm here to talk to you about, Dr. Reed."

He leaned forward on his desk. "I'm intrigued...and everybody calls me, Doc."

"I guess the best place to start is that my friend, Jackson Kelley, sent me a monograph you had written on the Manitou Formation."

Doc Reed's head tilted back and he laughed. "I remember Jack. Hard to forget. First-rate student. One of my favorites. Tell me where did he end up?"

"Director of the Scott Aquarium in Omaha. I spoke with him less than two weeks ago. He's the same old Jack."

"That says it all, doesn't it? So, what's this all about?"

Kira laid it all out for him, everything from the miscarriages to the T-gene to the brachiopod fossils and their connection to a cure. He took in what Kira had to say with keen interest, occasionally asking for clarification on a few points.

"Yes! Yes! That would follow," Reed said when she explained the re-differentiating effect of the SF-81 on the HeLa cells. "Like Derek and yourself, I have held the belief for many years that biological evolution had clear directionality. Not in the teleological sense, but as an unfolding of ever-greater biological capacities."

"Dr. Yoshi Yamato and I believe that this is something more though," Kira continued. "We believe now that this is all tied into cosmic and material evolution, even cultural and consciousness evolution."

"Remarkable." Reed tapped the bowl of his pipe on the ashtray and wiped the dottle clear. He steepled his fingers and looked skyward for a few moments. "Well, I know just how I can help with this." Picking up the phone, he made a few calls. It seemed only seconds before his room was filled with young geology students. Eagerness played across their faces.

In no time Kira, the professor and ten geology students were in two vans driving along Colorado's Highway 24. "Where are we headed?" she asked Reed.

"Just outside of Woodland Park to a place north of Mount Deception called Rainbow Falls."

Apropos name, Kira thought.

The drive took a little more than hour and she spotted the place before Doc said anything. They entered a valley of red rock. Rainbows formed over the spray of waterfalls at the far end. Reed hopped out and unlocked a gate to a private road. "I have special collecting privileges," he said with a wink.

Kira looked out upon the landscape. The road cut deeply into the mountain, revealing Earth's past in geological strata. Nothing promising popped out at her yet. There were a few outcroppings of the Manitou, its coarse rust hue contrasting starkly with the dull brown gravel and dirt of the road. But none of the fragments showed signs of *brachiopod* shells.

"Here!" Reed shouted, and the vans stopped abruptly. The students clambered out.

"I don't see anything," Kira said, as she inspected the rock surface.

Immediately Doc began splitting a rock with his hammer and chisel. "These dolomites are extremely dense," he explained.

The rock fractured horizontally into two flat planes. An abundance of pearly white shells were on one of the slabs. "Bingo," Reed said, with a big smile. "Here we go. Have at it."

Soon the area was filled with the sounds of hammers splitting rocks. Doc leaned against one of the vans and offered Kira a water bottle. "Shouldn't take long," he said.

"Not with all these kids you've got helping you," a voice called out.

Kira looked in the direction of the voice and saw a dark-haired young woman striding toward them. A cowboy hat was pushed back on her head. A canteen hanging from a strap banged against her left hip, and she carried a rifle in her right hand like she knew how to use it.

Kira felt the muscles tense in her belly and looked to Doc. He laughed.

"Hey Theresa, checking to make certain we aren't drunk teenagers."

"Never too early in the day for that." Doc Reed introduced the woman as Theresa Lopez. Her grip was strong. She studied the students banging away at the rocks. "Another field trip, huh," Theresa said. "There's been a lot of strange people up here in the last couple of weeks."

"We'll be out of your hair in a couple of hours, I figure," Doc said.

She waved his explanation away. "Take your time. You're always welcome." She went back the way she came and disappeared over a small ridge.

By early afternoon the students had collected enough rock to fill both vans.

The ride down was filled with laughter and Kira found herself joining in the good-natured bantering. It had been some time since she had let herself go like this. *Maybe I never did.*

The final step was to take the slabs into the geology lab. Using dental tools Kira guided the students in removing the shelly material. With everyone working, it took them only a couple of hours to accumulate over twenty grams of the ancient biochemistry. The white flakes were placed into a sterilized Tupperware container and sealed. Then the container was placed inside a sealable baggie.

At the visitor's parking lot, Doc shook Kira's hand. "We can always get more if you need it," he said.

Kira nodded and got into the rental car. Driving away, she looked back and saw pipe smoke swirling above his head as he gave her a farewell thumbs-up. A feeling of love welled up in her for the wonderful old geologist who had just helped her. *One step at a time.*

Chapter 60

Hawke stood by the service counter in the brightly-lit terminal for private planes at Gatwick Airport. It was neat and huge with a private VIP lounge and bar. Windows showed the airport, and beyond the London skyline. The setting sun reminded him he hadn't slept in almost thirty-six hours and had logged two flights across the Atlantic. *I'm tired.* The nameplate on the service counter desk read, Liddy Ross. She was in her fifties, heavyset, with rust-colored hair. Her perfume was very strong and he resisted the urge to hold a handkerchief to his nose and mouth.

"Ms. Ross," Hawke said, handing the woman his ID, containing his top-secret clearance.

The woman handed back the card. "How can I help you?" she said, her British accent clipped and professional.

Hawke accepted the ID and in the same motion laid his smart phone on the counter. Its specialized Bluetooth technology would download everything the woman brought up on her computer. "I'm sorry to bother you, but I'm looking for this woman." Hawke showed her a picture of Kira Taylor.

"Sure, I remember her," Liddy said immediately. "She was here with another man, sort of Asian-looking. They were a strange couple, in a hurry, no baggage. Luckily for them, everything was in order." Liddy handed the photo back and lowered her voice to a whisper. "Is she wanted by the U.S. government?"

Hawke shook his head. "Nothing like that. She has information we need. The man she was with, do you recall what he looked like?"

"I can do better than that. Everyone has to show us their passports if they are leaving the country. We scan them and then check them against the database for Britain's 'Do Not Fly List.'" She tapped her computer keyboard. "Voila." She turned the monitor so that Hawke could see the picture.

Hawke gasped. It was Yoshi Yamato. *He's supposed to be dead.*

"Is everything alright, sir? Is this man wanted?" Liddy said anxiously.

Recovering quickly, Hawke shook his head. He stared at the Japanese passport and read the name – Chosin Yamato. "I'm sorry. I didn't mean to alarm you. He's one of ours and I didn't realize someone was already on this case. Thank you, Ms. Ross. You've been a great help."

Hawke walked away from the counter. He found a place where he could sit down unobserved. He tried to rub the fatigue from his eyes, but didn't succeed. The amphetamines he'd taken for the flight back across the Atlantic were wearing off. *Just a few more minutes, then I'll board the plane and sleep.*

He activated the information his phone pulled from the woman's computer. Once more he marveled at the similarity between Chosin Yamato and Dr. Yamato. They were the same age, born in the same place, a small fishing village in Hokkaido, Japan, and the eyes were exactly the same, golden irises with specks of green in them. *Christ, they could be the same person. Maybe Yoshi got a fake passport in order to leave the country. Or maybe he had a twin brother*. Hawke knew he was too tired to figure it out now. He took a deep breath and brought up the flight information: Gulfstream 650; Transponder Yamato Communications – 192 Alpha; Original destination Sioux City, Iowa, USA; Updated destination Colorado Springs, Colorado, USA; Departure 3:02 a.m.; Estimated arrival 5:32 a.m. local time, which meant they had already landed.

She's gone home.

Hawke checked the time. He was a half day behind them and it was only going to increase. But that couldn't be helped. Right now he needed sleep. He did have a few things working in his favor, though. An Air Force buddy working for NORAD at Cheyenne Mountain Directorate out of Colorado Springs owed him a big favor. It shouldn't be hard to track the Gulfstream's transponder signal.

The bigger problem was Jurgenczak, who was expecting a report on Kira Taylor. Hawke typed in a short message on his phone. "Taylor is alive but I lost her trail in London. I'll call when I pick it up again." He punched send and watched the text disappear. *It's done. I've forsaken Jurgenczak.* Somehow the realization wasn't as freeing as he thought it would be.

Chapter 61

Kira parked the rental car in front of the motel's restaurant. She spotted Chosin sitting at a booth with a coffee cup in front of him. *If only I could do more than ease his symptoms.* Fortunately she was still licensed in Colorado, and prescribed morphine for the pain in his body, Lasix to remove the fluid from his lungs, and Heparin to thin his blood so that his heart did not have to work so hard. His breathing improved almost immediately. Without these drugs, the rarefied mountain air of Colorado would have killed him.

She joined him in the booth.

"Mint tea," he said, glancing at his cup.

"Sure. How's the pain?" she asked.

Chosin said, "I can control it."

Kira was relieved to see him taking care of himself, but even so she recognized that the cancer was taking its toll. His breathing was labored though not unbearable.

Chosin shoved her smart phone across the table. "Take it," he said.

"I thought Jurgenczak could track us through the GPS?"

"Not any more."

She gave him a puzzled look.

"An American company here has been working on technology to cloak a smart phone's signal, making it untraceable.

"And Yamato Communications just happens to have access to this technology." Kira smiled. "Well, I have some good news of my own. I got the fossil shells we need."

"Then we are set for tomorrow," Chosin said. "We're taking a commercial flight to Madison, Wisconsin early in the morning."

"A commercial flight?"

"I'm sending the corporate jet back to Hokkaido. We'll be more invisible using the airlines."

"What's in Madison?"

"Dr. Sonya Speyer. She does stem cell research. Her lab will have all the equipment you need. Plus, she has graduate students that can help with the preparation."

"Can we trust her?"

Chosin slid a sheet of paper across the table to her. On it was a list of names. Sonya Speyer's was at the top. "These are the people who have had profound non-dual experiences like yours and mine. When I contacted her, she immediately understood what's at stake."

Looking at Chosin, Kira again felt overwhelming compassion for the man she knew was so close to death.

"I am well enough for this," he said, as if reading her mind.

"Then we're off to Madison, tomorrow." Kira kept her face expressionless, but couldn't make the sinking feeling in her gut go away. What she failed to tell him was that the *brachiopods* were the wrong age. They were from the Ordovician. It had been bothering ever since Doc Reed broke open the first slab of rock. Yet she felt deep in her bones that she had to keep going. *I have to trust something good will come out of this.*

Chapter 62

The SF-81 looked promising, what little there was of it. The two Asian technicians helping Arne Jurgenczak had prepared as much of the shelly material as they could from the meager supply of brachiopod fossils delivered to the lab.

The five different species from seven different sites provided little more than half a gram for processing. Jurgenczak knew that he should have kept them separated, but in an impulsive movement he decided to combine them all, since it was the only way to duplicate the tests that were run in the Caernarfon lab.

He carefully watched as the technicians began the long procedure separating the SF-81 into its separate biochemical elements. But even as he watched, Jurgenczak could not help but feel that his holy dream was unraveling.

The deaths of so many clouded his thought processes. He had never felt so alone and afraid. It was as if the strength and certainty he had gotten from God was eroding away.

When the technicians finished, he told them to leave. He would run the test on the HeLa cells himself. Following them out into the Nebraska twilight, he watched the first stars of evening show themselves in the deep dark blues of night. Doubts filled him and he asked, *Why are you deserting me, Adonay?*

He heard no answer.

Chapter 63

Kira and Chosin stood on the redwood deck enjoying the warm morning on the shores of Lake Mendota, a large recreational body of water extending out from Shorewood Hill, a picturesque village neighboring the University of Wisconsin in Madison. Behind them stretched the prairie-style home of Dr. Sonya Speyer. Everything about the house blended effortlessly into the lakeside setting.

Sonya's husband, John, joined them carrying a tray with four glasses of iced tea. He was a tall, lanky man, with a shock of silver hair. On the ride from the airport, he had apologized for his wife's absence. "Sonya had to stay home. She's leading a webinar on a stem cell ethics."

John handed out the tea and set the tray on the railing. He smiled. "The webinar should be winding up in a few minutes, everyone's starting to repeat themselves. Cheers," he toasted.

Kira sipped the tea and let herself relax into the peaceful essence of the surroundings. She concentrated on the sailboats, windsurfers and pleasure craft crisscrossing the blue water. The bright sun and warm air made Caernarfon seem so far away, like another lifetime. She wished herself to be here forever in this idyllic place – no Terminator Gene, no explosion.

"Here she is now," John said interrupting Kira's reverie.

Kira turned around as Sonya emerged onto the deck. She was a petite woman in her early fifties, just over five feet tall. The fine bones of her face stood out clearly under a dark tan.

"Sorry to keep everyone waiting," she said, her voice filled with exuberance.

To Kira's surprise, Chosin almost leapt out of his chair and embraced her.

Sonya stood back a half step and carefully looked the Japanese information broker over. Frowning she said, "My, my.

Chosin, I may have an idea for you." Her gaze, falling on Kira, radiated an intense energy that drew Kira forward. "And you're Kira," she said. "Welcome, welcome." Sonya cupped Kira's hands in her own. A jolt of warmth spread quickly through Kira's body.

The deck's round glass table gave the impression that all of them were dining at a small cafe, listening intently to one another, instead of outside enjoying the warm afternoon. Kira found herself listening raptly as Sonya told the story of how she and Chosin met. John sat back smiling, having heard all of it before, but happy to relive it.

"I was a speaker at the first global conference on conscious evolution and global politics in Tokyo," Sonya was saying. "Chosin came up to me after my talk and said, 'Why bother with any of this?'"

Kira shot the Japanese a questioning look, surprised he would say anything so directly. "It's true," he affirmed.

"At the time I thought he was just another existential nihilist, rejecting the fruits of modernism. I started to give him my song and dance about waking up. He held up his hand to silence me and said, 'I woke up and everything is already perfect.' We've stayed in touch ever since. I keep trying to convince him that the new cultural evolutionary perspective is the true awakening, and he, politely of course, ignores everything I have to say."

"I can sympathize," Kira said dryly.

For the first time a slight smile crossed Chosin's face as he realized he was being ganged up on by the two women.

Sonya's face turned solemn and her eyes fastened on Kira. "So, this is a big deal we have here, a very big deal. I've had three miscarriages. How about you?"

Kira said, "One."

"I looked at the statistics. It's staggering. How could everybody have missed this? And then on the de-differentiation of the embryo, I can find nothing." She shook her head slowly side to side. "Amazing...just amazing."

Kira checked her phone and was pleased to see the images of the Jacobsen embryo de-differentiating were still there. "Here's what it looked like," she said, handing the phone to Sonya. "The exact mechanism of why this occurs was never understood by anyone at the Caernarfon lab."

Sonya studied the images, her forehead furrowed in thought. "It's got to be some sort of timing sequence issue."

"What do you mean?"

"If you look at the developmental sequence of a fertilized egg to a fetus, it's a series of systems growing out of earlier stages. Each stage needs to follow the previous one precisely, one after another. Something's messing that order up. At least, that's my guess."

Kira exchanged glances with Chosin. "Chosin's brother, Yoshi, saw this as a new species trying to emerge and that the problem was not genetic but some sort of morphogenic shift."

"So what do you want from me?" Sonya asked.

"I would like you to help me duplicate what we were doing at the Caernarfon lab."

"Why not just go public with this?"

Chosin spoke up for the first time. "One person already tried that before the explosion, and he was killed." He went on to explain Jurgenczak's responsibility in the destruction of the Caernarfon complex.

"You really think he's that powerful?" John asked.

"Not just him, the people he's working with." Chosin explained the connection with George Drake of Keewatin Industrial and with Bartnum Haggerty.

Sonya shifted back in her chair, the surprise clearly registering in the sudden stiffness of her movements. "It sounds like we're the only good guys that know about this. I mean, what the hell is going on here?"

"That's my point. We don't know," Chosin said.

Sonya glanced at her husband. The smile had long since

disappeared from his face. "In other words, you can't guarantee John's and my safety if it gets out I'm helping you with this?"

"True," Chosin answered.

Sonya stared out at the western shore of the lake, a dark band green and silver going into shadow as the sun swung over into afternoon. John placed his right hand on her arm. He nodded to her.

"Ok," Sonya said. "I suggest a compromise. Let's see where Kira's *brachiopods* take us. In return I get to tell a number of my evolutionary colleagues about this extraordinary piece of information."

Chosin and Kira nodded at one another. "Agreed," he said.

Kira said, "Let me tell you what I'm going to need."

Chapter 64

Kira was alone on the deck. Chosin had gone to the guest room to rest and Sonya had to attend to matters that could only be solved by phone calls. John had gone into the kitchen. "Rustlin' up some grub," he said with a wink.

The afternoon turned hot. Kira watched a light breeze send ripples across the blue and silver water of the lake. She breathed in deeply and let it out slowly. Sonya Speyer was not what she expected. *What a force of nature.* For the first time since Yoshi's death, Kira felt a sense of release. She no longer had to carry the burden of saving humanity. It was an impossible task anyway; an improbability that she could have pulled it off. *My job is done,* she sighed with relief. *I've done what I needed to do.*

"Ready?" a voice behind her asked. Kira whirled and saw Sonya standing there. She shook a brown paper bag held in her left hand. "John made us some sandwiches for lunch," Sonya said.

"Are you sure you need me?"

Sonya's lips turned down in a little pout and she said with exaggerated disdain. "Feeling a little sorry for yourself are you?" She smiled quickly, taking the sting out of her words. "It's understandable. Come on. I walk to the lab whenever I can." Tossing the Tupperware container of brachiopod flakes to Kira, she turned and headed through the house.

Kira had no choice but to hurry after her.

Sonya set a brisk pace along the tree-lined streets and Kira nearly had to jog to keep up. Periodically, the lake glimmered through the trees.

"That's quite a story of yours," Sonya said. She laughed at Kira's puzzled expression. "Chosin told me of your non-dual experience. And you never had a spiritual teacher. Amazing. It's just the kind of vague awareness we call the evolutionary pulse.

Just amazing."

"For a while after I arrived in Caernarfon, I felt almost all powerful, that I could do anything. And then it all fell apart after Derek's death."

Sonya nodded. "That's the way of things. The way of conscious evolution."

"What do you mean? I didn't ask for any of this?"

"It's not personal, although you probably have a hard time believing that. It's a kind of synchronicity, a bringing together of circumstances – your inner life, your external conditions, maybe even your brain patterns. It can feel like you're being manipulated by a higher power." She smiled. "A little bit of that going on, maybe?"

"A lot of that."

"But not personal. Right?"

"Something bigger," Kira said. "But it's also very clear it's not personal ."

"That's it," Sonya agreed. She peered at Kira and nodded as if she saw something. "You know, I have a number of colleagues who would love to study you."

Kira's jaw dropped. "What?"

"Just kidding, dear."

"So what about you?" Kira asked. Sonya shrugged and said matter-of-factly, "Child prodigy, MIT at fourteen, by twenty-four I had two PhDs and one M.D. I guess you could say I was a classic overachiever. Then one evening a friend took me to a workshop with a Hindu teacher, Guru Ma. That night with my head in her lap I felt for the first time unconditional love. I felt a power greater than anything else, greater than anything imaginable. For the next six years I became Ma's disciple. I went everywhere with her – India, Europe, South America, all over the United States. More and more kundalini energy, primal energy was spewing out of my whole being." She laughed. "I was one hot potato."

"But now you're here, running a medical research lab."

"True. Seems almost too worldly, huh? Well, here I was this hot potato, the tantric energy roaring through me so powerfully that men were practically having orgasms just kissing me. It was intoxicating, but at the same time I wasn't doing anything for the world. I had no context for my experiences. So Ma in all her wisdom saw what I needed. She kicked me out.

"At first, devastated, lost, depressed, I wandered around. Months later, I came across an American guru. Like Ma he was a student of Sri Aurobindo. Only he had become a conscious evolutionist."

"The overmind," Kira interjected.

"You know of Aurobindo's work? Fascinating."

"I don't know much. I tried reading it once but couldn't get what he was talking about."

"Doesn't matter."

Kira chewed on this for a moment, then, "You and Chosin have both mentioned a group of evolutionaries. What are they?"

"Yes, there are a couple thousand of us now, in all walks of life, all disciplines. It's a sort of club. We're equals. Each in our own way devoted to bringing about cultural change that raises consciousness, expands consciousness. Our main theory is that biological evolution ended when humans developed culture. Out of culture came something new – the Noosphere, the world of meaning, values, discovery and ideas. The Noosphere has been evolving at breakneck speeds ever since. Until consciousness has now become aware of itself, evolution has become aware of itself."

"Derek and Yoshi were always talking about that. How the Terminator Gene was really somehow about conscious evolution."

Sonya nodded vigorously. "And they were right to do so. It's so incredible. When Chosin first told me about the Terminator Gene, I knew instantly it was the means, the device that has brought humanity right to the edge of the cliff. And to think it was right there under our noses. Ah, here we are."

They walked up a narrow drive and arrived at a five-story circular building on the northernmost edge of the University of Wisconsin campus. Sonya's lab was on the top floor.

Sonya dropped the brown paper bag on her desk and went directly into the lab. For the next two hours she virtually floated like a butterfly flitting from bench to bench. First, she directed the maceration of the shelly material. Then using a state-of-the-art gas chromatography machine, she separated the SF-81 into its separate biochemical constituents. All the time she was working, she hummed to herself.

Kira had never met a woman like Sonya. All her life she had been looking for a teacher and never really knew it until now. Sonya's presence and energy seemed to complete something deep inside Kira. But what was more, the two of them worked in concert together. It was like being part of a world-class surgical team, anticipating each other's movements, each other's requests. By late afternoon they were ready to run the tests.

Chapter 65

It was the same setup Yoshi had run in Caernarfon, using both HeLa cells and cancerous *neuroblastoma* cells, as well as the two synthetic polymers for controls. Kira examined the polymers, peptides and mineralizations Sonya's lab assistants had quickly isolated. A knot formed in the pit of her stomach. They were identical to those tested in Yoshi's lab. *This shouldn't be.* Ever since identifying the *brach* fossils in Colorado, Kira knew they were from an earlier period.

She walked over to Sonya. "Can we talk for a moment?"

Sonya looked up from her phone. "Of course."

"The *brachiopods* whose shells we're testing are a species of *lingula,* from the Lower Ordovician, around 40 million years later than the Cambrian."

Sonya's eyes narrowed. "And that means…what?"

"I just reviewed all of our tests samples and they're identical to the ones Yoshi and I isolated in Caernarfon."

"Why do I get the feeling you think this isn't good?"

"Our hypothesis, the hypothesis for our whole line of research, is based on the assumption that the mechanism of biological evolution for multi-cellular organisms changed at the Cambrian/Ordovician boundary."

"So you're surprised the biochemistry for these Ordovician *brachs* is the same as the Cambrian ones from Wisconsin?"

"They shouldn't be the same."

"You didn't tell me about this, why?"

"I had a good feeling in my gut about it, so I just kept quiet."

"Okay. I get it."

Fascinated by Sonya's equanimity, Kira said, "You're…you're not mad?"

"Of course not. Now that I've had some time to think about all this, I can see it's not adding up. There's something we're missing. We're in the trees and cannot see the forest."

Kira smiled ruefully. "That's what Derek told me, the day before he died."

"Smart man. So, what does your gut tell you to do next?"

"Run the tests," Kira said with confidence.

"I knew that's what you were going to say," Sonya said, putting her arm around Kira's shoulders and giving her a squeeze.

Relief filled Kira, but still she was riddled with doubts.

Sonya let go and returned to the tests. "I'll do the HeLa cells if you do the *neuroblastomas*. I still need you to tell me what Yoshi was thinking when he insisted upon running the same set of tests on these cells."

"I'll do my best. He believed that some sort of change, a biological change in the human nervous system occurred when we became highly social, changed from roaming family groups to tribal structures."

"He must have thought it had something to do with the sympathetic nervous system."

Kira nodded.

"Fascinating, just fascinating." She looked at the lab bench. "To work."

Chapter 66

Sonya and Kira were walking back home in the evening, and the sun hung just above the western horizon. Kira's stomach rumbled in protest of hours in the lab with only a sandwich to eat.

"John will have something ready for us when we get home, I'm sure," Sonya said.

Through gaps in the trees, the lake was a mirror of still water, the sun skipping off it in blinding halos of light. Kira watched Sonya shimmer in the bright reflection, a giant smile growing across her face. Suddenly the older woman began laughing. She laughed so hard, tears rolled down her animated face.

The laughter was so infectious that Kira couldn't help herself from joining in. She let the laughter roll through her and all the sadness and disquiet were replaced with a feeling of well-being. It was wonderful. When she could laugh no more, Kira felt cleansed.

Sonya used her fingers to dry her eyes. "It's all just so absurd."

They glanced at each other, began laughing all over again. They were both bent over, hands on knees. Had anyone seen them, they would have thought they were little girls laughing at some strange thing only kids find funny.

When at last they caught their breath, Sonya said through teeth clenched to keep from laughing "I've come to think of you as the eyes through which evolution is looking at itself."

"How absurd is that?" Kira asked. She understood the cosmic joke. Only humans laugh. It is the ultimate way of becoming one with another. In those moments of mutual laughter the boundaries between the two women had melted away and Kira knew what true love was for the first time, love that passed all understanding. "Thank you," she said with all her heart.

"You're welcome."

Chapter 67

John met them at the front door. His shock of white hair looked molten under the soft glow of the porch light.

"Good timing," Sonya said cheerily.

"I was watching for you," John answered, his voice solemn.

"What's wrong?" Sonya and Kira asked in unison.

John led them to the couple's spacious kitchen. Food was spread out on the counter buffet-style. He poured wine into crystal stemware. "I'll tell you while you eat."

While Kira and Sonya were at the lab, John had taken Chosin to visit one of the university's leading oncologists. "The prognosis isn't good," John said. "He has only a couple of weeks, maybe only days to live."

"We shouldn't give up yet," Kira stated.

"We'll have to do something radical," Sonya said.

"What's next?" Chosin asked from the doorway. All of them turned to stare at him. Pointedly ignoring their looks, Chosin walked to the counter and helped himself to some food. "No one's going to die,"

Kira flashbacked to a time when she had to give the worst news to a couple. She had to tell the young woman that the cause of her seizures was a *glio bastoma,* an always fatal brain tumor. For the first time Kira understood what the woman said when she turned to her husband and said, "Why not me?" It was an affirmation of life, not a denial of death.

"What's next?" Chosin repeated.

John glanced at the clock on the wall. "It's the Fourth of July. The fireworks are starting."

"We have a great view from our deck," Sonya added.

They took their food and wine to the table and watched the colorful patterns of the deafening explosions. Kira had always loved fireworks. But for the first time the sky-filled conflagrations were a perfect expression of the great mystery, the heart of the cosmic joke, coming out of nowhere, beautiful, powerful, and totally ephemeral. Nothing to grasp and hold on to.

In their silence all four knew the very existence of humanity depended on tomorrow's test results.

Chapter 68

Hawke sat in the Air Force Academy football stadium watching the fireworks. The grandstands were filled with cadets and their families as well as people from Colorado Springs and the surrounding communities. It was the end to a day filled with ceremonies honoring the nation's birth and the founding of the academy. Hawke did not share the "oohs" and "aahs" from the people surrounding him. He had come to a dead end in his search for Kira and Chosin. Arriving back in the States, he pursued them here only to find that Chosin and Kira had disappeared. The Yamato Communications plane had returned to Japan without them aboard.

He sat in the stadium trying to think what his next move was. A series of concussive explosions brought him back to the fireworks display. The last time he had seen them was here with Caitlin Yee. Hawke closed his eyes and saw her in his memory – short black hair framing her elfin face...twin snow leopards tattooed on her thighs, the smoke gray fur with black rosettes setting off the creamy whiteness of her skin...Caitlin's pale green eyes were like the cats themselves.

It was here at the stadium, in this spot, the next night, that he and Caitlin pledged eternal love, they would be together forever. But that was a long time ago. A different lifetime, when Hawke was a different man.

The image of Caitlin was swept away by another barrage of rockets. In its wake was Dr. Kira Taylor. He remembered that moment of complete acceptance in her eyes. He had not known that feeling since Caitlin walked out of his life almost twenty years ago. *If Kira discovers a cure for the Terminator Gene and announces it to the world, then all is completed and my part in all of this will be done.* He swallowed hard and clenched his fists. *What will happen to me then?*

Hawke let the thought play out, felt a darkness in his soul that he had never felt before, a darkness borne of Jurgenczak and the explosion at Caernarfon. A shudder swept through him. He saw himself on Ray Howe's boat...the scientist was sliding into the cold waters of the Irish Sea. Hawke felt as though he were standing on the edge of an abyss. *I've killed innocent people in the cause of a man I can no longer trust.*

Hawke knew that eventually he would be hunted down. He willed for Kira to be successful, for Jurgenczak's nightmare to be ended. The darkness in his soul abruptly parted and he saw what it was hiding – the desire to kill himself and take himself out of Kira's way. He grasped for the strength of will to kill himself here, in the only place he had ever truly been happy.

The startling climax of the fireworks display filled the night sky with blinding flashes of light and the roar of titanic explosions. Hawke flinched, thinking he was back in the battle for Baghdad. When the final cannonade ended and the last firework embers paled against the night sky, he straightened. Thoughts of suicide passed and he was once more in control. Of course, he would not kill himself, there was still more for him to do. Hawke didn't know what, but he had to trust in a future that held something important for him. He had to go back to Omaha and Jurgenczak. *My fate awaits me there.*

Chapter 69

Kira slept soundly with a sense of peace. She awakened slowly, letting the morning unfold in its sunny brightness. Her ribs hurt from laughing so hard. She even thought about going out for a run. Surely Sonya or John had some old work-out clothes they could lend her.

Kira glanced at the clock: 9:13 am. *The tests!* She bolted out of bed and threw on the clothes she had been wearing for the last three days and hurried downstairs.

Chosin and John were sharing a pot of green tea in the kitchen's breakfast nook. Chosin was staring out at the lake, watching the early morning sailboarders skimming across the choppy water. Their dazzling colored sails flashed brightly in the sun. "Sonya left hours ago," he said when Kira burst into the room.

John said, "She just called. She insisted that we let you sleep and bring you only after you've had a shower and something to eat." He smiled. "She has some very interesting results."

Kira hugged Chosin and grabbed a croissant. As she ran for the shower, her mind began racing over what the results could be.

"Come, take a look," Sonya said, beckoning Kira over. On a big smart board Kira could see that the HeLa and *neuroblastoma* cells had re-differentiated and were combining to form viable tissue – just like they had twelve years ago at Yale.

Chapter 70

The young Korean lab tech looked up from the microscope. The slight epicanthic folds of his eyes crinkled as he depressed a key on the keyboard beside his station. Instantly, the slide he was studying flashed upon the smart board above his lab bench, along with the other six. "That's all of them, Dr. Jurgenczak," he said.

"Yes," Jurgenczak said, unable to keep the dismay out of his voice. Yamato's lab in Caernarfon had isolated seven polymers and four peptides from Kira's SF-81. Unfortunately, here in Omaha, Jurgenczak didn't have enough of the *brachiopod* fossils to do more than a skeleton approach. He had to choose those samples whose biochemistry seemed most likely to re-differentiate the HeLa cells. The cellular biologist stood up from the lab stool and studied the board. His dark blue eyes darted anxiously from one image to another. He hadn't left the lab in three days. His long white hair, normally tied back with a simple black ribbon, stuck out at all angles. His face was haggard and his clothes were slept in. Nothing was working – and hope diminished with each failure.

Why let me come this far only to fail, Adonay?

Jurgenczak came to the last petri dish, heart hammering in his chest. Then he saw it. The cancer cells had re-differentiated just like Dr. Kira Taylor said they would. His hands fell limply to his sides and he sat down heavily.

The last one. It was a test of my faith. I'm sorry I ever doubted you, Adonay.

He checked the chemical composition: a *depsipeptide* – a bicyclic peptide.

He looked over at the lab tech. The young man was grinning. "You did it, sir. You did it." "Thank you, Tommy," Jurgenczak answered, smiling weakly. "You can go home now. I'll wrap up here."

"You sure? I don't mind staying."

"I appreciate that, but you deserve a rest. You've been here over thirty-six hours."

"So have you, sir."

Jurgenczak felt his strength returning. The knowledge that Jehovah was still there supporting him filled him with renewed energy and a surety of purpose he had felt before. "I feel better, now that we succeeded, than I have in the last few days," he admitted. "And I want to relish the moment." *Besides, I have people to contact and I don't want you reporting to Drake what you see.*

"Thanks, sir." The young man slipped off the stool and walked to the lab door. He turned and said, "Congratulations, Dr. Jurgenczak." He slapped the open key and the door swung inward. It hissed closed behind him.

Jurgenczak retrieved his smart phone from his pocket and punched a sequence. Before hitting send, he turned it off and placed it on the bench. *From now on, I must be stealthy. No one can know of my movements.* He pulled a prepaid cell phone from his briefcase. It was a secure, encrypted phone and he was certain Drake couldn't break it. The number rang twice and a deep voice answered. "I've been expecting your call."

"Yes, your Eminence. I have what I promised," Jurgenczak said.

"Come to the abbey."

The line went dead.

Chapter 71

Sonya Speyer tapped a pencil against the smart board's liquid crystal display. With each tap the screen's liquid gel quivered like rain hitting a quiet pond.

"What's wrong?" Kira asked.

Sonya shook her head. "Nothing's wrong, I'm just puzzled with this *depsipeptide* that's causing the cancer cell cultures to re-differentiate. I've seen this chemical structure before; I just can't recall the details. It's something important, though." She sighed. "It'll come."

"All the same, you're worried. I can see it."

Sonya pointed her pencil at a stack of papers on her desk. ""What I am worried about is that list you gave me of animals expressing the Terminator Gene. I checked around and it's not going to be easy getting test embryos."

Surprise flickered across Kira's face. "They had over a thousand at the Caernarfon lab."

" I'm working on it. Meanwhile, I need you to do something."

"Anything."

"I know a healer in Oklahoma – a Comanche. A Siddha Yoga master, a member of our evolutionary community, had an incurable carcinoma. He went down to this healer and…well, I can't explain it, but he's been cancer free for five years."

"I think I see where you're going with this," Kira said. "But I don't think Chosin will go."

"I believe he will, especially if you accompany him," Sonya replied.

"I don't see how I would make a difference."

"From what you tell me, and from what he's shared with me, I'm certain a shift took place when his brother first contacted him. I don't think Chosin even realizes it."

"You think the Terminator Gene has given him purpose

again?" Kira asked.

"Not exactly," Sonya said. "Ordinary purpose comes from the needs, fears and wants of the self, the personality. You know, what got you through childhood, school, career – all the stuff of ordinary life. Then when the self falls away, well, you know what happened to you, for a brief period of time there is no meaning. Meaning had to do with the self, so why do anything, right?"

"I felt that way, but it only lasted for a few hours."

"For some it lasts for a lifetime. But for others like Chosin, a new operating principle takes over. In non-dual literature it's called 'Do the next right thing.' It's like—"

"It's like the scallions in miso soup," Kira interrupted. "The dish will tell you what's right if you can see clearly. What's correct for you is correct by being correct for everyone."

Sonya laughed. "A brilliant analogy."

"It's not mine," Kira said. "It was one of the last things Yoshi said to me."

"Fascinating, Yoshi and Chosin were twins in so many more ways than just appearances. At any rate, I believe Chosin was already moving into this state when the two of us met in Tokyo four years ago."

"And Yoshi's phone call accelerated his transition."

Sonya nodded. "For me, it's evolution at work. He'll go if you ask, because like me, he'll know it's the next right thing to do."

Kira thought about all the work to be done in testing the embryos. "I can't leave you to do all this work on your own."

"No worries there," Sonya said. "I'll keep you informed about everything that's happening here. In the mean time, I have something else for you." Sonya went over to a closet at the far end of the lab and pulled out a couple of Kohl's Department store bags. She handed them to Kira. "I stopped by before I went to work. Early bird specials. There's a few more items at home."

In the bags Kira found running clothes and a pair of long distance shoes. "I'll pay you back."

Sonya shook her head. "I won't hear of it. I've…" Her throat constricted and she fought to keep tears from her eyes.

"I always wanted a daughter to buy clothes for," Sonya said, her voice a low rasp.

"Me too," Kira echoed.

Impulsively they hugged. The dark cloud of the Terminator Gene settled over the two women. They both recognized in the other, the sad toll that the T-gene miscarriages had taken from their lives...and the billions of miscarriages facing women all over the world.

Letting go, Sonya said, "I suppose you'll want to jog home?"

"I think I'll take a long run."

From the top of the fifth floor, Sonja watched Kira take off in a direction that would lead away from the house. *A long run is just what she needs.*

Sitting down at her desk, Sonya finally remembered where she had seen that chemical structure. It was one of the most promising discoveries from the worldwide search of the oceanic biota for agents that could advance the well-being of man. She quickly skimmed the literature. *Didemnins* were group of peptides derived from tunicates, a primitive family of chordates. They formed some of the earliest and simplest animals with backbones and nervous systems. *Didemnins* showed a powerful ability to fight leukemia cells, *adenocarcinoma* of the kidney, advanced epithelial ovarian cancer and metastatic breast cancer. At the end of the article she found what she was looking for. "Large amounts of chemically-synthesized *Didemnin B* have shown in laboratory tests to halt the growth of cancer cells. The National Cancer Institute is now planning Stage One trials."

It seemed obvious to Sonya the anticancer effect of the *Didemnins* was responsible for the re-differentiation of the HeLa cells not some ancient biochemistry from the Cambrian period.

Sonya leaned back in her chair. *This is not good. Not good at all.* She felt sorry for Kira if her long journey led to this dead end –

no cure for the Terminator Gene. *Still, I must get some embryos and run the experiments. Who knows?*

But in her mind Sonya had already begun formulating a plan to let the world know of the impending catastrophe.

Chapter 72

Leroy Parker could feel the throb of the drum deep in his bones like the heartbeat of the world. He was in the sun circle of the Comanche Homecoming in Lawton, Oklahoma, where he drummed with the other elders of the tribe. It was night and the arena was awash with lights. Red, white and blue streamers floated overhead on wires.

As a dance leader, Leroy knew the meaning behind the drum. Constructed from cottonwood and animal skins, it was round like Mother Earth. The beaters were cottonwood with wet rawhide wrapped around one end that dried hard and stiff as stone. When they struck the skin, the drum came alive with the marrow of the world, its presence bringing the dancers to life.

Beside the drummers, singers chanted songs, a descant to the deeper melody of the drum.

The resonant sounds of the drum stirred Leroy's muscles, making his own legs step in time to the dance. He was drumming for the first time in ten years, since the arthritis had crippled his joints and made movement in his fingers and hands painful. But now that the arthritis was gone, he felt alive as never before, even as a young man home from the war in Vietnam – alive and unscarred.

Tonight, Leroy led the drummers in the high-spirited fancy dance – the whirling, leaping dance of young warriors bent on a quest. As the leader, Leroy set the pace of the dance. In the middle of the song, when the beat was at its most energetic, a young male dancer carrying a shield and lance appeared suddenly in front of Leroy. A wolf skin, with the head and upper fangs draped over his jet-black hair, cascaded past his shoulders to his waist. The pelt writhed with the man's leaps and gyrations, looking as though it too were alive. The wolf dancer's face was painted completely white. Three slanting spears of red slashed each cheek. He wore only a breechclout and calf-high moccasins trimmed with wolf fur. From the heel of each moccasin trailed a wolf tail that brushed the Earth with each step. The young dancer moved gracefully and powerfully, mimicking a wolf hunting.

Leroy glanced at the other drummers, but none of them paid any attention to the young Indian. The young man moved closer to Leroy and tapped the rim of the drum with his spear. Then he spun to his right and leaped high, twisting his head and upper torso to the left to stare at Leroy. In his mind Leroy heard the words, "Follow me, old man." The dancer then began whirling rapidly, his legs pumping furiously. Leroy followed. He could see nothing but a blur of colors and he heard only the deep throbbing stamp of the drum.

Leroy first noticed that the arena had vanished. He looked down and saw that his own body had altered into a filament of light. The churn of life enveloped him, melding with his spirit. He experienced a new level of awareness that went beyond the sweat lodge and the smoke of the pipe.

Leroy often thought of the ancient warrior shamans of the Comanche Nation and what their journeys to this other world must have been like. He expected a feeling of delirium and joy, but now that he was here, he was a bit disappointed. There was no passion, only being. There was no struggle, only existence.

Then he and the wolf dancer were flying above Mother Earth until they came to the plain of Leroy's vision and the shadowless humans fighting one another. At first Leroy shied away. But the wolf dancer tapped him with the lance and pointed it at the humans. His mouth opened and Leroy heard the death song of the Comanche. The meaning of the vision became clear to Leroy. It was of the end of the world for all humans.

Abruptly, Leroy felt a pounding from deep inside the Earth. He was back at the Comanche Homecoming. The dance had ended. The wolf dancer was gone. In his place stood Leroy's granddaughter, Lucille. She stared at him with great love. New elders came forward to take up the beaters for the next dance. Leroy moved aside like a man who had been asleep and finally saw the world for what it really was. He knew he had just witnessed the end of the Comanche experience. A terrible pain swept through him as Lucille walked toward him. His beautiful granddaughter would never know what it was like to have a son or daughter, would never experience the cycle of death and rebirth.

Lucille came up to him. She opened her mouth to speak, but Leroy put his fingers to her lips, quieting her. "Someone comes tomorrow," he told his granddaughter. "I have to go now and prepare."

Chapter 73

Leroy Parker sat beneath the ramada at the old weathered picnic table beside his house. Hot coffee spun swirls of steam into the dawn chill from the ancient cup beside him. The sun was just rising, turning the prairie grass a dusky red. He sighed and took a sip, grimacing at the bitter taste, but needing it. The drumming and the vision of the night before had taken their toll and he was tired.

Rubbing his face with his hands to get rid of the worst of the fatigue, Leroy studied the Oklahoma ranch that had been in his family since his great grandfather, Quanah Parker, settled here at the end of the 19th century. The old clapboard house had been replaced twenty years earlier with a modern brick one. Pickup trucks filled the area in front and several Comanche elders waited patiently. Behind, surrounded by a copse of small willow trees, was the sweat lodge. Leroy cast a long glance at it and shook his head. It was not time for the sweat lodge. Today would require something greater. The phone call from the woman shaman in Madison said as much.

"Leroy," the voice on the phone two days ago had said, "I have a favor to ask of you."

Leroy recognized Sonya Speyer. "Whatever I can do," he answered.

"Another member of our evolutionary group is sick and needs your help."

Leroy smiled. He did not know what her group did, but Sonya was an honorary member of his Comanche clan and he could not refuse her this favor.

"He's Japanese and his name is Chosin Yamato," Sonya said. "He's very sick. He's an empty man with a dark soul. His father and the death of his younger sister have affected him greatly."

"We will do what we can," Leroy replied, "but ultimately it is up to him."

"There's something more." Sonya said. "He'll be arriving with a woman. She has the eyes of Coyote Woman and will bring light to what you have seen, my good friend." Sonya had hung up then without saying goodbye.

Leroy poured the remains of his lukewarm coffee onto the ground and walked over to where the other Comanche elders sat on foldout plastic chairs around a small glass table. "They will be here in a few minutes," he said. The men nodded and went back to talking among themselves. Leroy had called this meeting and now they waited to see why.

Lucille came out of the house with more hot coffee for everyone.

Leroy shook his head. He sighed. *Coyote Woman*. The idea put him on edge. It was Coyote who brought life to the Comanche by freeing the buffalo for them to hunt. But Coyote was also a trickster. After his vision last night, he could not help but feel anxious about what this Coyote Woman would do.

A white van topped a rise on the long twisting drive to his place. Its tires sent a brown tail of dust spinning upward behind. A minute later it ground to halt in front of Leroy's Dodge Ram pickup. The dust floated to the side away from everyone. A woman with long, red gold hair got out of the driver's side and went around the van to help her male passenger.

Leroy stepped forward. The other Comanche stayed put waiting to see what Leroy would do. He saw that the woman had retrieved a wheelchair from the back of the van and had helped the man into it.

The passenger was bent over, trying to stop the coughing that racked his body. When he straightened, he looked at Leroy and recognition splashed across his face. *You're the one.* "Sonya, says the answer is here," he said.

Leroy nodded and held out his hand. "Welcome, Chosin Yamato. I'm Leroy Parker." It was a signal and the other elders came forward. They took Chosin's luggage and wheeled him toward the house.

Leroy watched the sick man disappear, then turned his attention to the woman. She stood in light tan slacks and matching blouse. Her hair was pulled back and her blue eyes studied his face. Taking her hand in his, he said softly, "I have been waiting for you, Kira Taylor."

Chapter 74

The next morning was cold and gloomy. Storm clouds feathered the eastern horizon; lightning scattered through them.

Kira wrapped her arms around her herself, wishing she had brought a sweater. She had no idea Oklahoma could be so chilly in the summer. The reception had been chilly too. After meeting the shaman yesterday, he had abandoned her. Fortunately, Leroy's wife, Wilma, had come to her rescue. She was a trim Kiowa woman in her late sixties. Her silver hair was cut short and she wore a bright red sweater and Levi's. A silver pendant was the only jewelry she wore.

Wilma had taken Kira inside and set her up in a modest room in the home's basement. "It is the Comanche way," Wilma said, answering Kira's unasked question. "The men separate themselves from the women." She laughed at the expression of astonishment on Kira's face. "I know. They miss out on so much that way." She winked and left Kira to herself.

Kira had used the rest of the day to get caught up. Chosin's supplies of morphine, Heparin and Lasix were running low, so she contacted a small clinic in Lawton. When she explained she was at Leroy Parker's place, the attending physician became a whole lot friendlier. "No problem," he said. "It'll be waiting at the front desk for you tomorrow when you come in."

Next she went through her messages on her phone. There was nothing from Sonya yet, which didn't worry her since it had been less than twenty-four hours since leaving Madison. Her parents were worried so she texted, "I'm fine, love you." The rest of the messages were from Jack. They all were variations of "Alone and alive in Omaha. Where are you? Contact me." Though tempted to call, she decided not to.

While tapping her phone to close it, Kira inadvertently brought up the image of Mrs. Jacobson's miscarriage. Now the hopes of millions of women across the globe depended upon a single isolated chemical Kira had first distilled twelve years ago in her SF-81. It seemed impossible, that she and Sonya were on the verge of saving humanity. Even back in Caernarfon Kira had wondered how the action of the single isolated chemical could affect the differentiating sequence of an embryo. She tried to imagine various scenarios but had to admit it was well beyond her knowledge of cellular biology. She had to trust that Sonya would know what to do.

This morning as Kira watched the storm disappear over the Wichita Mountains, she found herself believing Sonya would be successful. She pulled out her smart phone to check for messages, when Leroy came out of the house with two elders pushing Chosin in his wheelchair. Kira watched as the quartet headed toward a circle of men forming just beyond the sweat lodge.

Messages forgotten, Kira stared intently at the healing ceremony as it unfolded. Chosin was pushed to the center of the ring of Comanche elders. One man began beating a single drum in a slow steady rhythm. Leroy was speaking softly, and Kira strained to make out the words. Over her career as a doctor, Kira had witnessed what she could only call miracles from the alternative medicine that had found its way into the western model. She wished now that she had taken the time to be trained in qigong and acupuncture.

I have to find out what's going on. Kira took a step forward, when a hand gently lay across her shoulders.

"You cannot attend," Wilma Parker said.

Kira sighed. "OK. So what's going to happen?"

Wilma gestured to the plastic chairs and the two women sat down. "Most non-Indians do not understand what goes on in Leroy's healing ceremony. It has been described as a kind of shadow work and is based on storytelling. In this case the stories of Chosin's life have been messed up in some way, and the cause of his disease is that his storytelling is out of balance. In order to be cured, Chosin needs to remember them and retell them correctly so that they can be rewoven and make him whole again."

"Will it take long?"

Wilma laughed. "He will be here for many days. Chosin first has to learn to speak from the disease – let the disease tell its story. If he succeeds, then over several weeks the disease will begin to separate from his body. He'll put it in an object like this." Wilma held up the tooth of a coyote. "When that happens, he will see it for what it is and he will be healed."

Kira studied the circle of men with Chosin in the middle, sitting in his wheelchair. She surprised herself by silently praying the ritual would work.

"Thank you," Kira said, squeezing Wilma's hand. Love and gratitude flowed between the two women.

Kira stood. "I need to go into Lawton to the clinic and pick up some medicine for Chosin. I'll be back this evening."

Chapter 75

When Kira returned to the Parker ranch with the medicine, dusk was a red smear on the horizon. She stayed in the van, watching the cloak of darkness rapidly approach. The chirring sounds of cicadas echoed back and forth from cottonwood to cottonwood. A sudden chill from the distant storm whooshed through the Wichita Mountains and goose bumps covered her arms and legs. Kira felt really alone, with a kind of freedom she hadn't known in several weeks. But rather than be at peace, her mind dwelled on what she had seen in Lawton.

The town was modern enough, as was the clinic. But the streets were filled with many Native Americans who appeared as though they owned only the clothes on their back. They shuffled around, moving like old people do. Yet, these were young men and women in the thirties and forties. Kira had read how hard life was on the reservation, but the stark reality of it scraped her senses.

Kira found herself reflecting on the world's problems. Books and magazine articles devoted billions of words to the genocide in places like Dafur, to suicide bombers, wars from Afghanistan to Chechnya, global warming, third world poverty and disease. *A world with no solutions.*

She shook her head trying to dispel these thoughts. Yet, at the same time, she remained curious as to why they came up in the first place. Then the source surfaced. She wanted to shy away from it but forced herself to confront it. The question had been there from the moment she boarded the plane for Caernarfon. *Is humanity worth saving?* Kira's smart phone chirped. It was a text message from Sonya: "Located embryos, begun running tests. Call tonight."

Feeling as though she had just been reprieved, Kira texted back, "Excellent."

She stepped out of the van and went into the house. No one was around, so Kira went to Chosin's room. After the morning ritual, he had slept through the afternoon. He woke up as she entered.

"How are you doing?" Chosin moved each bit of his body a little, then made a big stretch and sat up. "This was the right thing to do."

Wilma Parker appeared in the doorway carrying a steaming cup of what smelled to Kira like herbal tea. "I think he's looking better," she said. She patted Chosin on the shoulder and left.

"You are looking better," Kira said, trying not to sound surprised. Taking a small flashlight from her pocket, she checked his eyes. The golden irises with their green flecks were equal and reactive. His forehead was cool to her touch. "Are you feeling any pain?" she asked.

"I had many strange dreams," Chosin said cryptically.

"You're not going to tell me." Kira smiled, suddenly understanding. "Of course, there's no you."

Chosin made a face as he sipped the tea. "Want some? I'm sure they have more."

Smiling, Kira shook her head. "I'm sure it's prescribed only for you. Speaking of prescriptions, I got these for you." She put the morphine, Heparin and Lasix on a nightstand beside the bed. "Ceremony or not, you should still be taking these."

Chosin nodded, "Have you heard from Sonya?"

"She's located embryos."

"Then you're free to go home."

"I only wish that was true," Kira said.

"You need to let go, let go or you will get a sickness worse than mine."

"Thanks."

"Have you spoken with Leroy Parker?"

"Not really. His wife tells me what's happening."

"Shut the door," Chosin said. He motioned Kira to come

close. "He's the one that appeared in the vision right after Yoshi died. The one who said 'metamorphosis' to me."

Kira was taken aback. This was the first she's heard about it. "What are you saying?"

Chosin related the vision he'd experienced the night Yoshi died.

"Leroy Parker? Are you sure?" Kira asked, dumbfounded.

"I've known from the moment I saw him." Chosin studied her face and shook his head slowly. "I know what you're thinking, but he didn't know me."

"That's odd," Kira said. "He acted like he knew me."

"Ever since we met, the world is becoming strange and unpredictable. I repeat: 'you don't have to stay.' I am more than ready to die here."

"You're not going to die."

Chosin smiled. "Living would be okay, too."

She said, "I have to ask, did you actually start telling your stories?"

Chosin ignored the question and closed his eyes. Within seconds he was asleep.

Kira felt his pulse. It was good and strong. His breathing was more even and his color was ruddier than the day before so there didn't appear to be any ischemia. She smiled. Whatever the Comanche elders were doing was working. She tiptoed out of the room and closed the door softly behind her.

Chapter 76

What's happening with the embryos?

As if answering, Kira's phone chirped. Sonya's face appeared on the screen. "How's Chosin?" she asked first thing.

"Stronger," Kira said.

Sonya smiled. "Excellent. What do you think of Leroy?"

"He really hasn't spoken with me since the moment I arrived."

"Fascinating. Well, it is what it is." Her smile disappeared.

Kira felt a great pang deep in her stomach. *The news isn't good.*

"The news isn't good," Sonya echoed. "The chemical that re-differentiated the cancer cultures is actually a new cancer-fighting peptide. It's from a family of chemicals known as depsipeptides. It's commonly derived from of all things, tunicates. Fascinating that it also shows up in the shelly material of the fossil *lingula*. I suspect you could also get it from modern living *lingula*. By the way, do you know what tunicates are?"

Kira was no longer listening. Her mind flashed to her teenage discovery in Nevada, a discovery that had led to a life-long obsession of these early forms of chordates. She also recalled seeing the living tunicates in Jack Kelley's aquarium.

"Hey, Kira."

"Wh...what?"

"Where did you go just now?"

"Uh...ummm...tunicates have been a passion of mine. Some paleontologists love trilobites, others dinosaurs. Me, I love tunicates. So, what does this mean for the tests on the embryos?" Kira knew that modern day tunicates were common enough that it could mean a universal cure for the T-gene. But she kept this to herself.

"Well, here's the really bad news," Sonya said. "Even a small amount of *depsipeptide* turns out to be lethal to the embryos."

Kira's mind was shouting at her. *Fuck! This was our only fucking hope!*

Chapter 77

Kira's phone chirped again. It was Sonya Speyer. She turned it off. *This shouldn't be.* All along Kira had believed she was doing what she was supposed to be doing – following the evolutionary pulse. But it had all gone horribly wrong.

I have no life. I'm not a good thinker. At best I'm an average doctor. The tipping point for mankind will come and go without a solution...and there's nothing within my power to fix any of it. I am powerless. I have always been powerless.

She was totally empty.

A gentle hand touched her shoulder. Kira brushed it away. Leroy Parker went around the low table and stood facing her. "I need you to follow me," he said softly.

Kira didn't answer.

Leroy took her limp hand in his. "You must come with me. Now."

They were in the sweat lodge. Steam burned Kira's bare skin but she did not flinch. She steeled herself against the pain. Then, as she looked deep into the glowing stones, her life began peeling away layer by layer: Sonya...the Terminator Gene...Caernarfon...Sioux City...Yale...childhood...parents. All disappeared one after another until she was left feeling as though she floated in the dark well of a dream. There was only one thing left for her to do – she ate her own brain. Then there was nothing.

I am dead.

More superheated steam rose from the rocks. Leroy held baby Kira. Her breath came in shallow gasps.

I can't be dead. A young Indian girl is looking down at me. She marveled at the little girl's angelic face. The dark brown liquid eyes shone with a fluorescent light of their own. *I am so much more than I ever thought I was.*

"Why are you laughing?"

"Humanity must die," Kira said.

The Indian girl held out her hand. "Come into my house."

Kira was standing in a dark room. The only sense of place was the little girl's hand in her own. *"Where am I?"*

"Is," the girl answered. The house was suddenly filled with the same ethereal fluorescence as the girl's eyes. The light came from millions of tiny larval-like creatures floating in the air.

The Indian girl vanished...the house disappeared...the lodge faded away. Kira was staring into the bright afternoon at the sun-drenched Wichita Mountains. The healing circle beside the sweat lodge was ending and the Comanche elders were wheeling Chosin toward the house. Leroy Parker stayed in the circle, staring at her intently.

I know the meaning of metamorphosis.

Chapter 78

Bishop Hilario sat in a high-backed leather chair in the Interregnum Catholic Mission's book-lined library. It was a small room with plush carpeting and dark oiled wood paneling. Expensive paintings hung in lighted alcoves secluded among the shelves.

A servant poured fresh coffee into sheer porcelain cups. The bishop spoke curtly in Portuguese and the man left. "We're alone now," he said in fluent English to his visitor. "Please tell me about this plan of yours to save humanity."

Arne Jurgenczak studied the bishop. He was small and well-tanned. The evidence of his Portuguese ancestry was spread across his narrow, ascetic face – thin lips, hawk nose and black eyes. He sat behind a large oak desk, placing it like a barrier between them. To Jurgenczak, the bishop was everything he hoped for – a strict religious conservative who steadfastly believed in the right of God to govern the lives of men.

The truth was Jurgenczak, in spite of his strong faith in God, was slightly intimidated by the man. *Give me strength, Adonay.*

"Your Grace," Jurgenczak began. "What I have to tell you is a fantastic tale, but I assure you, every bit of it is true – and I can prove it." He slid a thin manila envelope across the desk. "Here is the science to back up what I am about to tell you."

Jurgenczak waited until the bishop spread the papers in front of him. "Nearly ten years ago while working on the Human Genome Project, I was led by God's hand to uncover a pestilence that could wipe out all of humanity. I have called it the Terminator Gene. Its workings are insidiously simple. After a finite number of generations, this mechanism makes it impossible for women to bear any more children. Right now, humans are nearing the tipping point and soon no women will be able to give birth. Mankind stands on the edge of the abyss. Fortunately,

Gentel has uncovered a solution to this plague, a means to end this T-gene's impact on women."

"Why tell me?" Bishop Hilario asked. "Why aren't you giving this information to the United Nations and enlisting scientists from every country to stop this plague, as you call it?"

"Because we have a divine opportunity to use this plague to create a world in preparation for the second coming of Jesus, to enact God's law on Earth."

A frown crossed the bishop's face, but Jurgenczak didn't notice and hurried on, carried forward by his own religious fervor. "I have harvested over 25,000 human embryos, enough to create a new world of god-fearing people. With the solution, we can make sure these embryos are carried to term, become vibrant living children. Then with the Interregnum Catholic Mission's help, together, we can raise these children in the name of God and make this planet into his kingdom as God intended."

"How do you propose we help you with this?" the bishop asked, his face now a mask of concern.

Jurgenczak could hardy believe his ears. It should be painfully obvious what he was talking about. It made him wonder if the bishop wasn't as smart or far-seeing as he had been led to believe. "Your Grace, I'm asking that the Mission help me raise these children. With your resources, we can raise them under the eye of God."

The bishop tapped a large ring against the folder. To him, Arne Jurgenczak represented everything he despised in humanity. A fanatic who meddled in church affairs. Even worse, he was a scientist who trusted science over God. And now he came to Interregnum Catholic Mission with a preposterous tale and an even more preposterous plan to save only a few thousand people.

Bishop Hilario stuffed the papers back into the envelope. "Even if I accepted your wild fanciful story about the end of humanity, God would never let his children die." The bishop crumpled the envelope in his hand and shook it at Jurgenczak. "And this...this so-called science of yours is madness. You should be condemned to the seventh circle of Hell with Judas Iscariot for your barbarous lies."

Bishop Hilario threw the envelope back across the desk. "Get out!" he thundered. "Get out of this abbey before my servants throw you out." He swiveled his chair around, signaling Jurgenczak to leave.

Dazed by the rebuff, Jurgenczak stumbled out of the room. Minutes later he was standing by his dark blue Mercedes. His hands were shaking. *Adonay...why? Why bring us this far only to fail.*

Jurgenczak knew he was beaten, knew that God had withdrawn his favor because of something he had done. Looking into the Omaha twilight, he heard a hawk screeching in the distance. The sound was like a death knell, keening across his plans. Then it came to him, why God had taken forsaken him – Dr. Kira Taylor. It was all going well before she came in. *Adonay, I know now why you took your presence away. It's because Kira Taylor is still alive.*

Jurgenczak leaned against the car. Sweat coated his face and his body shook with rage. *I have to find her. Kill her. Then Adonay will bless my plans again.*

To find her, he needed to find Jack Kelley.

Chapter 79

Everything around Kira glowed with the evolutionary pulse – the chirruping of the grasshoppers, the coarse flaked bark of the cottonwoods. She was a dust grain floating at the will of the breeze. She was both the wind and the dust in an endless dance of love. The mystic poet Rumi, flashed in Kira's thoughts: "And then my heart pulled itself apart and filled to the brim with a new light overflowed with fresh life; now even the heavens are thankful that because of love I have become the giver of light."

Kira was all this as she keyed Sonya's number on her smart phone. Sonya appeared on the screen, her face a mask of concern. "Kira! I've been worried. Are you alright?" Sonya took in a breath and her concern turned into a puzzled look and then happiness as a smile spread across her face. "You're glowing, Kira."

"I know the answer," Kira said calmly. "I can't tell you how but it's obvious. It was there all the time." She ticked off the pieces to the puzzle. "Yoshi's focus on Hox genes and the sympathetic nervous system, Derek's Green Gene theories, my deep understanding of tunicates, your intuition about morphological sequencing."

"By the grace of God," Sonya said.

"Only by the grace of God. I always thought it was about me. Now I know it's not."

"It's about life. So what do we do next?" Sonya asked.

"My friend, Jack Kelley, has what we need."

Chapter 80

The building was a nondescript, one-story office complex located in a strip mall. The only thing that told Hawke he was in the right place was the sign above the front entrance – Gentel Pharmaceuticals. In all the times he had accompanied Arne Jurgenczak to Gentel's home offices in Omaha, he had never once been to this address.

Hawke parked his rented SUV in the lot across the street and waited. Mercury vapor lamps lighted the building's entryway, making it as bright as day. He would easily be able to spot Arne Jurgenczak if he showed up. It was a long shot, but the only chance he had.

Back in Colorado Springs, Hawke had once again used his top-secret clearance to access military satellites in order to find the old man. But for the past twelve hours Jurgenczak's smart phone had been turned off, so Hawke had done the next best thing. He tracked the phone's whereabouts through the satellite's GPS log for the past four days. Three and a half of those days had been spent at this storefront. Hawke Googled the business name and found out that Gentel Pharmaceuticals had been started by Jurgenczak more than a decade ago, before Gentel Systems had begun its meteoric rise in the biochemical industry.

Hawke leaned back in the drivers seat. It was just after 10 p.m. and the strip mall was quiet except for a pizza place and a twenty-four hour grocery store. Cars came and went, but no one turned into Gentel Pharmaceuticals. He realized he might be sitting here all night, but if he was going to find Jurgenczak, this was where to start.

Hawke still didn't know what he should do. The secret of the T-gene he had kept so well for ten years haunted him now. Had he done the right thing? He wanted to tell Jurgenczak that he felt used, lied to, that he was going to tell the U.S. government everything, tell everyone about the Terminator Gene, to see how the old man would react.

Thirty minutes later a classic Volkswagen Karmen Ghia pulled into the parking lot. A young Asian man got out. Hawke was out of his car in an instant and across the street before the young man reached the front door.

"Excuse me," Hawke said, flashing his Gentel Systems Security ID. "You must be..."

"Tommy Seung," the young man said, looking askance at the African American image on the ID. "Who wants to know?"

"You're just as Dr. Jurgenczak described," Hawke said smoothly. "He asked me to meet you here." He put away his wallet and extended his hand. "Sorry, the name's Hawke. Dr. Jurgenczak wants you to show me the building's security system, see what it needs in the way of upgrades."

"Kinda late, isn't it?"

Hawke let a shrug cross his features. "You know, especially after the Caernarfon disaster."

Tommy Seung smiled ruefully. "C'mon, I'll show you where everything is."

The guard at the front desk, impressed by Hawke's credentials, let both men through with a wave.

Hawke followed Tommy down a well-lit hall. "The guard at the front and a retinal scanner are the only security we have," the tech explained as he led them into a large lab and to a door at far end. Tommy put his eyes to the scanner. The lock clicked. He dumped his backpack on a lab bench in the center of the room and added, "I'm here only for a few minutes to make certain some experiments are proceeding well, but feel free to look around as much as you want."

Hawke nodded and scanned the room. He was dumbfounded by what he saw. It was replica of Yoshi Yamato's lab in Caernarfon except for the large industrial freezer at the other end. "What do you store in there?" he asked, pointing at the cabinet.

Tommy glanced over his shoulder, followed the finger. "Human embryos."

"How many?"

"Over 25,000 – with more coming in every week."

Hawke whistled. *Human embryos; that's different.* The large number nagged at him with a sense of unease, but he shoved the feeling aside and concentrated on what Tommy Seung was doing. "What experiments are you running now?"

Tommy adjusted the resolution on a microscope. "I've been running an analysis on the peptide that re-differentiated the HeLa cells."

"Good news, then?"

"It belongs to a group of bio-chemicals that's being tested as a cancer cure. Unfortunately, we're out of shelly material from the *brachs,* and until we find more, we can't go to the next step. I'll let him know right away; he said he wouldn't be back in tonight." Tommy logged onto the computer and began entering notes on a web page.

Hawke asked, "When will Jurgenczak get this information?"

"Whenever he logs in to this URL," the tech answered. "It's called a mirror site. He can use any computer to see what we're seeing, or in this case, the results I'm entering."

"Can anybody just log in?"

"Impossible. It's a double encryption. The URL is encrypted as well as the password."

"That's good," Hawke said.

"Thanks. I designed it myself." Tommy noted the time: 10:53 p.m. and logged off. He gathered his backpack and headed for the door. "Look, you may be security and all, but I can't let you stay here unsupervised, and I'm leaving."

Hawke smiled. "I've seen everything I need to. Tomorrow I'll make some recommendations to Dr. Jurgenczak."

The two men walked out.

Hawke watched Tommy Seung drive away, then retreated to his own vehicle. He settled into the seat. Thousands of human embryos...Suddenly he knew what was really happening with Jurgenczak's so-called plan for the Terminator Gene solution. He'd never had any intention of distributing a cure to the entire world. *He's going let people like me die out, start his own group of humans cured of the T-gene.*

I can't let that happen.

Hawke forced himself to be calm and analyzed his options. He had to find Jurgenczak and stop him. Recalling the *brach* image from Jackson Kelley to Kira Taylor, he came to the only conclusion that made sense. *Jurgenczak needs more shelly material and the only person who knows where to find it is Kira's friend.*

Hawke opened the GPS app on his smart phone and asked for Jackson Kelley's address. Two places came up. His home was by the Missouri River over thirty minutes away. His work was Omaha's Scott Aquarium, half the time from the strip mall. A sense of urgency swept through Hawke. He punched in the aquarium's address and tore out of the parking lot.

Chapter 81

Kira parked her rental in the Scott Aquarium parking lot. She saw Jack's Hybrid beside a dark blue Mercedes but no Jack. *He must be inside.* She checked the time: 11:15 p.m. She was grateful he agreed to meet her here this late. She smiled at the synchronicity. *It's fitting since Jack has a big role to play in bringing new life into the world.*

Crossing the asphalt, Kira was reminded that the search for her own answers had begun here just weeks ago. An interesting thought arose. *Could Jack have somehow engineered everything that had happened to me?* Certainly he had set her on the path to removing the obstacles necessary for her to solve this riddle.

The front door was cleared of all the scaffolding and tools that had barred her way on her last visit. She easily strode through the lobby, past the entrance to the Shark Tunnel. She took the stairs two at a time to the top floor and Jack's office. Pushing open the door, she had to adjust her eyes to the dim light within. The suite was still the same – plush and huge. The smart board cast an opaque glow that lighted the curved aquarium beneath it. In the room's silence she could hear the gentle sweep of waves. Kira had to look carefully to make sure the tunicates were still there. She spotted three of them floating ethereally in the clear water.

Jack, his back to her, sat at the conference table staring out at the distinctive Omaha skyline. Keewatin Industrial, Bartnum Haggerty and Gentel lit up the night with spires that seemed to reach to the heavens.

"Jack?" Kira said. He didn't turn. She walked over to him – and saw a deep gash across the back of his head. She placed two fingers across his carotid pulse. *He's alive!*

Kira's medical training took over. She found the room's lighting and turned it up full. She needed saline solution to clean the wound and sterile gauze to stop the bleeding, neither of which she had. A quick glance around the office revealed a half-empty water bottle. Jack's shirt was 100% cotton and she ripped it off him, tearing it into strips. She cleaned the wound and made a compress to stop the bleeding.

Kira forced her voice to remain calm. "Jack, can you hear me?"

"He can't hear you," a soft voice whispered from behind.

Kira whirled and saw Jurgenczak step out of the shadows, a revolver in his right hand.

Chapter 82

The Scott Aquarium's name was in three-foot tall metal letters above the entrance. It had taken Hawke twelve minutes to get here. There were three cars in the parking lot. Two he didn't recognize. The third was Jurgenczak's Mercedes.

Years of habit made Hawke move cautiously. He eased out of his car, scanning the area for any signs of the old man. A shadow of movement in a third-floor window caught his attention. The silhouette had an amber glow surrounding it. Hawke knew it instantly – Kira Taylor.

Hawke glanced at the Mercedes and his mind flashed to what Jurgenczak had asked him on the plane: "Can you kill her?" He ran for the front doors. Years of working for the old man gave a Hawke a good idea of what Jurgenczak would do if he confronted the woman he considered his nemesis.

The front doors were unlocked. They opened silently and Hawke closed them the same way. Jurgenczak could be anywhere, but Kira was on the third floor and he would go there. He sprinted for the stairs, hoping he wasn't already too late.

Chapter 83

"Jack needs an ambulance," Kira said. "I'm calling 911."

"He'll have one after he tells me what I need to know." Jurgenczak motioned her with the pistol to move toward the aquarium. *Thank you, Adonay, You've answered my prayers and brought her to me. With this woman out of the way, I can prepare the world for the return of your son.*

Jurgenczak sighed. He cocked the revolver's hammer and aimed it.

Kira heard the sound before she saw any movement. She glanced at the door and a compact shadow lunged into the room. Jurgenczak saw it also and instinctively turned to meet the new threat. In that instant Kira recognized the newcomer – Hawke. The security chief threw himself on Jurgenczak just as the gun went off. The roar was deafening.

The two men fell to the ground in a heap. The pistol spun across the floor and stopped at Kira's feet.

Hawke rolled off Jurgenczak. Blood was spreading across his shirt.

Jurgenczak staggered to his feet. He saw Hawke lying on the carpet. Shock filled his face as he recognized his assailant. "Hawke...no...no...What have you done?"

Hawke gasped and said, "I stopped you."

Kira picked up the gun. She did not aim at Jurgenczak. "It's over," she said softly.

Slowly the old man backed toward the door. *I must escape to save the world.*

"It's over," Kira repeated.

Jurgenczak shook his head. He stumbled and grabbed the doorjamb for support.

Kira felt overwhelming compassion for the old man who would have killed her. "There's nothing you can do now. I know the solution and life will go on." With her other hand she pulled her phone from her pocket and dialed the police.

Jurgenczak fell to his knees and began praying.

Kira went over to Hawke. The bullet had caught him in the center of his chest. Blood trickled down his chin. He leveraged himself up on one elbow. "Forgive me," he said to Kira.

You are perfect as you are, Kira thought and squeezed his hand with all her love.

"It's going to be all right?"

Kira nodded.

Hawke smiled and closed his eyes and slumped backward. "Caitlin," he whispered.

In death, Hawke looked more peaceful than he ever looked when alive.

Chapter 83

Omaha, Nebraska

George Drake sat in the penthouse atop the Keewatin Industrial spire that dominated the Omaha landscape. It was his private suite, and as founder and CEO of the company, he had the only key to the elevator from the garage twenty-five stories below to the top. The whole office was glass, an aerie that gave him a panoramic view from the Missouri River to the rolling hills of the western suburbs, where his mansion lay sequestered on a hundred private acres of restored prairie. The view made him feel as if he was king.

Goddammit! I am Lord of all I survey! He swallowed and felt the hackles rise on the back of his neck. *So why should I be on edge?*

He knew the answer even before the intercom buzzed and his private secretary said, "Your ten o'clock appointment's here, sir."

Drake had been rattled ever since he got the call from Kira Taylor, "Send them in," Drake said curtly.

Kira Taylor walked in followed by Sonya Speyer. The appearance of the two shook Drake even more.

Kira's head was shaven. She wore plain clothes in subdued colors. Yet an aura of gentle sweetness made everything about her alive and vibrant. By contrast, Sonya was the picture of the professional woman. Her business suit was tailored. She had drawn her white hair back severely and she wore just enough makeup to remind anyone looking at her that she was feminine. She carried an old leather briefcase, the handle polished smooth from use.

Drake hid his surprise by motioning the two women over to an ornate conference table of maple inlaid with Etruscan marble, the edges so perfect there were no gaps between wood and stone.

He'd had it specially made to awe anyone who made it this far to his private office.

"Why the hell are you here?" Drake asked Kira.

Sonya answered, "I thought you were trying to find her."

"I cut my losses after the debacle at the aquarium," Drake said. "So, again, she's here because?"

"We know everything," Sonya said quietly. "Your hiding of the Terminator Gene. Your explosives that destroyed the Caernarfon lab. Your backing of Dr. Jurgenczak and the 25,000 human embryos warehoused here in Omaha." She paused, then said, "So here's what you're going to do."

"What I'm going to do? Just who the hell are you tell me what to do?"

Sonya smiled. "One answer would be a good friend of Chosin Yamato."

Christ! Drake thought, unable to hide his dismay. *I thought Chosin was dying*. "Is he well?" he asked.

"He will be." Sonya let the words sink in. Then, "So, I repeat, here's what you're going to do." She pulled another sheet of paper from the briefcase and slid it across the table. It contained graphics and specs for a vaginal suppository. "You're going to manufacture these."

Drake studied the paper. "You found a solution to the Terminator Gene. Congratulations."

"Yes, we did. You will have your biochemists synthesize what's on this." She handed him a flash-drive. "On Labor Day you will make an announcement to the world about the Terminator Gene. And you will tell them that you have found a solution...that the solution will be provided free in honor of those men and women who died in the Caernarfon blast. Then you will release to the scientific community all the information concerning the solution."

"Why would anyone believe me?" Drake asked.

"They will believe because it is you." Sonya answered.

Drake thought about the enormous time and cost that Keewatin would have to bear. "This'll be expensive, if I agree."

"You will. It's your chance to be the hero, the savior of humanity. That's what you've always wanted."

Drake sensed that Dr. Sonya Speyer was holding something back. "What aren't you telling me?"

Sonya glanced at Kira who sat silently in her chair, "Scientists will analyze the chemical composition of the solution. However, they won't be able to figure out how it works. They will trace critical markers to the *tunicates*. But that'll be it."

"Because it doesn't actually work, does it?" Drake said.

"It works," Sonya assured him. "In an inexplicable way it's Kira. She has become the vehicle for the next stage of evolution. Her realization has created a morphogenic field for a new species."

"I...I can't believe this," Drake said, denial thick in his voice.

Sonya met Drake's skepticism with a gentle promise. "You will."

"But won't doctors and scientists see that it isn't really happening?"

"Doctors will investigate these new children and find that the dominance of the sympathetic nervous system over the parasympathetic nervous system has been reversed. That's the one and only physiological change they will discover," Sonya explained.

"What does that mean?"

"The nearly constant background tone of fear and danger that lies behind everyone's awareness will be gone. In its place will be ease and calm."

Kira looked at Drake and spoke for the first time. "It will change the quality of every human relationship. It's where evolution wants to go next."

Epilogue

Lawton, Oklahoma

Dr. Kira Taylor watched the contraction ripple across the mother's swollen belly. The monitors were hooked up and the steady rhythms of maternal and infant heartbeats filled the room. "Push!" she commanded.

The woman responded, her breath whistling through clenched teeth. After forty seconds, the contraction subsided and she lay back, limp.

"Your baby will be born very soon, Lucille, I promise," Kira said. "The head nearly crowned this time. Now concentrate on your love for your baby."

The clinic's obstetrics room was clean and white. Kira had personally seen to it that the latest equipment was available so that if there were any complications, they could deal with it. But Leroy Parker's granddaughter's pregnancy had been perfect and now the birth was going smoothly.

Lucille's back arched and her great belly surged upward as another contraction surged through her. Kira saw the baby's head and said very calmly and slowly, "You're doing fine. Focus on relaxing and on your breath." Lucille breathed deeply and slowly. The contraction peaked.

"Okay. One more push like the last and the baby will be here." Lucille pushed and started screaming as the baby slipped into the world. A gush of amniotic fluid coated Kira's surgical gown and her shoes. "It's a girl," she said to the mother. Lucille's screams turned to sobs of joy. Kira cut the umbilical cord and carefully set it aside. Next, Kira handed the wet baby to a nurse who wrapped it in a warm towel.

The nurse set the tiny newborn at the pediatrician's station and checked her vitals. The nurse gave Kira a thumbs-up.

Lucille reached out to hold her new baby. Kira nodded to the nurse who carefully laid the infant in the mother's arms. The girl started crying lustily and Lucille crooned, "Oh baby, I'm so glad you made it."

The baby opened her eyes and for a moment they locked on Kira. Complete trust and compassion flowed outward and flooded her thoughts. Kira looked around the room. *Births are normally happy, but this is different.* It was as if the baby's trust and openness were affecting everyone with a pervasive sense of equanimity, arising from a deep awareness and acceptance of the present moment. Kira knew these feelings were something never experienced in a normal delivery.

They were something new evolution had brought forth.

Lucille smiled through her tears and said, "It happened just like you said it would, Dr. Taylor."

Kira laughed at the memory Lucille's words brought up. She had been explaining to Lucille and her husband what they had to do before making love. She handed Lucille a suppository the size of a grape. "Insert this inside your vagina fifteen minutes before the two of you decide to make love."

"Is there anything special we have to do?" Lucille had asked.

"Just what humans have been doing for hundreds of thousands of years."

The baby started to squirm and move her mouth in suckling motions. Kira marveled at this moment of ultimate creativity, this moment of being the evolutionary pulse. It had been nearly a year since she awoke in her home in Sioux City with that surreal feeling coursing through her. Kira smiled.

Now I am that.

Kira Taylor walked up the steep hill to where Leroy Parker sat on a stone outcropping that overlooked a meadow in the Wichita Mountains. At his feet was a small fire. He carried a sacred pipe with the bowl carved in the shape of a horse's head.

"It's been two weeks now and your granddaughter is doing well and the baby is fine," Kira said.

Leroy beamed. "It is the month of the red grass, when the world begins anew." He indicated that Kira should sit across from him. And when she was situated comfortably, he said, "You have a question."

"Something I need to know. When I showed a picture of you to my friend Jackson Kelley, he recognized you immediately. Said he saw you in a dream...danced with you actually."

The Comanche elder smiled and said, "Is that so."

ROUNDFIRE BOOKS

Roundfire Books put simply, publish great stories. Whether it's literary or popular, a gentle tale or a pulsating thriller, the connecting theme in all Roundfire fiction titles is that once you pick them up you won't want to put them down.